The Dispossessed

The Dispossessed

A Story of Asylum at the US-Mexican Border and Beyond

John Washington

VERSO
London • New York

First published by Verso 2020
© John Washington 2020

1 3 5 7 9 10 8 6 4 2

Verso
UK: 6 Meard Street, London W1F 0EG
US: 20 Jay Street, Suite 1010, Brooklyn, NY 11201
versobooks.com

Verso is the imprint of New Left Books

ISBN-13: 978-1-78873-472-1
ISBN-13: 978-1-78873-475-2 (US EBK)
ISBN-13: 978-1-78873-474-5 (UK EBK)

British Library Cataloguing in Publication Data
A catalogue record for this book is available from the British Library

Library of Congress Cataloging-in-Publication Data
A catalog record for this book is available from the Library of Congress
Library of Congress Control Number: 2020932718

Typeset in Sabon by MJ & N Gavan, Truro, Cornwall
Printed in the UK by CPI Group (UK) Ltd, Croydon CR0 4YY

There are walls behind the walls.
                    —Ursula K. Le Guin

But 'tis a single Hair —
A filament — a law —
A Cobweb — wove in Adamant —
A Battlement — of Straw —

A limit like the Veil
Unto the Lady's face —
But every Mesh — a Citadel —
And Dragons — in the Crease —
                    —Emily Dickinson

Contents

Prologue

Sometimes it adds wings to the heels ... sometimes it nails them
to the ground.

—Montaigne, "On Fear"

Piedras Negras, Coahuila, Mexico

Fourteen men were slumped on mattresses and chairs, smoking
inside the warehouse, watching over the migrants. One of the
men had a pistol tucked into his waistband; another had a pistol
resting on his lap. The men were fussing with their phones,
ribbing each other, killing the morning. A slight waft of marijuana smoke lingered in the air. Someone hocked noisily, spat.

Arnovis, a thin, strong, hard-gazing twenty-four-year-old
Salvadoran man, nonchalantly grabbed his black knockoff
Puma backpack—the one his mother had bought for him back
in Jiquilisco—wove through a maze of the sitting and slumped
bodies, and walked out onto the patio.

Hey, vato, where you going? one of the men called.

Just to shower, Arnovis said. That okay?

And your backpack?

My clothes.

The shower was a five-gallon paint bucket filled with water,
a plastic bowl floating on the surface. It was set next to the
tall concrete wall. A few wires crisscrossed the sky above the

patio. A couple of the fourteen coyotes—Arnovis had counted them—could see him through a large window. He grabbed the bucket and hauled it over to the door, where he plugged a coiled heating rod into an outlet, ran it back outside, and dropped it into the bucket. He stepped out again and, as the water began to warm, scanned the yard. The walls were about twelve feet high: definitely higher than he could jump. A branch of a mango tree growing on the other side of the wall dipped down far enough he thought he might be able to reach it. But he wasn't sure if it would hold his weight.

That branch, he thought, my only hope.

Arnovis's brother, living in a suburb of Kansas City, had wired money to the wrong coyote, a man named Gustavo. Well, his brother didn't wire the money; his brother's friend did. His brother doesn't have papers, and couldn't send money on his own, which may have been why there was the mix-up. Gustavo—the wrong coyote—got seven hundred for doing nothing, and he didn't see any good reason to give it back. The problem—and for Arnovis it was a life-and-death problem—was that the family didn't have any more money. After a deportation to El Salvador from Mexico a few weeks earlier, and a down payment on the six-thousand-dollar smuggling fee—the family sold a prized goat for three hundred bucks to help pay for the first trip—there was nothing left.

El Suri—the coyote who did not get the money—was the guy actually planning to take Arnovis across the border. The two of them had hit it off, joking around on the migrant trails; earlier, El Suri had even suggested Arnovis stay in Mexico and work with him. Arnovis got along with everyone. He liked to tell jokes to quell tension, and rarely complained—that is, he was just being himself, and wasn't angling for a job in human smuggling. Maybe if it was just between El Suri and Arnovis they could have worked something out. But El Suri had a boss. The boss wanted his money.

~

2

As El Suri made a couple calls, Arnovis was hovering nervously. He remembers one call on speakerphone. Someone was trying to convince El Suri to head back south to take the next load. I'm waiting, El Suri said, for this one last kid to pay up. We're trying to get his brother to wire us. The man on the other end of the line suggested El Suri chop off one of Arnovis's fingers and send it to his brother.

Yeah, maybe.

El Suri hung up. Arnovis leaned up against the warehouse wall. He felt his future rushing at him like an oncoming train. A loud crescendo, and then—not boom but silence, death.

After another call, El Suri explained the situation: I got no problem with you, man. You're only two hundred bucks to me. But the jefe, El Suri said, he doesn't fuck around. He wants your money by ten tomorrow morning, and if you don't have it by then, he's going to come by, and what he's going to do to you—he's going to cut you into pieces.

Arnovis nodded, trying to take it in, trying to think. Trying to get out of the way of the train.

No money, and he was dead. That simple.

After a while El Suri called Arnovis's brother again, trying to convince him to drum up the money.

If you don't send three hundred dollars, we're going to have to take care of your brother.

There were about seventy-five people crashed, sprawled and breathing on the open warehouse floor. Arnovis found an open spot and slumped down to try to think. After a while he tried calling his brother again, but couldn't get through. Then he tried Gustavo, the coyote who pocketed the money for doing nothing. Surprisingly, he answered.

Gustavo! Arnovis explained the situation. It was all a mistake. He was going to be hacked into pieces if he didn't pay his coyote tomorrow, and they had meant to wire El Suri, but had

3

accidentally sent the money to him, so if he could just return the money …

I don't have it, Gustavo said.

What do you mean you don't have it?

I don't have it.

The seven hundred dollars my brother wired you?

Yeah, don't have it anymore. And, just a word of advice, Gustavo added, if they told you they were going to hack you into pieces, you better pay, or find a way to get out of there. And then he said something Arnovis already knew. These people don't fuck around.

Arnovis went back to El Suri. He told him he'd work for him, do whatever he wanted. El Suri told him that was great. Terrific. He'd be glad to have him.

But, he still needed to pay.

He had twelve hours to figure a way out. That night was long, the floor hard and cold. Arnovis sat in a daze, hugging his knees, listening to the snores and moans of his fellow migrants crowding the open floor. It was like they were in a mass grave, but still alive. In his anguish, he still felt hope; he still rejected the fact that his final truth would come to him the next morning: that train, then silence.

In the morning, walking out to take a shower on the cold patio, where fourteen coyotes were smoking and checking their phones, he found his salvation: a branch.

If he could reach it, and if it didn't break, he could pull himself up to the edge of the wall, grab on, and—maybe—get over. He didn't know what was on the other side, but it was almost certainly better than what was on this side.

After plugging in the water heater and looking up at the mango branch for another moment, he walked over to it and jumped.

Back in Corral de Mulas, in the Usulután Department on the western coast of El Salvador, when he wasn't plowing fields with oxen, laying bricks, mixing cement, harvesting corn, or working for a pittance at a sea turtle hatchery (for $180 a month), Arnovis would earn extra money climbing coconut trees. He'd kick off his sandals—if he was wearing any—wind an old rope around one wrist, toss it around the trunk of the palm, wind it around the other wrist, and shuttle up a forty-foot tree in a few seconds. He would then haul up his machete, which he had tied to the far end of the rope. Amid the scratch of fronds, he'd straddle one of the green branches, tie up a bundle of coconuts, hack it off, and lower the bunch to the ground. Getting down from the tree was trickier than getting up. He'd wind the rope twice around his waist, loop it over the space where a thick frond grew out of the trunk, and lower himself. No belay devices, no locks, no pulleys; nothing but rope, palm, and his wicked grip. Back on the ground, if he was thirsty, he'd wedge a coconut onto a stump with his hand, whack and twist the shell off in a flurry of machete hacks, pinprick the white flesh with the tip of the blade, and throw his head back and guzzle.

With his squarish face, high forehead, and narrow eyes, his down-turned lips tend to spring into an almost goofy face-wide smile when you catch his eye. But when his gaze locks, as it does in photographs, his eyes burn with worry and resolve. He wears a flattop buzz cut and a thin mustache, and is trim, with strong arms and shoulders. He also has a light step and an antsy energy: if there's work to be done, such as a bundle of coconuts to harvest, he'll kick off his sandals and be up the tree in seconds.

Coconuts go for about twenty cents apiece in Corral de Mulas, so if you want to make any money you have to climb a lot of trees. Sometimes four or five family members would head out together, leaving the house as early as three in the morning with two oxen pulling a tottering cart along the beach, heading south. The men climbed for coconuts and the women gathered pink cashew fruits until the heat started burning through the trees. Sometimes they would see small planes cruising low over a nearby airfield cut out of the jungle, spitting out wrapped bundles without touching down, and then buzzing back into the sky. These were the kinds of things they would see, hear, and not say a word about. Ver, oír, callar: a common saying and survival strategy in the Northern Triangle of Central America.

The mango branch held. Arnovis reached up his other arm and clutched the next branch, planted his feet against the concrete wall. In another heave he had a hold on the top edge. He braced his feet, yanked himself up, and then swung a leg over the wall. That was when he heard one of the coyotes. *What the fuck!*

This fucking vato! another shrieked.

Arnovis looked down the other side of the wall and saw a few dozen kids in uniforms crossing the patio of an elementary school. The mango tree was too far for him to reach the trunk to shimmy down. There was nothing to do but fall twelve feet onto the hard concrete in his black hand-me-down dress shoes.

Arnovis didn't hesitate. He didn't have time. He didn't even jump. He just let go.

Gimme Shelter

> Who kindly sets a wanderer on his way
> Does e'en as if he lit another's lamp by his:
> No less shines his, when he his friends hath lit.
>
> —Ennius

The basic idea of asylum is simple. Someone comes to your door because they are in danger, because they are afraid. You open your door, and you share your roof. But within this simple idea lies a labyrinth constructed of different sorts of fear: some fear is grounded in immediate physical danger, some is diffused in general conditions of oppression; some is exaggerated, some completely imagined. Some fears are unrealized, some send you to your grave.

As a legal construct, asylum is less simple. According to the 1951 UN Refugee Convention, which set the original international standard for defining refugees and asylum seekers, an asylum seeker is someone who, "owing to a well-founded fear of being persecuted for reasons of race, religion, nationality, membership of a particular social group or political opinion, is outside the country of his nationality and is unable or, owing to such fear, is unwilling to avail himself of the protection of that country; or who, not having a nationality and being outside the country of his former habitual residence as a result of such events, is unable or, owing to such fear, is unwilling to return to it."

Fear is the requisite for asylum, but the definition is based on a fear of a specific entity, the state—a fear of being persecuted by the state or its representatives. But the fear must be "well founded," and many of today's asylum seekers, especially those from Central America and Mexico (where, taken together, most people seeking asylum in the United States are from), are fleeing non-state persecutors. The single country from which most asylum seekers come to the United States in recent years has been China, though in 2018 Venezuela topped the list for the first time.

According to the United Nations High Commissioner for Refugees' (UNHCR) *Handbook on Procedures and Criteria for Determining Refugee Status*, "in general, the applicant's fear should be considered well founded if he can establish, to a reasonable degree, that his continued stay in his country of origin has become intolerable to him."

The US Supreme Court also wrestled with the definition of *well-founded fear* after adopting the language of the Refugee Convention into law with the 1980 Refugee Act. During the oral argument for a 1987 case, *Immigration and Naturalization Service v. Cardoza-Fonseca*, in which a Nicaraguan woman who overstayed her visa appealed to the United States for asylum, attorney Dana Leigh Marks (now an immigration judge) suggested defining such fear according to the "reasonable person" standard: would a "reasonable person" in this same factual situation fear persecution upon return to their country? But the justices sought a more quantifiable criterion than reasonableness —they tried to pin down the quivering subjectivity of fear. In his majority opinion Justice John Paul Stevens wrote, "One can certainly have a well-founded fear of an event happening when there is less than a 50 percent chance of the occurrence taking place."

Justice Harry Blackmun argued in a concurring opinion that "the very language of the term 'well-founded fear' demands a particular type of analysis—an examination of the subjective feelings of an applicant for asylum coupled with an inquiry into the objective nature of the articulated reasons for the fear."

Justice Antonin Scalia tried throwing out a few examples, and here he and Marks, still in the oral argument, engage in some frightful repartee.

> SCALIA: Let's assume that the persecution in the country you're talking about is very ... it's horrible persecution, it's torture; it isn't just incarceration ... Now, suppose my chances of actually being subjected to that if I go back are one in a thousand. Would I have a well-founded fear of going back?
> MARKS: It depends on whether it would be reasonable to have that fear in view of the small chance that something is going to happen.
> SCALIA: I know it would, and what's the answer?
> MARKS: The answer is that the tryer of fact should look at the specific facts which you put forth to show the objective situation.
> SCALIA: You see, I don't know the answer to that. Is that a well-founded fear or not?
> MARKS: One in a thousand, I'm sure it's not.

In 1987 Marks was a thirty-two-year-old immigration attorney presenting her first case before the Supreme Court. Today she is an immigration judge and president emeritus of the National Association of Immigration Judges. When I spoke with her, in

2018, thirty-one years after she had argued *Cardoza-Fonseca*, she told me she had been heavily counseled to avoid any attempt at quantification, and that Scalia had "backed her into a numerical corner." Justice Stevens finally settled on what has become an unofficial *10 percent standard*: if an asylum applicant has at least a 10 percent chance of "being shot, tortured, or otherwise persecuted," they meet the requirements for being eligible for protection.

What we are left with: to be *well founded*, fear should be "subjectively genuine and objectively reasonable," and can be based on the one in ten probability of occurrence of persecution. Marks told me, however, that most judges and attorneys avoid the numerical standard, and that she personally sticks to defining fear as well founded if it is "subjectively genuine and objectively reasonable."

The legal grappling with this complex structure of a feeling hasn't exactly made matters more clear. And yet, when you feel it, nothing could be more lucid than fear—more all-consuming, more convincing, more instant.

It is an emotion relatively easy to invoke—a mere word or a glance, given the right context, can incite one of our most elemental, spine-straightening, snake-brain responses. And yet what many of us may have experienced in a movie theater, or perhaps while lost in an unfamiliar city at night, or in a moment of turbulence at thirty thousand feet—those fleeting moments that twang at the nervous system—pale next to the pervasive fear that does *not* pass when the curtain drops, you find your way, or the plane touches down. Fear—as it relates to asylum—is fear that remains, builds, and pushes you to flee. While Montaigne said that fear "dethrones our judgment," fear also thrones our drive to self-protection: wings to the heels. Incommensurability, too, is perhaps part of the nature of fear. You can't measure or weigh it—it is just there, pressing, breathless, total.

What we take to be fear, and fear responses, as neuroscientist Joseph LeDoux has shown, should really be broken up into unconscious *responses to threats* and conscious *feelings of fear*. According to LeDoux's scholarship, the amygdala—a little almond-shaped neural mass in the bowels of the brain that is commonly associated with fear—is not the center of fear itself, but rather where the brain responds to threat stimulation. The amygdala, that is, triggers the chemical response (read: objectively reasonable), and the subsequent sensation is the feeling of fear processed by the conscious brain (read: subjectively genuine).

"You can never be wrong about your experience of fear," LeDoux told me when we met to discuss his research. The fear an asylum seeker experienced might not be merited, but it's not wrong. When someone is removed from the danger, LeDoux explained, it's also tricky to ask them how they felt about their fear. The very act of remembering, or *reconsolidation*, in neuro-scientific terms, is liable to alter the memory. In other words, memory is not so much a thing—a file or code—as it is an act, which is a singular and new experience in itself. In terms of asylum, a more logical approach for immigration judges would be to measure the threat instead of measuring the fear. A careful editor to the 1951 Convention might replace "well-founded fear" with "well-founded threat."

But—in terms of asylum—fear cannot be considered only as it involves the individual. For example, if the solution to an indi-vidual's fear is to offer refuge—a neighbor opening their home —what if whole crowds are afraid and in need of refuge? At some point, it's no longer safe for the original householders or for those who previously found solace under the roof. Complications abound.

And yet if we recognize the complexity of those who are knocking on the door, we also need to scrutinize those who are behind the door, those who have the roof to offer. Why are we the ones inside rather than outside? Why do we get to decide who to open the door for, who to turn away—just because we have the key and the house title? How, and under what legiti-macy, were we the ones who were able to raise the roof? How did we obtain the land on which to build the house? Who was living there before? What are *we* afraid of?

Politically, the modern concept of asylum—though rooted in ancient religious traditions of sanctuary and primordial codes of welcoming the stranger—was formed in a period of political statecrafting and Cold War geopolitical braggadocio. Today's legal concepts of refugee and asylum laws are still based on definitions that were originally tightly circumscribed by anti-communist ideology.

Amid the postbellum shuffle and rethink, the asylum policies enshrined in the 1951 Refugee Convention only applied to Europeans who were forced to flee their homes by events occurring before January 1, 1951, though hundreds of thousands had been similarly uprooted and unroofed in Asia and Africa, and millions more would take wing in subsequent years. These geographical and temporal limitations were more about politics than about need or even capacity. As Matthew Gibney puts it, "No country knit together its definition of a refugee with escape from communism as tightly as the US. Before 1980, refugees from non-communist countries (with the sole exception of the Middle East) had no status under US law." Accepting refugees and asylum seekers was a way for the United States to leak the communist bloc of its citizens and undermine their governments. Those fleeing the rest of the world were simply left in the cold.

Today, there are two paths by which someone can gain refugee status in the United States—as a refugee or an asylee. Refugees apply from their own country (or a temporary place of resettlement), which must be of "special humanitarian concern" to the State Department. There are numerical limits, per region, on the number of refugees admitted each year. The 2018 ceiling for refugees from all of Latin America and the Caribbean was 1,500 people. But that was the ceiling. The actual number of refugees granted protection from all of Latin American and the Caribbean in 2018 was less than 1,000. Overall, in the same year, 22,491 refugees were resettled in the United States, and that number took another nosedive in 2019, with the annual ceiling set at 18,000, the lowest ever. White House officials have also purportedly considered shutting down the program altogether. In 1980, the total number of refugee admissions into the United States—the majority from Vietnam, Cambodia, Laos, as well as the Soviet Union—was nearly 250,000.

Asylees, meanwhile, for which there are no numerical limits, apply once they are inside the United States or when they show up at a port of entry. As the ceiling for refugees collapses—and as other pathways to immigration are foreclosed—more and more people fleeing danger are showing up to the US border and asking for protection through the asylum process. In 2017, 331,700 people applied for asylum in the United States, which was almost twice as many as applied in 2015, and roughly six times as many as applied in 2010. Just under thirty thousand cases were decided, however, meaning the backlog of pending cases is rising sharply. Worldwide, there were 837,445 asylum seekers in 2010, according to the UNHCR. By 2018, that number topped 3.5 million.

Under the umbrella of asylum—it might help to imagine an actual umbrella here, buffeted by hard wind and drenching rain—there are three different types of protection: asylum status, withholding of removal, and protection against deportation afforded by the Convention Against Torture (CAT). All three categories hark back to the guiding principle of asylum: non-refoulement, or the guarantee to *not return* somebody to a place where their life would be in danger. The first two options are based on the 1951 Convention, with "withholding of removal" applying to people who have not met the one-year filing deadline, or don't qualify for another reason, such as having been denied asylum previously or having committed a felony. The Convention Against Torture, meanwhile (signed by the United States in 1988, but not implemented into US law until a decade later) not only prohibits torture itself but prohibits the expulsion, or refoulement, of anybody where "there are substantial grounds for believing that he would be in danger of being subjected to torture." Both withholding of removal and the CAT claims have a higher bar than that for asylum: you need to prove that it is *more likely than not*—more than a 50 percent chance—you are going to face death, persecution, or torture upon return. To be eligible for asylum status, that threshold, thanks to Scalia and Stevens, is set at a 10 percent chance of future persecution.

To lay bare the political nature of asylum protections: during the 1980s the United States took in Cubans and Nicaraguans (fleeing Communist governments that the US openly opposed) but summarily denied Haitians, Guatemalans, and Salvadorans (fleeing US-backed authoritarian governments). In 1987, Nicaraguans were granted asylum at a rate of 84 percent. Meanwhile, for both Salvadorans and Guatemalans the asylum approval rate throughout the 1980s hovered between 1 and 3 percent. A 1982 Immigration and Naturalization Service memorandum revealed the government's flagrantly discriminatory interpretation of the 1980 Refugee Act and the 1951 Refugee Convention: "Different criteria sometimes may be applied to different nationalities ... In some cases, different levels of proof are required of different asylum applicants."

Asylum policy has remained both grimly discriminatory and starkly political. The United States denies almost 90 percent of Mexican claims, while granting nearly 90 percent of claims from Eritreans—a gaping and irreconcilable disparity. In part, the difference owes to the mutual economic dependency between the United States and Mexico; it would be a diplomatic sucker punch for the United States to openly acknowledge that Mexico either persecutes or cannot protect its own citizens, but it has no problem making that same assessment about Eritrea.

Although terrorism has replaced the Communist specter, it is still largely fear—the nation's—that drives hard-line immigration, asylum, and refugee policies. We codify the nation's fears into law, yet we delegitimize the fear of our neighbors, the fear of refugees and asylum seekers—many of whom are fleeing not abstract, future-oriented fear of possible demographic change, "replacement," or improbable violence but actual, immediate, duck-for-cover, jackboots-kicking-at-your-door, roof-is-collapsing fear.

Corey Robin called fear "the most electric of emotions." John Locke said it was "the strongest emotion which the mind is capable of feeling." Montaigne recognized that we (and our reason) are fear's subjects, and yet we also wield fear, politically, like a nightstick, and invoke it to bolt our doors or to batter them down.

After the 9/11 attacks, a common fear unified much of the country, serving as social cement, a reason to talk to a neighbor or stick a flag in your lawn. It also divided the country and led to the rounding up and imprisoning of thousands of Muslims, as well as dramatic changes in US immigration and asylum policy. We responded to our fear by invoking it in others. And it was largely fear, too, that led to a massive, multi-trillion-dollar flexing of hard power—the longest war in US history—which has killed and uprooted millions.

The marrow of civilization, Hobbes reasoned, is not mutual interest but rather mutual fear. We are frightened of each other, and so we draw each other close, establish rules of engagement: politics. You intuit the need to protect yourself, but you need to rationalize, or legislate, the need to protect your neighbor. In submitting our authority of self-protection to the state, we expect protection not only for ourselves, but for and with our compatriots. In other words, we are all safer if we are all safe.

But demarcating who is given room under the wing of the leviathan has been an ongoing controversy that has, in part, sparked conflict, conquest, and holocaust. It has also spurred the development of institutionalized state protections such as the Universal Declaration of Human Rights and the Refugee

Convention that today—at least on paper—extend rights and protection to every single human being on the planet. Sovereignty needs steel and statecraft; the extension of rights and protections needs incubation and cultural shifts. According to the "contact hypothesis," the best way to counteract prejudice—to diminish fear—between majority and minority groups, between residents and newcomers, is by integration and patience. Fear typically prompts the opposite of patience. As Corey Robin writes, "What makes fear such a source of political élan is either the memory or the expectation of political entropy." Nothing signifies political entropy more than—you can almost hear an Ennio Morricone theme—a stranger coming to town.

Two countervailing fears leave asylum seekers outside any state protections: the instigating fear that pushes people to flee their country, and the receiving population's fear that propels them to slam the door. What results is a global crisis of homelessness: millions of people left in the cold of statelessness. To be stateless, as Hannah Arendt cogently observed, is to be rightless. Since the origins of human rights in the late eighteenth century, laws and protections have been hitched closely to the state. That is, if you fall or are pushed out from under its wing, you fall into a political abyss.

In 1845 Frederick Douglass, after escaping slavery in Maryland, wrote that he "imagined watchmen everywhere. At every ferry a guard. On every bridge a sentinel. And in every wood a patrol of slavehunters." He captured the plight of the fugitive slave, in

> a land given up to be a hunting ground for slaveholders. Where he is every moment subjected to the terrible liability of being seized upon by his fellow-men, as the hideous crocodile seizes upon his prey!—I say, let him place himself in my situation—without home or friends—without money or credit—wanting shelter, and no one to give it—wanting bread, and no money to buy it,—and at the same time let him feel that he is pursued by

merciless men-hunters, and in total darkness as to what to do, where to go, or where to stay.

Douglass's history is different, but his fear is similar and context relevant to that suffered by many migrants and refugees —hunted in one state and denied protections from another— dodging the watchmen, men-hunters, and border guards of today.

First Attempt

1

To get to Corral de Mulas by land, head along the Pacific coast two hours southeast from San Salvador, cross the bridge over the Lempa River—a broad, shallow, puddly thing during the drought when I first crossed it—which winds its way north until it marks the border between El Salvador and Honduras for about twenty miles, and then dips back into the department of Chalatenango. The bridge across the Lempa is the Puente de Oro, the Bridge of Gold, which guerrilla fighters bombed on October 15, 1981, in a sapper operation during the country's civil war. By dynamiting power stations, snipping electrical wires, burning over a thousand buses, and blowing up bridges, the guerrillas were trying to provoke an economic collapse and convince the people that the government wasn't in control. The government was struggling—desperately—to control at least one thing: violence. "The Lempa River," a Salvadoran refugee told journalist Robert S. Kahn in 1984, "had been turned into a cemetery. It was full of bodies of students and murdered workers. They would tie heavy things to the corpses to keep them from rising. In order to eat fish, it was necessary to season them with garlic, because of the stink of human flesh. People would clean fish and find human fingers in them, and in spite of this, they ate them, because there was nothing else to eat." Today, as much or perhaps even more than during the civil war, the government is losing its control as the predominant wielder of violence.

Over the Bridge of Gold, take a jackknife right-hand turn off the two-lane highway into the small elbow town of San Marcos Lempa. In just a couple hundred yards you leave behind the pulperías—small corner stores—selling bananos, anonas, lychees, onions, chips, and soda, and enter a tunnel of ceiba, zorra, cedar, and breadnut trees that looks like a shade-dappled gateway into a tropical wonderland. To the west is the Nancuchiname forest, which abuts the Lempa River and has become a dumping ground for bodies, as revealed by the 2016 discovery of a mass grave.

On what locals refer to as *la carreterra*, or the highway, most of the traffic is horse-drawn carts loaded with corn or firewood, shirtless men slowly, wobblingly riding bicycles in dirty rubber boots with machetes across the handlebars, and occasional herds of skinny Brahman cattle. There are also listless dogs reluctant to heed oncoming cars and, above, draft-riding vultures or the occasional scream of green parrots. You have entered territory run by the Mara Salvatrucha—MS or MS-13. You are about to leave it and enter, a few miles down the road, Barrio 18 territory, and then leave that and enter, a few more clicks, back into MS territory. The signs are few, but if you were to trespass into one of the tiny communities—El Zamoran, El Marillo, Amando López—occasionally breaking the tranquility of the canopy of breadnuts and ceiba, or if you trudge off the road into the Nancuchiname forest, some young, thin toughs will almost certainly ask to see your ID (foreigners likely exempt) to check if you came from enemy territory.

And even if you don't see them, they see you.

Throughout my time in Central America I heard countless descriptions of the tremendous situational awareness of the gangs: they unobtrusively watch everything. They're unobtrusive, of course, until they obtrude. Young lookouts—*halcones*, *chequeos*, or *paros*—keeping an eye on all incomers. Scaled up, this situational awareness would be the envy of state surveillance regimes, calling to mind the dystopic dream of "operational control," as articulated in its 2007 national strategy and defined as "the ability to detect, respond, and interdict border penetrations in areas deemed as high priority for threat potential or other national security objectives." It could have been describing MS or Barrio 18's control over certain Central American neighborhoods.

Daniel Ghezelbash, in his book *Refuge Lost*, explains that the answer to why nations are obsessed with deterring migration "lies in sovereignty and the related desire to maximize control over who can enter a country's territorial boundaries." Swap "country" with "neighborhood," and he would be describing the sovereignty exercised by the gangs. They, too, seek to control irregular immigration.

Jockeying, as the gangs do—against both the state and rival cliques—for small islands of territorial control, as well as for position to loot and commandeer unaffiliated "civilians," is essentially terrestrial piracy. I saw clear evidence of such piracy firsthand in the Rivera Hernández neighborhood of San Pedro Sula, Honduras—often cited as the most violent city on the planet. Honduran journalist and illustrator German Andino and I visited a small outpost of the Barrio 18 gang one night in the summer of 2018, where we met a cluster of young "sympathizers" and novitiates, including El Mini-Me—the ranking member when we first arrived—all drinking tepid bottles of Barena beer on a dark corner in front of the pulpería Tienda Emily. After we exchanged greetings with the shaking of damp palms, one of the stumbling drunk youths uncapped a bottle of warm Barena with his teeth and handed it to me. We talked Trump and JOH (the much-hated and illegitimate Honduran president Juan Orlando Hernández), and it seemed we all were trying to put each other at ease. After a while, El Mortal—the *palabrero*, or local leader—made his appearance. The crew sniffed bumps of coke from a small baggy and got giggly, trying to convince German to give them a tattoo. After further small talk—the adrenaline had eased its grip, but I still wasn't quite at ease—we said good night and left.

The next morning we stopped by again and the crew were still at it, though now they had moved into the shade of Tienda Emily's storage area. They hadn't been invited in; they had just taken over the place. The sloppy, macho blustering I had witnessed the night before was even more present in the sweaty, mosquito-slapping shade. El Mortal and El Negro, one of the senior members (though he looked to be in his early twenties at most) were reclined on plastic-string chaise lounges. A flat-screen TV hung on the wall, a stereo system and a Playstation were propped on storage crates, and the place was cluttered and filthy. There were dozens of empty and half-empty Barena bottles on the floor, and the space reeked of sweating bodies and beer. At one point, one of the shirtless drunk boys accidentally kicked and shattered a bottle. Nobody thought to sweep up the shards. German had bought a bunch of baleadas—variations on beans, eggs, and cream in folded flour tortillas, a Honduran specialty—and the kids, none of whom had eaten since the night before, ravenously tore into them.

The family who lived and worked in the house connected to Tienda Emily was busy running the pulpería. But they also had to tend to the clique, for whom the store was convenient because it was situated at a T in the road, providing them with strategic field of vision. They stashed their prized AK-47 in a back room. Not far away, another upstart gang had simply moved into a woman's house—suddenly adding about a dozen armed and elbowy gangsters to the residence.

Sometimes, instead of simply moving into a home unannounced, the gangs will post blunt eviction notices: "On behalf of the gang Barrio 18 we give you twenty-four hours that you float on out of here, otherwise you'll regret it, lives will be dropped just for opening your doors ..."

The gangs conduct the same piratical commandeering in El Salvador. Jesus, a gay Salvadoran man routinely hounded, extorted, and once gang-raped by Mara Salvatrucha members, told me his story one afternoon in a Mister Donut shop in a

San Salvadoran mall over plates of pork chops. Jesus showed me the thick scars on his wrists—the hardened flesh looked braided—from when gang members had once tied him up to rape him. After he had fled to the United States, only to be denied asylum and deported, he found a job with the mayor's office—going into impoverished neighborhoods and working on community development projects. But even though he enjoyed his work and found some stability, he couldn't escape the gangs. They swore that his by then ex-partner (whom he had traveled to the United States with, and who *was* granted asylum) was sending him money. That wasn't true, but he couldn't convince the gangs, and had to pay them one hundred dollars a month in "rent," as well as deal with them occasionally dropping by his house to mess with him. At one point, they took his refrigerator. And then they booted him out because one of the gang leaders wanted the house for his girlfriend. Jesus now rents a small shack he shares with two roommates, a couple chickens, and his dog, Pepa.

In another notoriously dangerous neighborhood, the Mejicanos barrio of San Salvador, a community organizer, jack-of-all-trades activist, and gang member I got to know, Beto, pointed out to me a handful of houses that had been commandeered by the gangs. (He himself grew up on the periphery of the gangs and had recently been forced—during a brutal eighteen-second jumping in—to join their ranks.) They might take your refrigerator and TV if they don't want your home, he told me. Only a week before one of our meetings, Beto's upstairs neighbors had been evicted out of their family home when one of the higher-level gang members wanted it. Thank you for your collaboration, the gang member had told the departing family.

Juan José Martínez, a Salvadoran anthropologist and writer who, along with Andino, conducted research in San Pedro Sula, describes the houses they interviewed gang members in as "vestiges of an ancient war. Vegetation was growing inside them. The ceilings and the doors had been removed months ago. Inside, all that remained were the walls, painted with the graffiti of dead gang members. One of the houses had a room flooded with greenish water swarming with mosquitoes. It was like a big factory for chikungunya, the malaria-like illness plaguing Rivera Hernandez."

It was seeking protections against piracy that led to the establishment of the earliest asylum policies. As maritime technology developed around three thousand years ago, the Greek islands became increasingly interconnected through trade and plundering incursions—the stories of which Homer memorably sung. In the eyes of some ancient Greeks, the seagoing ship itself was, as Hellenic scholar Geoffrey Bakewell put it, "that wretched instrument that first breached divinely sanctioned natural boundaries in search of gain." Pillaging and invasions became such a nagging problem that laws were put in place to demarcate sacred spaces that would be off-limits to the marauders. These sanctuaries eventually became spaces where people charged with crimes, or even political enemies, could find refuge.

The etymology of the word *asylum* touches on the same history: the need for protections from piracy. *Sylos* is Greek for plundering. *A-sylos* is a space off-limits from such plundering. As scholar Philippe Gauthier explains, "the term *sylan* designates a violent action, which consists of seizing a person or the goods belonging to a person." *Sylan* is despoiling, pillaging. A-*sylan* is freedom from pillaging, freedom from piracy. The word later took on the sense of "inviolability." According to Linda Rabben, "sanctuaries functioned as legally acknowledged places of refuge … for runaway slaves, ousted politicians on the run, and other individuals who were being pursued. To assassinate someone who had taken refuge in a sanctuary was considered a heinous enough crime for the gods to inflict a scourge (a plague, for instance) on the whole city as a punishment."

But freedom from despoilment leads to other vulnerabilities, as Hobbes noted, especially when you submit yourself to the state for protection. Philosopher Daniel Heller-Roazen writes that public space itself can be seen as a form of asylum, a collective agreement on "the cessation of acts of plunder." And yet, he also notes, that agreement establishes "a means for systematic depredations all the more effective for being planned." That is to say, asylum is not only an act of protecting, but a political maneuver that can affect the opposite of protection. The delimitation of spaces where *sylos* was forbidden didn't just protect those spaces, it also consecrated the very act of delimitation: the rise of state bordering not just in the geographic sense but, centuries later, in the distinctions between citizen and slave, legal resident and undocumented, or even refugee and economic migrant. This is one of the inherent paradoxes of asylum and refugee principles: that the delimiting of protection from a state reinscribed the need for a state, even if it was a different one, to offer that very protection. But it isn't just the pirates who are pillaging outside the sylos-free zones; it's also the colonial and neocolonial and corporate state itself that pushes, and breaches, lines of agreement to seize resources and establish new forms of territorial control. It is the state that is the ultimate pirate.

The locals refer to the area as islands, but San Juan del Gozo, dangling between the roar of the Pacific and the calm of Jiquilisco Bay, is actually a peninsula. Straight across that bay from Corral de Mulas (there are actually two separate communities, Corral Uno and Corral Dos, but they're often referred to by the one name), where Arnovis was born, is the Isla de Madresal, Mothersalt Island—an actual island—and hovering behind it is the gray, perfect profile of the Chaparrastique volcano, often tenderly scarved in white lenticular clouds. Where the bay hits the sea is another island: Isla La Pirraya. One of the things these islands are known for, besides being a refuge for guerrilla exiles during the civil war and for gangsters today, is soccer. The internationally competitive Salvadoran national beach soccer team trains on La Pirraya, and every village on the islands has multiple fields, many of them neatly maintained with grass and regulation-size fish-netted goals. Compared with the many soccer fields I've seen and sometimes played on in Central America, the pitches on San Juan del Gozo (or Joyous Saint John) peninsula stand out. The local soccer leagues are competitive, and, though he didn't have much time to practice after work, Arnovis was a good player. I watched a high school game one heat-stilled afternoon with Arnovis's father and about thirty spectators. The Corral team, shirtless, played against their San Marcos rivals, and it was an entertaining game—a win for the skins. It was on a soccer pitch just a few miles from this one where trouble first started for Arnovis, where the fire sparked that forced him to flee.

In the summer of 2016, Arnovis and a group of friends from Corral de Mulas formed a team, Arsenal. They wore knockoff yellow Brazil national team jerseys, and, despite it being their first season, by late October they were at the top of the league and preparing for their biggest game yet: a rematch against Juventus. The teams had played the week before, but Arsenal only had seven players, and, despite scrapping hard for a tie, the game didn't have enough players to make it official. Arnovis would later tell me that he had had a bad feeling about the rematch, and didn't want to play. Juventus players weren't pleased that Arsenal had eked out that first tie. The rematch, he knew, was going to be physical.

It was a searing Sunday afternoon, and nearly a hundred people gathered in the spotted shade around the field to watch. There's not much to do on the islands, and attending local soccer matches is popular entertainment. Juventus came out gunning, and scored first. Not much later Arnovis, who was playing wing, scored a tying goal off a corner kick.

A few minutes later, Juventus's goalie punted the ball into Arsenal's half. It took a bounce and then Arnovis and the

Juventus forward, Frank (known as El Monkey, because he had once broken his leg and now walked, supposedly, like a monkey), both went up for it. They smacked together in the air, Arnovis's elbow clunking into El Monkey's mouth. It wasn't intentional, Arnovis told me. But intent hardly matters in the heat of a game. Even flagrant fouls aren't *intentional* in the same way that premeditated malice can be intentional off a field.

As he was describing the incident to me, Arnovis and I were sitting in his open-air, dirt-floor kitchen, and he stood up to offer a reenactment, pretending to jump, but leaving his feet nailed to the ground, and knocking into an imaginary El Monkey. I stood up and filled the role: Show me how you hit him.

I don't remember—maybe like this. And he swiped his elbow against the side of my face. There wasn't even a whistle, he said. But El Monkey was pissed.

You don't always recognize moments of consequence when they occur. The end of Arnovis's ulna cracking against El Monkey's molars: and then two years of flight, Arnovis chased and detained by the merciless men-hunters, trying three times to enter the United States, twice deported, his daughter taken from him, lingering years of dread and occasional moments of panic.

El Monkey picked himself up and got into Arnovis's face. Arnovis stood him down. "Discutimos," is how he first described the incident to me. They "had words." The ref finally blew his whistle to try to break it up, and, after a couple shoves, the benches were cleared as the two players continued to *discutir*. When the ref—or *profe*, as they call them in El Salvador—took back control, he gave both Arnovis and Frank red cards, ejecting them from the game. They weren't even allowed to stay on the sidelines. Arnovis walked off the field, trying to calm himself. El Monkey followed, and they each took up poses about twenty yards apart to watch the match from the other side of the fence.

After a few minutes, Arnovis heard someone calling out: Hey, man. Hey, loco.

One of the guys who had been talking to El Monkey strolled up to Arnovis.

What?

The guy looked at him, chucked his chin, and then said, Sos tumba.

What? Arnovis said again.

Sos cadáver. You're dead.

I asked anthropologist Juan José Martínez, who has studied and written about Central American gangs for years, about the specific phrasing of the threat. *Sos tumba*—literally, *You are a tomb*—sounded odd to me. He told me it wasn't unusual in the gang world. You're "living dead" is basically what it means, and he offered a number of other colorful Salvadoran idioms that signify the same: *Tonight you're family is going to dress in mourning. You're going to put on your wooden suit.* Or: *Tomorrow you're going to wake up with flies in your mouth.*

It turns out that the forward whose mouth caught Arnovis's elbow, El Monkey, was the brother of the palabrero of the local Barrio 18 clique.

Sos tumba.

According to the United States Customs and Immigration Services, you are eligible for asylum only if you have suffered persecution *on account of an immutable characteristic*—your race, religion, nationality, political opinion, or your membership in a particular social group—and the government in your country of origin is either unwilling or unable to protect you. As Arnovis's life soon became unlivable on the islands, it became clear that relocating to another town or city, as he and many others explained to me, would not usher him to safety. The inability to relocate—and escape the fear—is another of the prerequisites for asylum. Arnovis's only hope, as he saw it, was to find protection under a new roof.

The impetus of persecution against Arnovis—which began with that threat, *Sos tumba*—was not because of his religion, race, or nationality. And though at first glance it might not seem that Arnovis's persecution was because of his "political opinion" —he would be hounded by El Monkey's brother and the 18s, not the police, the state, or the army—it's important to consider what entity had actual political jurisdiction in Corral. In March of 2016, the United Nations High Commissioner for Refugees published *Eligibility Guidelines for Assessing the International Protection Needs of Asylum Seekers from El Salvador*, in which the UNHCR explains that contradicting a gang is a political action. The gangs, after all, have de facto political control over certain Salvadoran cities and towns, such as El Limon, the small village outside of San Salvador where a mass grave was discovered in 2019, or Corral de Mulas. The gangs in these places charge taxes, they offer protection, they enact capital punishment, and they even evict and dispossess people living within their territory.

In 2018, Attorney General Jeff Sessions wrote in a decision, "Generally, claims by aliens pertaining to domestic violence or gang violence perpetrated by non-governmental actors will not qualify for asylum." Karen Musalo, director of the Center for Gender and Refugee Studies, told me, "Asylum can and should accommodate people who are targeted by gangs." The question comes down to the elasticity of the very institution of asylum. Essentially, what does it mean to govern, and specifically, to whom is a government responsible?

It was like a bomb exploded in my life, Arnovis told me. He tried to ignore it at first, but you can't ignore a bomb.

A couple days later, he said, this kid—El Monkey—showed up at my brother's house and said he was looking for me. I went and talked with him, told him I was sorry, that I hadn't meant to hit him, all that.

They talked a bit, and then El Monkey got around to saying what he had wanted to say. Don't worry, it's all fine with me, he told Arnovis. No hay bronca. But I need to let you know that I don't trust my brother. Or his people. They're not going to let it go.

And then he told him something else about El Monkey's brother, the head of the 18s in Puerto Triunfo: Raúl thinks you're with MS.

That was the bomb.

Maybe, *maybe* he could have ducked out of the 18s' sights for accidentally elbowing the palabrero's brother in the mouth, but if they thought he was MS, he was just plunged into another realm of danger.

If I were you, El Monkey told him, I would leave.

The timeline has been blurred by the months, but soon after El Monkey's visit—the same day? the next morning?—Arnovis got a call when he was at work. He doesn't know how they got his number.

Sos tumba, someone told him again.

He hung up. His inclination was to go home, go into hiding. But at home were his then partner, Mirna, and his young daughter, Meybelín, who had just turned four years old. If they came for him and found him in his home ... he didn't want to think about what would happen if they found him with his daughter.

The phone call convinced him: it was too dangerous to stay. He went to find refuge in a spatchcock shack on the original plot of his family's land, which was about twenty minutes down a series of narrow, thorn-weed, sandy alleyways. Arnovis's father, Pedro, grows corn and cashews on the plot, and they have a dilapidated one-room shack Arnovis's parents used to live in—and where he was born—before the family grew. Now, the dirt-floor shack has nothing but a homemade rope bed, a hammock, a few rudimentary farm tools, and bugs. Cell service is spotty there, the nearest neighbor is out of earshot, and, as has always been the case, there are no lights or electricity to attract attention. And as he leaned into the hammock and watched the evening descend, the hot silence of the day shredded by the ringing of insects and the stirring of a slight breeze, he already

knew what he had to do. He knew what his only option was—
flight—and yet he resisted. He stared into the darkness for a
long time and, he told me, he felt very alone.

In the following days, Arnovis received a few more calls, all
with some version of the same message: sos tumba, sos cadáver,
te matamos, you're gonna wake up with flies in your mouth.

And then he got a call from a number he recognized. It was
Peluca (Wig), an old acquaintance who got involved with the
18s when they were still teenagers. Since then, Arnovis had tried
to keep him at a distance. They'd see each other sometimes,
and say What's up? ¿Qué ondas?, but that was it.

¿Qué ondas, loco? Peluca said. Where you at?

Around.

What are you doing tomorrow?

Nothing. Why?

I need to talk to you about something.

What?

Look, Peluca said. I just got a call from the vatos in Puerto.
They told me you had a problem with someone on the field.

Yeah.

And that I was supposed to take care of it. They told me
you joined up.

The "vatos from Puerto" were the MS leadership from Puerto
Triunfo, the nearest mainland town with a gas station—about
a twenty-five-minute boat ride away—that was literally divided
down the middle by rival gangs. MS leadership had heard about
the dispute on the island because they hear about everything,
and, like any decent politicians, they used the minor conflict to
press their agenda. They saw two openings: another reason to
attack their rivals, and a possible new recruit. The 18s, meanwhile, had sent Peluca as envoy to suss out Arnovis's position.

But Arnovis hadn't joined MS, and he wasn't going to join
MS. He told Peluca as much over the phone.

Yeah, yeah, Peluca said. But, you know, when they say something, that's how it is.

Peluca insisted that they get together the next day. Arnovis wasn't sure if it was a setup, but he couldn't say no. He'd already talked to his brother in Kansas about heading north, but they needed to raise the money first.

In the last year or so Peluca had been stopping by the turtle hatchery, where Arnovis worked nights, earning his $180 a month. The work was easy, but tiring—basically standing guard over sand-buried eggs, counting the coin-sized flippering babies when they hatched, and then hoofing them down to the shore—and he supplemented it with day labor he picked up when he could. The hatchery was isolated, miles down the beach from any paved road. You could get there by motor-cycle in about fifteen minutes on the hard littoral slick, or by way of a half-hour hack through thorns and weeds in the low jungle. Peluca would come around some nights because it was isolated, and he occasionally needed a place to lay low. He'd ask Arnovis for a cigarette, or some food, and if Arnovis had anything to share, he would. He couldn't exactly say no. Alone together for sometimes a couple hours, sometimes a whole night, next to the incubating turtles, they got to talking and became friendly. But Arnovis was nervous about being seen with him.

I asked him: But at night, in the hatchery, how would anybody even realize that Peluca was stopping by? They know, he told me. They know everything.

Operational control.

Arnovis told his partner where he was going to meet with Peluca the next day. He wanted someone to know his last whereabouts if he went missing. Those days, he later recounted, when he would sneak back to his house during the day, he was spending so much time clinging to Meybelín she was getting annoyed with him. Papá, let me go, she'd say, and he'd grip her tighter. Papá, stop! He'd win her over into a fit of giggling and, eventually, he'd let her go.

~

The next day Arnovis and Peluca were in an abandoned road-side shack that provided just enough shade to save them from the scorch of the sun. Arnovis could see the bulge of the pistol under Peluca's shirt. It was late afternoon.

You joined up, didn't you? Peluca said. You joined the Mierda Seca.

Mierda Seca, literally "Dry Shit," is one of the 18s' derogatory terms for MS. MS members, meanwhile, have their own terms for the 18s, among them Los Diecihoyos, or the Eightholes.

I'm supposed to take care of the situation, Peluca told him. But, I respect you. I respect your dad.

Peluca, as Arnovis described him to me, was a tough-looking guy. He was short, strong, had a couple of gold teeth and a huge "18" tattooed on his back. I'm not going to mess with you, Peluca told him, but when the next vatos come and wonder why I didn't fuck you up, you got to tell them something for me. You got to tell them that I showed up with a shotgun and two pistols, and that I put you on your knees and stuck one of my pistols in your mouth and rattled it around, and that you cried and cried and begged me not to kill you. You got to tell them all that—that I tried to get you to join. All right? Otherwise, I'm fucked. And so are you.

Arnovis agreed.

But if I were you I would just get out of here, if you know what I mean.

Arnovis knew what he meant. I asked him if he thought Peluca was trying to protect him. He was, he said, and he appreciated the favor, but he also knew that Peluca wasn't in charge, and he might have been able to stall a hit, but not deflect it entirely.

Arnovis knew that he was most vulnerable at night, which is why he had been sleeping away from home, spending the sour, dark nights in the damp shack or on the beach. But during the day, as he and his family planned his imminent escape, he needed to eat, and he wanted to sneak in more time with Meybelín. The day after his talk with Peluca, and after another sleepless night on the beach, Arnovis showed up at his parents' house around midmorning.

The family plot is divided by a small chicken fence, with two small one-room shacks on his parents' side, and a two-room home that includes a small corner store on his older brother's side. Each side has an outdoor kitchen, a small corral for the animals, plus outdoor storage for the plows, pumps, lumber, carts, bikes, and tools that the family and some neighbors share. It's all dappled by tropical shade from the palm, lime, avocado, anona, mango, coconut, and cashew trees growing in the sandy dirt that they rake every morning into piles of windfall branches and fronds to later be burned along with their garbage. The family also recently planted a dozen small chocolate trees in the coconut shade.

When I first visited, there were eight people living on his parents' half of the plot and around six—though with all the family traffic it was hard to get a straight count—living on his older brother's half. The mater- and paterfamilias were Pedro and Sonia, and then there were, between the two plots, three of their children, various in-laws, and five grandchildren. There were also eight dogs, a cat with a new litter, one rabbit, one parrot, two goats, about two dozen chickens with chicks, a handful of ducks with ducklings, and one piglet. In the heat of afternoons, the dogs would scratch off the hot top layer of dirt and splay themselves out for naps in the cooler dermal layers. Little rivulets of graywater from washing clothes and dishes trickled into a puddle between the plots, but, outside of rainy season, there were few mosquitoes. Slightly unkempt gardens—hard to control a plant in volcanic soil under the equatorial sun—were bursting in flower around both houses.

The actual houses are all small, with life revolving around the outdoor kitchens and the hammocks. Meal times were drawn out—the father eating in his hammock, Arnovis and Meybelín at the hot pink plastic table set up in the dirt shade, with Joana, Arnovis's partner, serving over the hot plate, and

Cecilia, Arnovis's fourteen-year-old niece, tending the wood fire and the tortillas. Family members and visitors milled, contributed, ate, netted themselves into hammocks, borrowed the bicycle, or merely passed through to say hello, drop off a chainsaw, borrow a hose, drink some water, and share news or gossip.

Arnovis had built his own one-room, dirt-floor home about thirty feet from his parents' house. His hut has concrete corner pillars with slat-board and bamboo walls—to allow the breeze through—and a corrugated metal roof. Inside are two rope-knot beds, a pink dresser for Meybelín, a hammock, an oar he carved himself, and one small wooden table, which he also built.

When Arnovis came onto the property the day after meeting with Peluca, he could tell something was wrong. Maybe, he thought, his family was just as nervous as he was. Maybe they had somehow heard about his meeting with a member of the 18s. Whatever it was, his brother-in-law, Miguel, came right up to him and told him he had to leave. For a moment Arnovis thought he had somehow offended him.

Just leave, Miguel told him. Just get out. You need to leave.

Yeah, I'm going.

Go soon.

Okay.

Miguel went back to a neighboring plot, and then Arnovis's mom told him what had happened the night before. Three guys had come looking for him. They saw a man about Arnovis's age who happened to be wearing a yellow Brazil jersey. Not the same jersey, but close to the one his Arsenal team wore the day Arnovis's elbow met El Monkey's mouth. That was convincing enough for the three men. They pulled Miguel out into the street and put a gun against his head.

You're dead, they told him.

You got the wrong guy.

You're Arnovis.

No. That's not me. You're making a mistake. Look at my ID.

Then where is he? One of the men raised a machete over his head, ready to swing.

I don't know.

Instead of killing him, they gave him a hard kick, and then took off.

Arnovis knew if they had found him instead of his brother-in-law, he'd already be dead.

And then things got worse, again. One of the three men who had pulled Miguel into the street thinking it was Arnovis was arrested the next day. They don't know why he was arrested, but, the family knew, the gang was going to think that Arnovis or Miguel had called the cops—that the arrest was their fault.

Later that day Arnovis saw a gangster named Gaveta on the road. ¿Qué pedo, chero? Gaveta said. What's up?

Arnovis gave him a thumbs up, tried to keep walking.

Hey, loco, Gaveta said. I want to talk to you.

MS was making another offer. Join up, Gaveta said. We'll protect you.

I don't know, Arnovis said.

Think about it.

But Arnovis didn't have to think. The threats were adding up, his situation spiraling. It was just a matter of time before they found him, before they went from warning to gunshot.

And yet you also wonder, for someone so poor that he had to borrow clothes for his high school graduation, and had to take a year off from school to work, did it ever did cross his mind to linger on those offers? After all, he shook hands and bumped fists with some of the guys who were already starting to collect renta, already sporting Nike Cortezes, already packing pistols. Arnovis wanted to be a soldier, he once told me, and the draw to the military doesn't seem far from the draw to the gangs—fraternity, regimen, violence. Another time, I noticed that the cover image for Arnovis's WhatsApp profile was a pair of white Nikes, a status symbol for gang members. I asked him about it. I like them, he told me.

That's it?

That's it.

But they're gang shoes, I pressed.

I just like the style.

I'd heard similar stories elsewhere on the migrant trails from other young men on the run. They had a few tattoos, dressed cholo style, hung out in cliques, sometimes even carried pistols —none of which Arnovis did—and swore they weren't gang members. Sometimes, it seemed the truth. Sometimes, they admitted they had been involved. Sometimes, style itself is a step toward status, or protection.

It didn't matter if Arnovis had thought about joining or if he did more than think about it. He had slipped into that total darkness: nowhere to go, nowhere to stay, and the merciless men-hunters were hunting.

He needed to leave now, with whatever money he had scraped together. To raise a bit more the family had sold a goat for three hundred dollars. And that would have to do. The problem, however, was that the easiest way off the island is by lancha—fiberglass motorboats with shade-cloths that ferry people through the mangrove inlets to Puerto Triunfo. Every morning, the lanchas depart every half hour from 4:30 to 7:00 a.m., in full view of the beach community—too conspicuous for someone trying to escape.

The exit route by land, a forty-minute haul through the dappled shade tunnel, wasn't much less visible or less risky. He didn't know how he was going to leave, but he knew he needed to leave before the 18s made good on their promise that he was tumba, or before MS got tired of him turning down their recruitment efforts, or before one of the guys who put a pistol against Miguel's head came looking for his own.

2

"Then fear drove out all intelligence from my mind," Ennius wrote. This is a common response for the individual, to choose muscle over mind to mitigate danger, but what is true for an individual does not hold true for a nation. When a nation fears, the political solution should not merely be muscular—to recoil or strike—but to consider the nature or cause of the fear. "There is need of deep, saving thought to go down into the depths like a diver," the king of Argos proclaims, as he is deciding an asylum claim in Aeschylus's tragedy, *The Suppliants*.

In 1933 Franklin D. Roosevelt warned of the *fear of fear*—"the only thing we have to fear is fear itself—nameless, unreasoning, unjustified terror which paralyzes needed efforts to convert retreat into advance"—so as not to succumb to a tepid national response to the challenges of the Great Depression. Six years later, he would deny safe harbor to over nine hundred Jews whose fear was not abstract or merely political, but fear of Nazi concentration camps. In that same decade, US immigration officials sprayed Zyklon B on Mexicans crossing El Paso's Santa Fe Bridge to delouse them.

One of the principal reasons countries limit refugees and deny asylum seekers is fear—fear that those individuals will do citizens harm. According to a 2018 Cato Institute study, the chance that an immigrant would be "mistakenly" let into the United States after being vetted by authorities and proceed to commit a terrorist attack is about 1 in 29 million. The chance of an American being killed by such an improperly vetted immigrant is even less probable: 1 in 328 million. You are much more likely to be struck by lightning—twice. That is, offering refugees a roof doesn't threaten your life, but denying them one threatens theirs. When the Trump administration in 2018 announced a new cut in the refugee quota, Bob Carey, a former senior official who oversaw refugee resettlement during the Obama administration, responded, "People will be harmed," he said. "People will die."

Countries are left with a choice when receiving asylum seekers: let them in or send them back. It's simple, and yet policy makers also consider long-term political consequences: To whom is the state responsible? What are the conditions in the country of origin? What about the receiving community? What about media optics, the next election?

The "real and intractable clash," as Matthew Gibney puts it in *The Ethics and Politics of Asylum*, is "between the claims of states (to self-determination, to cultural autonomy) and the claims of outsiders (to basic security, to greater economic prospects)." Whereas Gibney argues that "humanitarianism is a modest, sober, and painstakingly realistic criterion" by which to set asylum policy, humanitarianism is often a smokescreen. Consider the "humanitarianism" that drove the United States to welcome Cuban refugees at the same time it staged a Cuban invasion and slammed the door shut on fleeing Haitians. So-called humanitarianism typically plays second fiddle to politics and economics. Even judges and asylum officers fall prey. One study, by Banks Miller, Linda Camp Keith, and Jennifer S. Holmes, found that the employment rate in the metropolitan area where an immigration judge presides affects asylum decisions. That is, the higher the unemployment, the less of a chance the judge—charged with considering only the merits of the claim itself—is willing to grant asylum. The same study also found that the number of NGOs in the area can have "a profound effect on the likelihood that an applicant will be granted asylum." Another study, *Lives in the Balance* by Andrew I. Schoenholtz, Philip G. Schrag, and Jaya Ramji-Nogales, considered how an asylum officer's ethnicity, age, gender, marital status, region of birth, and education all influence decision making, and concluded that "the outcome for an individual applicant appears to depend, to a large extent, on the identity of the asylum officer to whom the case is randomly assigned." The immigration court system can be about as neutral as a wind sock.

It's not only our refugee and asylum policy consigning people to fear, torture, poverty, and death, but the global system of financial and traditional warfare, transnational corporatism, and human-induced climate change that's to blame for inciting an increase in refugee claims. "The way the universe of capital," Slavoj Žižek writes in *Refugees, Terror, Neighbors and Violence*, "relates to the freedom of movement of individuals is thus inherently contradictory: it needs 'free' individuals as cheap labor forces, but it simultaneously needs to control their movement since it cannot afford the same freedoms and rights for all people."

Gibney asks: "Should the obligations we have to foreigners and those we have to our fellow citizens be weighed on a common scale? Or have we, for example, a special responsibility to our compatriots—such as to ensure they have access to a welfare state—that might trump the claims of the human community"—of those outside our borders, knocking on our doors and asking for protection? It's one of the central questions of the ethics of immigration. As Martha Nussbaum puts it: "Fear, genetically first among the emotions, persists beneath all and infects them all, nibbling around the edges of love and reciprocity." Fear drives one to flee, at the same time that it nibbles and gnaws on our willingness to offer protection. It's a conundrum not only at the heart of refugee policy, but at the very heart of the nation-state.

The king of Argos, in Aeschylus's play, finishes his speech with a rhetorical question: "Is it not clear we must think deeply, or we perish?"

While asylees and refugees are often lumped together in common discourse, politically, they are miles apart. Asylum seekers have more visibility because they ask for protection once inside the country or at the border, and thus are used as easy political fodder: to startle voters or, more rarely, to invoke compassion. Refugees, meanwhile, are settled from abroad, and only come into contact with those affording them protection once they have already been vetted and accepted. Danger is the principal deciding factor in qualifying as a refugee. Fear, *well-founded fear*, is the principal factor for asylees. So one situation deals with the present (current danger); the other, with the future (fear of return). The lines, of course, tend to twist and knot. In responding to a refugee crisis, one state will work to remove the immediate danger by granting travel to the receiving state or constructing a refuge—often cramped and squalid camps—to "protect" the refugee. Meanwhile, the protection of an asylum seeker requires less a positive act than an act of omission: don't send them home.

Article 33 of the 1951 Refugee Convention, the cornerstone of asylum law, enshrined the principle of non-refoulement, a wonderfully vowelly French term, decreeing: "No Contracting State shall expel or return ('refouler') a refugee in any manner whatsoever to the frontiers of territories where his life or freedom would be threatened on account of his race, religion, nationality, membership of a particular social group or political opinion."

Though traditions of sanctuary, refuge, and welcoming the stranger go back millennia, and probably as deep into history as humans descend, it wasn't until the twentieth century that refugee and asylum laws were internationally codified. Since then, the concept of asylum has vacillated, but even while the legal definition serves as a guide, what's critical to those in need of protection isn't what's on paper, it's whether or not we open the door. Over the years, the gap between the definition of asylum and the application of its principles has widened into a chasm. It's why, in 2018 and 2019, as illegally denied asylum seekers piled up in Tijuana and other Mexican border cities, we began to see de facto refugee camps along the US-Mexico border; why the United States could attach the name "Migrant Protection Protocols" to a policy that dumps asylum seekers into dangerous Mexican border towns, leaving them the opposite of protected; and why the United States and Guatemala, El Salvador, and Honduras can sign what are effectively "safe third country" agreements to force asylum seekers who pass through those countries to apply there, even though the countries are themselves expelling tens of thousands of asylum seekers and are neither safe nor remotely equipped to handle asylum claims.

Another telling example of the chasm between the law on the books and its application: in 2018 the Harvard Law School Immigrant Defense Project published a report on the US government's misinterpretation of the "particularly serious crime bar" to withholding asylum in asylum proceedings. According to the 1951 Refugee Convention, applicants who have committed "a particularly serious crime" can be denied asylum, even if they can prove a well-founded fear of persecution. The United States, however, has been barring people who have committed only minor offenses—including filing false tax returns or failing to show up for court—denying asylum claims to those who pose no threat to public security and yet are at risk of grave danger and even death if they are returned, or *refouled*, to their home countries.

One woman from Sierra Leone who suffered a partial forced clitoridectomy was denied asylum for a conviction of selling less than an ounce of cocaine. And she wasn't the only woman consigned to sexual violence because of a technicality in the application of US asylum law. As Schoenholtz, Schrag, and Ramji-Nogales show, one judge found an asylum applicant credible and observed there was "a reasonable possibility" that she

43

would undergo female genital mutilation if she were deported to Senegal, but he ordered her removed anyway because she applied for asylum after the one-year filing deadline. In 2018, Attorney General Jeff Sessions went to even greater lengths to press judges to deny asylum to nearly all women who were fleeing domestic violence. Looking to "close a loophole" and limit the number of people staking asylum claims, one could put Sessions in the "originalist" camp of refugee philosophy—trying to adhere closely to the framers' original intent—as he claimed that asylum law was not intended to protect such women. But, much like the US Constitution, the Refugee Convention is a living document; it was dramatically updated and expanded in 1967, and some of the malleability was built in, as with the famously slippery *particular social group* clause: those persecuted because of their membership in a particular social group can qualify for asylum. The core of asylum is, and always has been, to protect.

"A decade ago, 1 in 100 border crossers was seeking asylum or humanitarian relief ... Now it's 1 in 3," the *Washington Post* noted in 2018. Despite what today seems to be a seasonal pattern of media frenzy about border crossings in the United States, this issue is not new—Mae Ngai writes about the "crisis atmosphere" surrounding immigration debates in, for example, the 1920–21 Congress. The nation is not liable to collapse because of immigration. And, it is critical to note, today's refugee crisis is not exclusively, or even mostly, American, though US policies play an outsized role both in sparking refugee and asylum crises and shaping and influencing global immigration politics. More migrants, refugees, and asylum seekers today are heading to Europe or toward urban centers in Asia and Africa than are descending on Arizona, Texas, or the American hinterlands. The United States is not even in the top five countries receiving the most refugees. In 2017, Turkey accepted more refugees than any other country in the world, followed by

Pakistan, Lebanon, Iran, Ethiopia, Kenya, and Uganda. In the same year, Uganda—with a gross domestic product roughly equal to the gross metropolitan product of Detroit and with a landmass about the size of Wyoming—took in more refugees than the entire United States. Relative to its GDP, Ethiopia hosts the greatest number of refugees in the world, followed by Pakistan. Measured in per capita terms, as of 2018, forty-nine countries accepted more asylum seekers and refugees than the United States. And as for total immigrant population, the United States, as of 2014, ranked sixty-fifth among other countries in percentage of foreign-born immigrants.

Meanwhile, since the fall of the Berlin Wall, according to geographer Reece Jones, the number of walls or fences along international borders has risen from fifteen to seventy. The International Organization for Migration concludes that around 40,000 people died attempting to cross a border between 2005 and 2014. A 2018 Associated Press study tallied 56,800 migrants who have died or gone missing just since 2014. Taken together, that's around 100,000 migrants dead in less than fifteen years, and those numbers may be only a fraction of the actual deaths and disappearances.

As more and more people throughout the world are finding their lives unlivable and moving across borders for an increasingly wide variety of reasons, receiving countries, including the United States, need to answer: As long as we're continuing to set fires on distant shores, will we open our doors to those fleeing the flames?

> Fear passes from man to man
> Unknowing,
> As one leaf passes its shudder
> To another.
>
> All at once the whole tree is trembling,
> And there is no sign of the wind.
>
> —Charles Simic

"The refugee crisis is something of a misnomer," Patrick Kingsley writes in *The New Odyssey*, his book tracing a Syrian asylum seeker's years-long journey to safety in Europe. "There is a crisis," Kingsley continues, "but it's one caused largely by our response to the refugees, rather than by the refugees themselves." It's an important distinction that shifts responsibility off the refugees and onto receiving communities. And yet, it singularly re-centers the *response* to refugees and neglects the *cause* behind their forced displacement. Without addressing the cause, focusing only on the response both shirks responsibility and keeps us a deadly step behind any semblance of a solution.

Refugees do embody a crisis. The word itself, *crisis*, comes from the Greek, *krinein*, meaning to separate or to cut. That word's first recorded usage dates back to Hippocrates's reference of the breaking point in a disease, when one either begins their recovery or takes a turn toward death. Refugees and asylum seekers live at this crisis point: they are cut off from their homes, cut off from their very lives, and can either be granted a new home and new life, or be denied and pushed back toward persecution and peril. The word *critic* has the same root: to cut, to separate, to discern. Politicians and judges are the ones who *discern* asylum claims: who gets approved and who doesn't, who's in and who takes the turn toward death. Interestingly, *crisis* and *criminal* have the same Indo-European root, which refers to those who are judged, cut off, and set apart. It is on this critical knife-edge that the asylum seeker balances. Author Gloria Anzaldúa similarly locates the refugee:

> This is her home
> this thin edge of
> barbwire.

Worldwide, in 2018, there were more than 70 million forcibly displaced people living on that thin edge. Most of them, over 40 million, were internally displaced, while another 26 million were refugees—people already settled or in the process of being settled in camps or receiving countries. Approximately 3.5 million were asylum seekers, with around 10 million officially stateless. How many, one might wonder, were *unofficially* stateless? How many had no state—no wing or roof—to protect them? How many were forcibly displaced and then rejected and deported, pushed off the knife-edge and left to fend for themselves?

"As migration worldwide soars to record highs," Lori Hinnant and Bram Janssen report for the *Associated Press*, "far less visible has been its toll: The tens of thousands of people who die or simply disappear during their journeys, never to be seen again. In most cases, nobody is keeping track. Barely counted in life, these people don't register in death, as if they never lived at all." The refugee's predicament is to flee to safety or to die: el norte or sos tumba.

But it is not only the refugee who's on the move. There's a reductive and false dichotomy that people often subscribe to when discussing international migration today: the insistent distinction between "legitimate" asylum seekers and economic migrants posing as refugees, a division sometimes reduced to either "bona fide" or "bogus" claimants. British authors Alexander Betts and Paul Collier fall into the trap: "Migrants [are] lured by hope; refugees [are] fleeing fear. Migrants hope for honeypots; refugees need havens." The sharp distinction also appears in the German terms *arbeitsmigration* and *fluchtmigration*— "work migration" and "flight migration." In reality, there is much blending, leapfrogging, and catalysis between the two categories. Take Arnovis: if the turtle hatchery had paid more than $180 a month, he would have had savings and could potentially have moved out of harm's way. Living hand to mouth, however, he would have only been able to afford to move somewhere equally overrun by gangs, where he would have been quickly identified and newly targeted. Many migrants in search of "honeypots" have hardly honey at all in their home countries; that lack renders them vulnerable and pushes them into danger.

One of many such examples I came across was the story of an impoverished Salvadoran nineteen-year-old, Ernesto, who, as an orphan growing up abused and neglected by his aunt, was unable to afford rent in a safe neighborhood in the city of Sonsonate, and repeatedly fell prey to the gangs. Searching for either a haven, a honeypot, or anything at all to get him away from his persecutors, Ernesto fled to the United States, was detained for eight months, and was eventually denied asylum. After he was deported, with mere dollars to his name, he had no other recourse but to return to his old barrio where, again, he was threatened by both gangs and the police, who suspected he was a gang member because of where he lived and because he had a few tattoos. When they arrested him, without charging him of any crime—he had committed none—the gang then suspected he was collaborating with the police. Poverty thus relegated him to becoming a "bona fide" asylum seeker. He was preparing his second trip to the United States when I met him, and, knowing his chances of gaining asylum after a previous deportation were nil, was intending to cross over undetected—an increasingly deadly endeavor.

Many deportees I spoke with described facing intense discrimination after being deported: because people assumed they had gotten into trouble in the United States, it was now even harder for them to find jobs, and they were thus consigned to live in poverty-wracked neighborhoods where they were targeted as newcomers by the gangs—all sparking a (sometimes second) asylum claim.

In a violent and warming world the rich can afford to protect themselves—with gated neighborhoods, getaway homes, and walled nations—and the poor are left with few options but climbing over the barriers and sometimes cramming their life stories into a sympathetic narrative. As other doors have been slammed on migrants by successive administrations—the "line" to get in has become so long and serpentine, it effectively serves as another wall—claims of fear are increasing.

This fear—whether genuine, enhanced, or fabricated—is the only currency besides actual currency (wealth) that will buy you entrance into the United States and other so-called developed countries. And migrants know it; that fear is their ticket. And so they claim it. And yet it is also fear—even when there is no longer a "sign of the wind," as poet Charles Simic (himself multiply displaced from his native Belgrade during World War II) puts it—that sets the "whole tree trembling," with countries responding to claims of fear by claiming their own fear, refusing to offer refuge and targeting asylum seekers.

The first cause of the crisis is ongoing transnational corporate capitalist and neocolonial despoilment (much more on that later) that upheaves countries and unroofs their people. The second crisis is the uprootedness itself—the refusal of a state to provide shelter. As climate change bears down in coming decades, as the global population grows, as inequality continues to rise, simply making more space under the roof will not be enough. We need to address the first cause, the first crisis. We need a "deep, saving thought" as Aeschylus put it—followed by quicker action.

Uprooted, unroofed, and ultimately unhomed: the 70 million people on the run in 2019 is only a fraction of the quarter billion estimated to be displaced by 2050. Some forecasts project two or more times as many. In denying these hundreds of millions of people protection, we are denying them not only a home, but a means of and a space for being. When they arrive to the gates and ask for protection—when they say, with clarity, "I can't live there"—by denying them asylum we are telling them, "Nor can you live here." And when there is no longer any safe or viable *here*, a person begins to sink into what Giorgio Agamben refers to as "bare life," into sheer biological existence. Picture refugees' repeated act of protest—in Australia in 2002, in Greece in 2015, or in the "Jungle" camp in Calais, France, in 2016—of sewing their lips together, the muted speech-act exemplifying their political reduction to less-than-human. The invalidation of their story, through its repeated denial, denies them entrance into the human community. Bare and tenuous biological life is what a judge, an immigration officer, a president consigns a refugee to by refusing to believe or listen to their story—calling their claim a hoax, calling them frauds, trying to cinch closed—a needle piercing through the flesh of the lips—the "loopholes."

For asylum seekers, originally dispossessed through violence or persecution, refugee protocols demand they tell a story in order to find a new home. When a judge denies a person asylum, they are redispossessing them not only of their story, but of what connects them to their home, the place where *being human* flourishes. They are denied their story and they are denied their very place in the world. Federico García Lorca, the revolutionary poet assassinated in 1936 during the Spanish Civil War, neatly captured the spirit of the multiply dispossessed in a frank staccato burst: *Pero yo ya no soy yo, ni mi casa es ya mi casa / But yet I am no longer me, nor is my home now my home.*

The dispossession, Lorca says, is existential.

3

I'm leaving, Arnovis said to his daughter.

He leaned down to her. Be good, he said, pulling her into his chest. I love you.

What else was there to say? Meybelín could tell, he told me, that he wasn't just leaving for the day or a few weeks. He could see it in her eyes. She knew. I love you, he said again, and then he backed away. Arnovis swung his leg over the motorcycle, and he could hear her crying behind him. Papi, she called out. Papi! Papi! Don't leave, she cried.

The family had paid fifteen dollars to one of Arnovis's uncles to help him escape by motorcycle. They'd also borrowed a helmet with a tinted face screen so he would be less recognizable, and—still entre chien et loup on that early morning in November 2017—he and his uncle zipped their way toward San Marcos Lempa, the elbow town on this side of the river. Riding over speed humps and potholes, avoiding sauntering cattle on their way to pasture, Arnovis's helmet occasionally clunked awkwardly, intimately, into his uncle's. Arnovis wanted to watch, to take in the landscape, to snatch one last view of the still bay, the twisted ceiba tree, the matutinal, flat gray profile of the volcano, but instead he just stared at the back of his uncle's head.

I was thinking, he said to me a year later, púchica (a common regional phrase, meaning something like "shoot," that Arnovis uses a lot), if I leave, maybe I'll be able to see Meybelín again, but if I stay, and they kill me, I'll definitely never see her again.

You will leave everything loved most dearly, Dante wrote in the fourteenth century. This is the arrow that the bow of exile shoots first.

Arnovis's mom, Sonia—a stout woman and blunt talker who runs the house, kitchen, and garden through quick labor and sharp commands, and who has one of the heartiest, most body-shaking laughs I've ever witnessed—left the same morning, but by lancha, and the two met a couple hours later in the city of Usulután.

Sonia bought her son a black knockoff Puma backpack for his clothes—two pairs of socks, two underwear, and one extra T-shirt. He didn't want to carry too much and stick out as a migrant. He also had an old Siemens phone, without internet connection, and $250 sewn into the collar of his shirt, another $50 in his pocket. Together, mother and son went to a Western Union to receive one last infusion of pocket money that his brother's friend had wired from Kansas. And then, before Arnovis boarded a bus heading to the San Marcos terminal in San Salvador—$1.50 fare—he bought a bottle of water and said goodbye to his mother.

Afterward, Sonia made the most of her trip to the mainland, as she later told me, to buy a few things: some coffee, sugar, other essentials you can't buy in Corral. Then—laughing at the memory—she sat down on a concrete bench and cried.

From the San Marcos terminal, Arnovis hailed a taxi and went to the central station in San Salvador where he boarded a PuertoBus heading toward and then across the border to Guatemala City. These were the first steps of a journey that tens of thousands of Salvadorans take every year, during which they fall prey to robbery, beatings, drowning, kidnapping, dehydration, starvation, murder, rape, arrest, prolonged detention, solitary confinement, psychological torture, extortion, forced labor, humiliation, and feelings of insecurity, abandonment, loss, aimlessness, hopelessness, constant danger, joy, pride, solidarity, confusion, and fear—according to what I've been told. On trouble's wing, Aeschylus wrote, you will find no two plumes alike.

For the next two months, before reaching the US border, Arnovis's story would follow his own singular horrors and hardships. At first, as he explained it, he didn't even know how to get where he was going—he only knew that it would be hard, and it was. He arrived in Guatemala City at ten that same night, took a taxi to a nearby hotel and, before he got out, asked the driver where to catch a bus for Mexico. La Línea Dorada, The Gold Line, the cabbie told him. First bus leaves at 4 a.m.

He paid eighty quetzales for a hotel and skipped dinner. I asked if he was hungry that night. Well, he said, sure I was. Why didn't you eat? No sé.

The next morning he got to the bus station early, purchased his ticket, and walked outside. There was a young woman selling coffee out of a large soup pot, along with sweet bread from a basket covered by a checkered green cloth. He bought a light breakfast. When I passed through the same station in Guatemala City, on my own early-morning bus ride about a year after Arnovis's, I tried the coffee and bread and thought of him, thought of taking a bus to a place that I don't know, not knowing how to get where I was going but *seeing with my feet*, as a migrant once explained it to me. What was it like to leave a place and no longer have a home, no roof or bed to return to?

Caminante, wanderer—Spanish poet Antonio Machado wrote —there is no road, you make the road by walking.

The pre-sweetened coffee that the woman served with a soup ladle, together with the vanilla muffin, cost Arnovis less than a dollar. The muffin crumb soaked up the hot liquid. As the bus downshifted and motored along the path between the volcanoes, heading north just as the sky was beginning to lighten, three young men a couple rows in front of Arnovis started talking about crossing the border. They recognized him as a migrant and, with some knowing locking of eyes, invited him to follow. A number of migrants have mentioned to me how they recognize fellow migrants, even in crowds, as they head north. A certain haircut, a mended backpack, the worn shoes, the darting eyes. A few hours later, as the bus approached the Mexican border, one of the young men went up to the driver and asked if he could let them off a little bit before the station. Arnovis got off the bus before the station, too. He followed the three men down the streets of Tecún Umán, a border city filled with bordellos, bars, fruit stands, cell phone stores, internet cafes, and money changers standing on corners flashing stacks of pesos and quetzales, with the green heat of the surrounding jungle pressing in on the rapid streets and occasional cloudbursts offering short-lived relief. Miguel Ángel Asturias, the Guatemalan Nobel Prize winner in literature, wrote of the eponymous Mayan king, Tecún Umán, he of the green towers, he of the tall green towers green, green green of the tall green towers ...

Along the Suchiate River, men and boys on clusters of rafts loaded and unloaded people, market goods, and animals. It's one of the iconic images of northward Central American migration: barefoot young men with long, gondolier-like poles pushing migrants and baskets and chickens across the river on rafts made up of boards lashed to the black inner tubes of giant tractor-trailer tires. Looming sometimes directly above the rafts is the bridge and the official border crossing. Arnovis paid his ferryman and asked how to find a ride north. The ferryman, really a ferryboy, told him where to catch a van that would skirt the immigration checkpoints. I asked Arnovis how he knew there would be checkpoints, and he told me he just knew, that there's a common knowledge of the migrant trail, basic things that everybody knows. Some of them, he would learn, were wrong.

The ferryboy told him to duck through the market, cross two aisles, pop out at the third aisle, head toward the road, and then there would be a white van parked on the near side of the lot, waiting for him. He thanked the kid, but was nervous, concerned it was a trap. That was another generally known truth about the migrant trails—that in Mexico migrants get kidnapped, held for ransom fees, and, if you can't pay, you wake up the next morning in a clandestine grave with flies in your mouth. It wasn't a trap. Arnovis boarded the van with about ten other passengers, some of them migrants, and they rode along the coast to Puerto Madero, then inland to Huixtla, up to Escuintla, the sunset's pink bruise over the low jungle, north to Pijijiapan, just past Tonalá and almost to Arriaga, where he planned to catch the train, the Beast. There, with night dropping its grays and blacks and the thrum of the crepuscular jungle just starting its racket, they hit a checkpoint. Maybe the driver didn't know about the checkpoint. Maybe he didn't care. A female officer opened the side door of the van and shined a red laser into Arnovis's eyes, ordering him to get out. He thought she was a federal police officer and only wanted a bribe, but, it turned out, she was an immigration officer. He was the only one they pulled out of the van.

They were nice, he told me. They never even handcuffed me. They gave me some food. They asked why I was in Mexico. I told them.

He spent a night in a small room outside Escuintla. It didn't seem like a prison: there were locks on the doors, but they were just regular doors. It looked like a house. The next morning they sent him south to Tapachula where he was deposited into the notoriously crowded, unsanitary, barely controlled open-air detention center known as Estación Migratoria Siglo XXI, or Migration Station Century XXI. One migrant had been detained there for so long he had established a small store inside—like a little pulpería, Arnovis said. The man sold fellow detainees Maruchan Ramen, cigarettes, soda, and drugs.

I've been told stories of Siglo XXI. Some of them, I assume, are wildly exaggerated, but the fervor with which the exaggerations are issued, it seems, must hit at some kernel of hard truth: that Siglo XXI is an awful place to be. I remember the director

of a humanitarian program in Honduras who talked to me, off
the record, about when he himself was fleeing north about ten
years earlier, was caught in Mexico, and sent to Siglo XXI. He
explained how wretched his experience was: there were people
doing drugs, drinking, threatening each other and getting in
fights, he told me, and the guards gave us almost no food. I was
painfully hungry for ten days, eating nothing but bean slop and
thin tortillas, and there were no bathrooms.

I stopped him. What do you mean there were no bathrooms?

There were no bathrooms.

You mean the bathrooms were so filthy you didn't want to
use them?

No, there were no bathrooms. No toilets.

And you were there ten days?

There weren't enough Hondurans to fill up a bus, so we
had to wait.

And in those ten days, when you had to go to the bathroom,
where did you go?

In the corner, on the walls, on the floor. It was disgusting.

I didn't press any more. The director was driving me, along
with a few recently deported migrants, along a broken road
in a rural part of Honduras. He was a respectable man, a boss
and community leader with a stable job, a home, a family, and
he was hotly exaggerating. Or, was he trying to convey something that can't be understood unless you live it or caricature
it? No home, no ground to push off from, no roof to shelter
under, no toilet to flush your waste. What but unflushable,
unburiable feces could more poignantly express the feeling of
homelessness, statelessness?

Siglo XXI does have bathrooms. I wasn't granted access to
see for myself—there seems to be a blanket policy of denying
entrance to journalists—but I've asked other migrants, including
Arnovis, and he told me that yes, there are bathrooms, though
he said that there were no stalls, and he had to defecate in front
of dozens of other people.

Before they locked Arnovis into the main barrack, where people slept at night on thin mattresses on the floor and hugged the walls during the day, one of the officials told him who the narcos were, who to look out for. Some of the people inside were, you know, Arnovis said, really tough. And, that first night, they were just smoking pot right out in the open.

Mexico has been both a transit country for migrants traveling north, as well as a destination country for years. But it wasn't until 2014 that it initiated a drastic change in immigration policy in response to the sharp increase in families and unaccompanied minors heading to the United States. (While many were unaccompanied, some had been "designated" as unaccompanied only after the Border Patrol separated them from extended family members or trusted friends—the word *separated* has gone through the same kind of transitive verbalization as *disappeared*.) That year, Mexico ramped up its own violent crackdown on undocumented migrants, installing more checkpoints on roads, hiring more immigration officials, and even planning segments of a wall between Mexico and Guatemala. The United States pressured Mexico to carry out the crackdown, as well as paid for some of it. As a result of the heightened enforcement, many migrants were pushed into increasingly remote crossing zones, where they fell prey to robbery and kidnapping—or were handed over to, robbed, or murdered by the police or immigration officials themselves; 2015 marked the first year that Mexico actually deported more undocumented Central Americans than the United States. In the fall of 2018, as Trump made outlandish claims about migrant caravans, sent troops to the border, and threatened to cut aid to Honduras and Guatemala (which he finally did in the spring of 2019), Mexican officials turned a convention center in Tapachula, Mexico, into an extension of Siglo XXI and locked up over 1,700 migrants in the pop-up prison. Many of them, according to reports, were tricked into walking into the Siglo XXI annex by officials who told them they could apply for asylum inside; they were not informed that once they entered, they couldn't leave again—a Calypso's welcome. A photo was leaked showing hundreds of red and blue camping tents set up inside an enormous open-air room into which the migrants were crammed. The new refugee camp didn't have water for bathing for the first few days, and some migrants were forced to share tents with strangers. The Trump administration, at the same time, earmarked $20 million in foreign assistance funds to pay bus and plane fares so Mexico could deport more Central Americans. In 2019, conditions got so bad and overcrowded in the original Siglo XXI that the guards lost control and there were multiple mass escapes, with around 600 people breaking out in one instance.

Back in 2017, after five nights in Siglo XXI, Arnovis became one of the nearly 100,000 Central Americans that year who were loaded onto a bus and shipped south. They were sent back to the places they had just fled. The world, for some of them, had become uninhabitable.

4

"I comprehend in this word *fear*," Thomas Hobbes wrote in 1651, as Europe was still smoldering after the Thirty Years' War, "a certain foresight of future evil." Nearly a fifth of the German population had just been killed, the modern borders of Europe were being formed at the Treaty of Westphalia, and Hobbes was contemplating how mutually recognized sovereignties might coexist. In fear of each other, he concluded, which may preempt wanton aggression, but is basically a call for perpetual cold war and can hardly be a comforting thought. Incident to the experience of fear, Hobbes wrote, is the inclination "to distrust, suspect, take heed," and to "provide so that many do not fear." But what about this last inducement? Does fear spark us to take care of each other? Can fear be both a selfish and unselfish motivator?

Hobbes saw fear as a critical motivator of any nation-state: "Those who go to sleep, shut their doors," he wrote. "Kingdoms guard their coasts and frontiers with forts and castles; cities are compact with walls, and all for fear of neighboring kingdoms and towns." It's revealing that today, despite people's frequent boasting of civilizational progress, Hobbes's description of a kingdom fortifying its borders could describe dozens of contemporary nation-states, including the United States, the United Kingdom, Mexico, Australia, and the European Union, to name a few modern states or state systems whose border politics can sometimes look more like those of medieval fiefdoms than of globalized twenty-first-century democracies. To steal a phrase from Freud: "Phobia is erected like a frontier fortification against the anxiety"—of the nation as much as the person. Other characteristics of the contemporary Western nation-state seem to be constant bomb-hurling, out-spewing of carbon, disposal of plastics, and the deracinating and dispossessing of foreign populations.

Migration, as writer Nicholas De Genova puts it, is "a central and constitutive fact of our global postcolonial present"—as are Hobbesian/Freudian castles and walls. Only the bona fide may pass.

It was only a few years ago that Corral de Mulas might as well have been an actual island. Until the government laid the "highway" in 2006, the only way out of Corral—except an hours-long haul across a dirt and sand-shifting road—was by lancha, the outboard-motor fiberglass boats built locally on La Pirraya Island. Before the highway, it was rare to even see a newspaper in Corral (I never saw one, even in 2019). And cell phones, none of them smart, hardly got signal. If you wanted news beyond neighborhood chatter, you had to take a boat to Puerto Triunfo. But then suddenly, in 2006, after the highway was laid, the little pulperías could stock their dozen shelves with snacks they didn't need to ferry over, and fresh vegetables were available via pickup truck—little mobile markets that still pass by twice a day, and to which the gangs charge a daily "vendor license" fee of ten dollars. Any resident who has a car or motorcycle can now feasibly make it to the nearest cities by land, or some of the regional dairy farms for work.

But the connective tissue of the highway, besides offering goods and a conduit to employment, also ushered in the gangs. Could the islands have avoided the violence if they had remained unpaved? It's possible, but not likely. There are complicated reasons for the development of gangs in the Northern Triangle—unemployment, the massive inpouring of weapons (mostly from the United States), deeply sown distrust for the police and the military, and the inurement to violence from recent wars—but disaffection and poverty were elemental to the gangs' incubation.

Unlike other types of mafias—the Japanese Yakuza, Italian Camorra, or the paramilitary cartels in Mexico—the gangs in Central America are more about identity, status, community, and culture than they are about trafficking and profit. Few gang members in MS-13 or Barrio 18 get rich. It's one reason why the politics of deportation aerated the fields so successfully for gang development. Both sides of forced displacement—home violence spurring initial flight and then US refusal and deportation—tore people from their homes, families, jobs, countries, and identity, and then, desperate and isolated, many of the recently migrated or deported sought new means of anchoring themselves to community. Especially in the United States, where both Barrio 18 and Mara Salvatrucha gangs were formed, the identities (and safety) of future members were challenged by the simmering racial tension and gang conflicts in Los Angeles. Nascent gangs offered the new arrivals protection, a "family," and a sense of belonging. Roberto Valencia, in his book *Carta desde Zacatraz*, traces the story of the late Salvadoran gang leader El Directo, who, at thirteen years old, was kicked out of his family and kicked in (or jumped in) to a gang *on the same day*. "Being a gang member was to have the support of everybody in the gang, the company of the men that rolled with us," El Directo explained to Valencia. "I don't know, the way we dressed, the *respect* of the neighborhood." Tens of thousands of young men followed a similar path. Politically, economically, or socially exiled, they found welcome in the gangs where they weren't finding it anywhere else.

"The majority of new gang members didn't need—and still don't need—to be forced or threatened in order to join," the Martínez brothers, Juan and Óscar, argue in *The Hollywood Kid*. "Poverty in Central America pushed them right into the gang's arms. The general misery, lack of opportunity, violence, and the nearly medieval living conditions, turned joining up with MS-13 into a completely logical choice. It's a choice between being nobody and being part of something. Of being a victim or a victimizer."

So the "highway" to Corral de Mulas didn't only truck vegetables in and let day-workers leave; it also opened the gates for locals to emigrate and for the gangs to establish a foothold. Before the highway, few people headed north to the United States, or they left only for a couple years, saved up and sent home remittances, and then returned. After the highway, as Arnovis and his mother told me one night as I was rocking in a hammock in their kitchen, people started leaving and not coming back. There were other factors, of course, but the timing coincides with a general simultaneous trend of "development" and tightened immigration enforcement: the contradictory pull of maquiladoras along the Mexican border, as well as in Central American cities, coinciding with the increasing militarization of both the international border and those same cities. The result was an effective lockdown—people were trapped in slums (in notoriously dangerous cities such as San Pedro Sula or Ciudad Juárez) or, if they had made it across the border, in the shadows of American towns and cities.

The "highway" to Corral de Mulas, for Corralites, became a one-way street: it was suddenly a cinch to get off the island, but it had become much trickier to return. Even today, there are no street names or addresses in the villages. You can't send a package to Corral de Mulas, or even a letter, but it's only two dollars to leave by lancha.

One of the stipulations for being eligible for asylum under US law is that the government in the country of origin is either unwilling or unable to protect you. The police in the Northern Triangle of Central America and Mexico—perhaps in no small part because of the United States' longstanding favoring and financial support of strong-arm, iron-fist rule—are not only corrupt but ineffective: another argument showcasing the governments' lack of political control. In Mexico, for example, according to a 2016 report, 93 percent of crimes go unreported. Of the cases that are reported, only 5 percent result in convictions; taken together, these figures mean there is less than a 1 percent chance that any crime will lead to a conviction. El Salvador doesn't fare much better, with a criminal conviction rate of less than 5 percent and with state security forces themselves responsible for over 10 percent of all violent deaths in 2017. In Honduras, the same: about 4 percent of homicides result in a conviction. For some context, in the same year the overall homicide conviction rate in the United States was 61.6 percent, though it varied greatly if the victim was white (63 percent) or Black or Hispanic (47 percent).

While traveling in Central America I often asked people I met the question: If you saw a crime being committed, would you call the police? Almost everybody I spoke with in the Northern Triangle told me they would definitely *not* call the police. They gave various reasons: that would be the stupidest thing they could do; it would aggravate the situation; it would place more people in danger; or it would simply be a waste of time. Sometimes I asked a more acute version of the question: What if, say, you heard your neighbor being raped? Would you call the police then? (This is not to assume that calling the police, anywhere, is the right response to witnessing a crime—the police's racially targeted violence in the United States makes calling them a poignantly bad option for many Americans, but the pervasive distrust of Central Americans of the police betrays, it seems, a more diverse set of fears.) The answer, inevitably, was no—almost nobody would call the police, even if they heard a neighbor's desperate screams.

If you're having an emergency, and something is happening to you, Arnovis told me, the police won't come. They might come two hours later … but they're not coming in five or ten minutes.

In a shelter in the Mexican state of Tabasco, one Honduran who had fled home told me that the cops in the Choloma neighborhood of San Pedro Sula do show up at crime scenes, but typically *before* the crimes occur. They come to scope out the scene and gather intel, he explained. Neighborhood residents know to stay inside and lock their doors when cops come around. Usually, fast on their heels, is a hit on someone: some gang members trying to take out a rival. The cops clear their way, provide security.

Earlier in 2016, before Arnovis's elbow clunked El Monkey's mouth, on one heat-sopping afternoon after he had come home from work, he had just dropped into a hammock to rest when a friend came around and asked if he wanted to play soccer. After lingering another moment in the shade, Arnovis jumped on the family bicycle, and the two of them headed to the fields.

Neither Arnovis nor his friend knew that the police were on the hunt for a couple alleged miscreants and that, struggling to find them, they were open to whatever prey they could sink their teeth into. A police truck zipped around the bend and came to a quick stop next to the two of them on their bikes. One of the officers got out of the cab and told Arnovis and his friend to get against the fence. A typical stop-and-frisk, Arnovis thought. But the cop, whom he recognized, was in the mood for something else.

A couple other kids—they were close to the schoolhouse—came up to see what was going on, and they were ordered against the fence as well. When one of them hesitated, the cop pushed him, and then gave him a kick. Arnovis—who, I've learned, isn't shy about calling out something he doesn't like—asked the officer why he had kicked the other kid.

And who the hell are you? the officer asked, approaching Arnovis.

Not trying to disrespect you, Arnovis said. Just asking why you were kicking him.

The officer pulled off the hat Arnovis was wearing and stuck it on the fence. Then he smacked him, hard, right on the side of his head. Arnovis's back had been turned to him, because that was how they had lined them up against the fence, and Arnovis turned around and told him he wasn't going to hit him from behind.

The commotion drew neighbors out of their homes. School had recently let out, and more students circled over to watch.

The cop unholstered his pistol. He didn't raise it, but a quick motion and a squeeze of the trigger was all it would have taken. Arnovis's father, Pedro, who had come out into the street, told the officer to take it easy. As more neighbors approached, the situation seemed to be spiraling out of control. The officer told Arnovis he was going to take him into the station, and said for him to hold out his hands so he could handcuff him. Arnovis refused. He knew that if he was handcuffed he wouldn't be able to defend himself, and that cops sometimes tossed handcuffed victims into the back of their trucks and later beat the hell out of them.

What crime did I commit? Arnovis asked. If you tell me I'm under arrest I'll get in your truck, but you're not putting me in handcuffs.

At that point Arnovis's brother-in-law, Miguel, came up. Miguel looks a lot like Arnovis, but with about forty pounds of extra muscle. I once saw him toss a large outboard motor over his shoulder, walk up the beach and up a flight of steps to put it into storage. The motor weighed well over two hundred pounds and he carried it like a bundle of linen. Besides having the extra muscle, their mother once told me, Miguel is also extra stubborn, and when he saw a cop with a gun drawn standing in front of his brother, he yelled at him to back off. The crowd kept swelling and the cop, seeming to have lost his advantage, gave up on arresting Arnovis, but he leaned in, and whispered to him that one day he was going to find him alone.

~

65

Not only is the state unwilling or unable to protect its citizens in many circumstances in Central America, it often does the opposite of protecting them. There are cases, Juan Martínez explained to me, where people will not only be unwilling to call the cops—he called it *unthinkable* in many situations —but they will actually call the gangs to settle disputes, especially those involving robbery or interfamilial violence. Sarah Chayes echoed the same idea in her groundbreaking report *When Corruption Is the Operating System: The Case of Honduras*, explaining that "in some cases, gangs serve as police auxiliaries."

Comedian Chris Rock once joked about how, since he was Black, he was against the cops, but, since he owned property, as he put it, he felt compelled to seek their protection. "So when my house gets broken into," he explained, "I'm not calling the *Crips*!" Chris Rock won't call the Crips because they don't wield governable levels of control over the neighborhoods they inhabit.

Max Weber defines the state as the entity that claims the legitimate use of violence within a given territory, and it's the gangs in many Central American neighborhoods that wield that stick. Gangs also claim the other defining attribute of a state—the entity that collects taxes. In Corral, just like in thousands of other cities, towns, and villages throughout the Northern Triangle, the gangs charge renta—extortion fees to businesses, street vendors, taxi drivers, and sometimes individuals. In Corral they target the supply and vegetable trucks. The political situation in Honduras after the country's 2017 presidential election (widely criticized as fraudulent) perhaps offers an illustrative example of the fundamental fragility of the state and the resulting power void that the gangs are able to fill. Before the election, President Juan Orlando Hernández (accused in 2019 of funding his first presidential campaign with drug money) had altered the constitution to be able to run for a second term as president. As JOH speciously claimed victory, the country descended into weeks of chaos and tear gas, with violent clashes erupting between body-armored state forces with guns and bandana-clad protesters with rocks, the people shouting ¡Fuera JOH!—Get out, JOH! Without the weapons or organizational unity to mount a sustained resistance against the state, the people resorted to burning tollbooths throughout the country. They wanted to make the streets—at least temporarily or symbolically—free.

James C. Scott, writing about the early origins of the state in his book *Against the Grain*, explains how a piratical relationship between raiders and a community can turn into something more stable and begin to approximate state organization: knowing that destroying a community would be killing the host that provides for them, raiders and pirates "are most likely to adjust their strategy to something that looks more like a 'protection racket.' In return for a portion of the trade goods, harvest, livestock, and other valuables, the raiders 'protect' the traders and communities against other raiders and, of course, against themselves. The relationship is analogous to endemism in diseases in which the pathogen makes a steady living from the host rather than killing it off ... In extracting a sustainable surplus from sedentary communities and fending off external attacks to protect its base, a stable protection racket like this is hard to distinguish from the archaic state itself."

In *The Hollywood Kid*, the Martínez brothers write: "In El Salvador, gang extortion ... is so pervasive that some multinational and transport companies have contracted ex-military and ex-police officers to work as gang liaisons. They don't even try to avoid paying the gangs. They just try to pay a reasonable *renta*. Some companies, with the bad luck of being based between MS and 18 territory, have to pay both gangs."

The Martínezes also describe police submitting to the authority of the Mara Salvatrucha. "In reality," they write, "the gangs are the state in some neighborhoods, counties, and villages." Mauricio Ramírez Landaverde, El Salvador's minister of justice and security, admitted as much to the *Wall Street Journal* in

2018 when he said that the gangs are so pervasive "you don't know where the state ends and the criminal organization begins."

The point is a critical one in terms of asylum policy. If you are persecuted on account of your opposition to the gangs—for resisting their recruitment efforts, or for refusing to pay their taxes—you are, in effect, staking a political opinion.

The so-called Central American gangs were founded in the 1980s in California as mostly Salvadoran war refugees attempted to settle into Los Angeles in the midst of a low-intensity race war. But it wasn't just the toxic neighborhood conditions born out of the legacy of severe racial and economic discrimination that fomented the gangs' development and empowerment—it was also US incarceration and deportation policies, mixed with US imperial interventions in El Salvador, that made an entire generation of young Salvadorans vulnerable, stripped them of their land, and gifted guns and money to ultra-conservative, ultra-violent state death squads, turning multiple generations against the established state and desperate for some sense of security. The embryonic self-protection groups, the gangs, first incubated in US prisons where race relations were even more volatile than in the streets. Then, these incipient gangs were sent back, person by person, in the thousands, to countries where the United States was actively supporting genocide, giving rise to what Roberto Valencia calls the "maleficent hate that traveled to Central America when the US government started the deportation centrifuge." Given the conditions in both Central America and Los Angeles, it would have been miraculous if the gangs had *not* formed.

As Tom Hayden put it in "When Deportation Is a Death Sentence," a 2004 article in the *Los Angeles Times*: "These young deportees are the fruits of war. They came to the United States as child refugees from conflicts sponsored by Washington, then formed gangs as homeless youths on the streets of Pico-Union [a central L.A. neighborhood]. When rounded up and deported to Honduras (or other countries in Central America), they become targets for rivals, vigilantes and police."

Hayden was writing during the implementation of a set of Honduran policies known as Mano Dura, or Iron Fist—still in effect today—which then president Ricardo Maduro says he learned from former New York City mayor Rudolph Giuliani: "Instead of taking the long route of accumulating proof of types of crimes committed," Maduro explained, "we opted to make it illegal to belong to gangs." Under a law passed after Maduro's election, having a tattoo was sufficient grounds for an arrest, and an arrest in Honduras can mean a severe police beating, years in dungeon-like prisons without conviction, and even death. The state in Central America is either unwilling to help or even actively seeking to harm and, for many, simply best avoided.

In the fall of 2018 I sat through an asylum hearing on the twelfth floor of a federal building in lower Manhattan for Alicia, the wife of a Salvadoran man who witnessed the murder of his neighbor, a police officer, outside his home. As elsewhere, a crime that the police in El Salvador do actually investigate vigorously is the murder of a fellow officer. On the day of the murder, when, later, officers came to the witness's house, he and Alicia were extremely nervous about being seen speaking to them. The man claimed he had seen nothing, which was technically true, as he had arrived to the scene immediately after the shooting. The police themselves acknowledged that it was dangerous for the man to be talking to them, and gave him a card with a number he could call and anonymously confess to what he had witnessed.

He never called, but, after the police arrested a few gang members allegedly involved with the killing, the threats started coming in against the family. Gang members showed up at their house, demanded money, flashed pistols, "borrowed" their van. They even told them they were going to sleep in their home—potentially a first attempt at taking it over—though the husband convinced them they had to leave. After his anxiety had pushed him to the brink, he concluded that his mere presence was putting his family at risk, and he moved out. The gang members then shifted their attention to his son and his wife. "You know we're the ones in charge here," one gang member told Alicia. "Do what we ask, or you and your kids are going to die." Her son, only ten years old, started receiving threats from upstart gang members in his class. The family couldn't handle it anymore, and, after over a year of threats, extortion, constant anxiety, and growing fear, they fled to the United States.

Alicia's attorney, Anne Pilsbury, argued that anyone who merely *talked to the police* had a protected status—they belonged to a "particular social group" in El Salvador. Reporting a crime, the argument went, is an "imputed political opinion." In this case, the judge agreed. "The fear is objectively well founded," he ruled, and granted Alicia asylum. As another Salvadoran woman whose son and husband were killed put it pointedly to the *New York Times*, not only are the authorities unable to provide protection, but, in some cases, "Talking to the police is a death sentence."

When you're not working, there's not much to do in Corral de Mulas but chat, wait for the breeze to blow away the heat of the day, or watch soccer. In the summer of 2018 I visited Arnovis and his family on three separate occasions, and once again in 2019, tailing Arnovis around the family property, jumping on the back of his motorcycle, helping lay bricks for his sister's house, and eating the delicious and simple food his mother and sisters prepared for the family: thick homemade tortillas from the family's corn plots, beans, eggs, and fish complemented with limes, cashew fruit, coconut, and anonas. Their hospitality, at times, was overwhelming: Pedro, Arnovis's father, would implacably insist that I take his spot in a hammock. I would eat three or four hearty meals a day while I stayed with them, and spent a lot of the time in and around the kitchen—the family hearth—where they cooked on a broad, dented comal propped up on bricks over a wood fire. At night, after a coffee, Arnovis would smoke and he and I would linger for hours under the single bare light bulb, sometimes until late at night, with the puppies (Crak and Grecia) and the piglet cuddling on the dirt floor beneath us. Sometimes we'd be joined for a while by his father, sometimes his partner, Joana, or sometimes his sister, Ale, but mostly it was his mother, Sonia, adding to the conversation, often laughing at something, telling a quick joke, or just sitting and listening. In these late-night talks Arnovis would tell me about his childhood, his three trips toward el norte, his time in detention, and his plans to head north again. Sonia, when she felt chatty, told elaborate stories of family members and neighbors and their troubles, or, one night, about giving birth to her children, which she did in the family shack without a doctor or a midwife. Arnovis, she told me, was born on Holy Thursday, after only a half hour of labor. She squatted down alone in the family hut and, as she said, just pushed him out. Her husband arrived soon after he was born, and Sonia sent him to find someone to cut the cord. There is one medical facility in Corral de Mulas, but it's only staffed, by either a single doctor or nurse, Monday through Friday. Outside those hours, you're on your own. If you have a heart attack after working hours, one neighbor said to me, you're dead.

On one of these nights, Arnovis and his mother told me about Tomás, Arnovis's cousin, who was disappeared in 2013. The long and convoluted story begins when Tomás refused to join the MS in Ceiba Doblada, a village about five miles up the peninsula. After he repeatedly rejected their recruitment overtures, the gang made a threat: either you join us or you die. Tomás told them no, and that they could try to kill him, but he wasn't going to go down without a fight. In retaliation, they took Tomás's younger brother, hauled him out to a remote cemetery in the mountains, and ordered him to start digging his own grave. Somehow, he escaped, and the family sent him into hiding in San Miguel. The gang then turned their attention back to Tomás, snagging him one day outside the cow stables where he worked, and then disappearing him.

Two months later, without a word of his whereabouts, after the family's search parties turned up nothing, the police announced that they had found his body. Arnovis's father went to identify the corpse, but it turned out to be the wrong body. Then, seven months later, the police came to the family again and told them, again, that they had found Tomás's corpse. This time they were right; Tomás, along with his saddle, had been buried in a clandestine grave.

The circle of violence in Corral de Mulas kept tightening around the family. In 2013, another young man, Jonathan, a neighbor and friend, was shot and killed one morning just a couple hundred yards from Arnovis's parents' house. For multiple people I spoke with on the island, this was the moment they realized that these murders were no longer anomalies, but part of a pattern of extortion, recruitment, threat, and homicide. Jonathan was twenty-one when he was killed by an elementary school teacher from Isla de Mendez. The teacher, who everybody knew as Profe Ale, had become the leader of a local MS clique. Profe Ale had been hounding Jonathan ever since they'd gotten into a dispute that the family didn't quite understand—maybe Jonathan had insulted the teacher, maybe he resisted recruitment, or maybe he'd simply seen something he shouldn't have seen, and hadn't kept quiet about it.

A couple days before Jonathan was killed, Arnovis, Jonathan, and a group of friends were playing soccer on a local field they had just finished trimming by machete, when an MS crew showed up and started asking around for Jonathan. Fortunately for him, the crew didn't know what he looked like. Also, Arnovis overheard who they were after and quickly told them Jonathan wasn't playing that day.

Jonathan didn't know the crew's mission and kept on playing. A few minutes later, Arnovis made his way over to him and told him, on the sly, that he needed to split. Not wanting to draw attention, Jonathan waited a while and then called out that he was going to go get some water. He borrowed a bicycle, pedaled away, and didn't come back. He started planning to head north right away, to flee.

That's all it takes, Arnovis told me: They start asking around for you, and you don't wait to find out what they want. You just leave. If you want to live, you leave.

But Jonathan didn't get gone quickly enough. Two days after the soccer incident, gang members found Jonathan between Arnovis's parents' house and the school, and they shot him to death. As his killers were leaving the scene, Mirna, Meybelín's mother, happened to be walking by with Meybelín on her hip. Meybelín was eighteen months at the time—now already witness to murder. Arnovis told me he doesn't think she remembers. Jonathan had a child, too, a son, who was only three months old when his father was killed.

I asked if the killing, heralding a change in Corral de Mulas, had made it into the papers. I had looked for it to try to confirm some of the details.

No, Sonia told me. They kill people like dogs here. That's how it is. If you want to live, you don't talk. It doesn't make it into the news.

Another prerequisite in order to gain asylum is the claimant's inability to relocate inside the country of origin: if you were persecuted or threatened in Corral, and you're able to safely relocate to Puerto Triunfo, or Usulután, or San Salvador, that potential safety valve makes you ineligible for asylum. So, naturally, I posed the question to many of the returned or potential asylum seekers in the Northern Triangle: Were you able to relocate and find safety elsewhere? The answer was almost invariably some version of: that's impossible, if you show up somewhere new and the gangs don't recognize you, they ask for your ID.

Alicia, the woman whose case I heard in the New York City immigration court, told the judge during her hearing, "I know, and everybody in El Salvador knows, that the gangs communicate with each other on a national level." I've even heard rumors that in Mexico, Los Zetas have a database that they check when migrants pass through their so-called safe houses.

I asked Arnovis if he could have relocated to Puerto Triunfo or San Salvador.

No, he told me, because if you're from here and you show up somewhere and they don't recognize you, they start investigating. They make calls … they have a huge system to identify people. In five minutes, they even know your birthday.

And then?

And then that's it.

Second Attempt

5

After he was deported from Mexico back to El Salvador, the problem for Arnovis was that he couldn't be there.

He was scared, ashamed, tired, hungry, and only had fourteen dollars in his pocket. Before calling his family to tell them that he hadn't made it, he spent a night in a scuzzy motel, La Estación, on the outskirts of Jiquilisco, where he recognized the crisis point he had reached. He had been on that knife-edge since he had received the first threat, but he was at home and in a rush then—with family and all its distractions—and then he was on the road, and then in detention, so this was the first time, as he explained it to me, that he really had the space to think. What conclusion did he come to? That it wasn't worth the risk, that he was as good as dead if he went back to Corral, and as much as he wanted to go back and see Meybelín and Mirna, along with the rest of the family, he didn't want to be dead. That was what he came to after a few hours in that dingy motel: that he needed to try for el norte again.

When I passed by La Estación, months after Arnovis's revelation, I wanted to stop in and take a look. I told one of the cleaning women I was thinking of staying there, and she let me poke my head in one of the rooms and glance into the bathroom —it was so small you'd have to keep the door open to use the sink. The room smelled like warm bleach, and instead of a bar of soap on the towel folded on the bed, there was a condom. A room cost six dollars for three hours, or ten dollars for a night.

Arnovis told me that they were price gouging me as a gringo, that he only paid eight dollars for his night of reflection.

The next morning, he called his brother to tell him he was back in El Salvador, and that he needed to leave again.

Arnovis always had sandals growing up—even if he often didn't bother to put them on—but didn't always have shoes. By the time his mother took him on a resupply trip off the island for the first time, at eight years old, he had already started working with his father. By the same age he was doing actual wage labor for which the family grew to depend on him. Using a wooden plow his father carved himself—and which still leans against Arnovis's shack—he guided two oxen to plow the family milpa of corn and beans. By the time he was ten he could plow a hundred-furrow field by himself, earning twelve dollars. Ten of those dollars would go to his family, and, with what was left, he would buy himself clothes and save up for belt buckles—he was growing a small collection. One of his favorite buckles bore an embossed skull with wings over a background of crossed pistols. His mom showed me a picture with him proudly thrusting his hips forward to show off that very buckle. He was wearing a cowboy hat, and they estimated that he was eleven at the time of the photo—already a working man.

Besides plowing fields, he also worked as a scarecrow for his grandfather. He would spend entire days completely alone in remote fields clapping away birds or trying to peg them with pebbles with his slingshot. I asked him what he thought about as he spent long hours alone. He had no phone, no books, and nothing but the sky and the silence to stare back at him. He told me that he talked to himself on those days, speaking about what he saw. A few times, when we were together, I caught him mumbling quietly to himself, and wondered if it was a habit he had developed while aiming his slingshot.

When he was in sixth grade, at thirteen years old, he took a year off from school to work full-time—a common practice on the islands. His older brother, in Kansas, attended even less school and to this day can't read or write. Arnovis learned construction and bricklaying and began working with his dad at the turtle hatchery. I didn't really have a childhood, he told me. I didn't have a chance to act like a kid. I was always with my dad. If my dad went to the store, I went with him. If he went to work, I went to work.

When he returned to school the next year, he sank back into his studies. He liked school and had a penchant for drama, performing Juan Gabriel songs to great hilarity. His mom laughed her deep body-shaking laugh as she told me about a time he dressed in full drag and sang in a school production. When he graduated from primary school in ninth grade, nineteen years old and sporting a thin goatee, he already had a sweetheart, Mirna, and everything seemed in order. They moved together into the one-room house that Arnovis had built himself.

When Mirna got pregnant, the first thing Arnovis wanted to do was go back to school, and he enrolled in classes. But when Meybelín was born, reality hit him quickly, and the needs of his young family drove Arnovis to leave school, again, to concentrate on work. Maybe he wasn't going to be able to get through school and get a good job, but he would, he promised himself, do whatever he could to give his daughter that chance.

Short and muscular, Arnovis often strolls around the property shirtless, half in and half out of his sandals, kicking around in the dirt. He has a soft, susurrus voice—with a shadow of a lisp —except when he laughs and a high-pitched whoop chirrups out of his chest. When he tells jokes, which is often, his lisp intensifies and he speaks rapidly, the words tumbling over each other. His excitement typically grows and propels him toward the end of the joke—I often had to ask him to repeat punch lines.

The local slang in these parts is often marked by the emphatic fillers *hn!* or *haah!* Almost everybody has a nickname, or multiple nicknames and diminutives—Gordo, Negro, Jo, Joa, Chendo, Che, Ceci. So, for such a rare, three-syllable name as Arnovis, it was surprising that I almost never heard anyone call him anything but Arnovis. (The Spanish pronunciation is with the hard-rolling *r*, and the last syllable is pronounced *veese*.) The second time I visited Corral de Mulas, his hands—thick with work—were covered in small cuts and splinters from working with the branches of thorny mongollano trees, which served as the posts for a barbed-wire fence he installed. He shrugged off the scratches when I asked about them, and then showed me his shoulder, where he had stacked the branches to carry. The scab running from his clavicle, up his shoulder, and down his back, was as thick as tire tread.

The first day I met him, as we were talking Meybelín came up and, impishly catching my eye, whispered in her father's ear, Coco. She had been pestering him all morning for another coconut. She's addicted, Arnovis said to me. Meybelín seemed unsure if being a coconut addict was a good thing or a bad thing, and pursed her lips thoughtfully, her right cheek dimpling. When I told her I'd like to become a coconut addict, she smiled, revealing a dark spot on her left front incisor. Most of that morning Meybelín had appeared almost in a daze, displaying a sort of wariness that seemed to go beyond typical youthful timidity. She would freeze sometimes if someone asked her a question, and would only be shaken back to the moment when her father called her name: *Meybelín!*

Arnovis is extremely close with his family. He and his father often sit together in the evening to talk and occasionally work together in the corn, bean, or cashew fields. He and his mother laugh and gossip together, and he and his sister love to rib each other—Ale has a hard punch, and if Arnovis jokes too hard about her suitors, she delivers him resonant, closed-fist wallops on his arm—and they all often fall into hammocks with each other, with Meybelín or Pedrito or Jason, the little ones, piling on top and hooking their limbs into the tangle. Trying to get a sense of what life was like before he couldn't live it, as Arnovis once described it to me, I asked what he liked about Corral.

He replied with descriptions that sounded like bucolic personal dating ads:

Before, when I could leave the house, I would look at the volcanoes, or go swimming in the bay.

I was on the community water rescue squad, and I once saved a child from drowning.

At night, when it was still safe, I would stroll with my family on the street in the evenings, visiting with neighbors, watching the shepherds bring their cattle back home.

It seemed a little twee, I thought, a calloused mind remembering halcyon days, but then one early evening when I was visiting, as the sky deepened to a gloaming indigo and the breeze finally started cutting the heat and I was swinging in a hammock between two coconut trees, I saw a young shepherd boy pass by on the street. Balancing on his bike, instead of pedaling to propel himself, he was hitching a ride by the tail of his last cow as they made their way home. He raised a hand to me and waved.

Arnovis hadn't wanted to leave. He never wanted to take the one-way "highway" out of Corral. He had wanted to finish building his house, add another room, work his plot of land, and harvest his corn and beans and cashews for his family. He had wanted to fish, watch his daughter grow up, and hang in his hammock in the evenings or stroll down the street to visit neighbors. Sometimes, he told me, when he was in flight—in a detention center or on the top of a train—he would think about what he would be doing if he were back at home. I would be together with my family, he said, relaxing after work, maybe watching television. That was the life he wanted. It was not the one he got.

After one night in the concrete-and-tile sex motel of La Estación, after the call to his family to tell them that he had failed, that he had been deported back to El Salvador, and that he didn't even have enough money to spend another night at the motel, an uncle who lived in the nearby village of Salinas de Sisiguayo came and picked Arnovis up. He would spend the next eight days without leaving his uncle's house, waiting for his brother in Kansas to gather the funds so he could try to go north again. Meybelín and Mirna came to spend a few days with him. He told me he was in a daze that whole time, pacing around the house, hardly taking anything in. His aunt and uncle thought he needed to disguise himself better this time, so he could slip by immigration officials: he should look more like a Mexican on a bus trip than a Salvadoran fleeing for his life. His uncle found him a pair of black Adod dress shoes and gave him a thin, long-sleeved collared shirt.

His brother arranged for him to go with a coyote, putting him in touch with someone he would meet at soon as he crossed into Mexico. His brother also had his friend wire five hundred dollars, and then Arnovis was off again, dressed, as he put it to me, like he was on his way to church. This time, he felt, he knew what was coming. Or at least there was less he didn't know.

I love you, he told Meybelín again. Be good … I love you. She cried again, and for this departure, Arnovis didn't have a helmet to hide his own tears.

Instead of heading straight north from Guatemala City he headed northeast, toward the jungle, the Petén.

It's a beautiful, hot, green drive along bursting curves and broken roads. You get the sense that you only need to turn your head, and the jungle brush would sprout up and gulp down the road before you looked again. This is one of the green hearts of the Mayans, where there remain pyramids and ruins from the ancient city of Tikal, or Yax Mutal, settlements dating back to 1000 BCE and where urban populations peaked, between the sixth and eighth centuries, at over one hundred thousand. Today, the Petén is a hot spot for narcos, after the source of cocaine shipments heading north shifted from the Caribbean to Central America in the 1980s and '90s, and, during the Guatemalan civil war, the United States propped up drug-trafficking military officers. In 1991, five years before the war ended, parts of the Petén were declared to be off-limits for development, according to the Law of Protected Areas, and even indigenous locals who had been living in the newly "protected" areas were forcibly removed by the military. The Nature Conservancy, an American NGO, used funds from USAID to purchase another huge swath of land in the Petén, which is now restricted for both developers and locals. Supposed efforts to combat climate change have incentivized companies to plant more African palm, as they are given tax breaks and reduced tariffs for investing in projects that reduce greenhouse gas emissions. But, as journalist Martha Pskowski has pointed out, cultivation of African palm "has been environmentally devastating in Petén." As agricultural barons squeeze out more indigenous people, they are replacing jungle with huge monocrop farms and engaging in what critics are calling ecocide: in 2015, a massive overflow from palm oil oxidation ponds spilled into the Pasión River, killing tens of thousands of fish and threatening dozens of indigenous villages. According to Pskowski, "from 1982 to 2010, Petén lost over 1.3 million acres of forest, during a time period when palm production expanded by 110,000 acres"—all of it further pushing people to take to the migrant trails.

A fellow migrant had warned Arnovis to have a fifty-quetzal bill ready to pay off the cops who would inevitably shake him down. When his bus halted at a checkpoint in the middle of the humid sting of the jungle, a cop ordered him and four Honduran men to get off and line up on the side of the road. Arnovis and his fellow travelers had their fifty quetzales already folded behind their IDs. The cop took their IDs, gave them a perfunctory glance, and then handed them back. Muy bien, he said, pocketing the money. Get back on the bus.

I asked Arnovis about that moment. It was the first time he had ever bribed anybody, and he said he was nervous. The last time he'd been lined up by a police officer he got a smack to the head and a gun drawn on him. He hadn't known if the bribe was going to work, or how it was going to work, but afterward, he told me, it felt like an accomplishment. *I had to fight so hard to survive*, he said. *It makes you mad, but, at the same time you realize you're strong. You're stronger than you imagined.* Think about it, somebody could tell me, *If you don't leave right now, tomorrow you're going to be killed.* And I could leave. I put on my shoes and leave. I don't know how to get there, but I get there.

When he arrived to La Técnica, on the border with the state of Chiapas, he learned that the system of coyotes and smuggling services was operated through the hotels. *You just show up at the hotel,* as he explained it to me, *and they ask you, Are you going north? (Everybody is going north.) You have to pay half up front, one hundred fifty quetzales, and then the other half before you get on the boat.*

Early the next morning, in Técnica, he joined a group of migrants gathered around a row of narrow lanchas: pregnant women, old people, little kids, and other young men like him standing in the humid, predawn darkness. Arnovis thought they were going to divide up into the different lanchas, but they all piled into one, all thirty of them, or maybe more than thirty, he guessed. They were packed in tight, and the lancha was riding low, the gunwale almost level with the tepid brown river water. *And then we just took off,* he said, *riding so fast. I think we rode for about four hours, and then we stopped in a little village close to Villahermosa. It was an indigenous village, almost nobody there spoke Spanish.*

About eight months after Arnovis crossed into Mexico for the second time, I tried to trace his footsteps, finding the isolated spot along the Usumacinta River where, given his descriptions, I approximated the point where he crossed. After a bumping, zigzagging tuk-tuk ride down a broken, narrow dirt road, I met a fifteen-year-old lanchero named Alberto. He looked no older than twelve, but he'd been working that river, he told me, since he was a kid. He would charge twenty pesos to motor me to the next village upriver. A woman and her young son were waiting patiently in the lancha, and after coming to terms that we'd be his only passengers for a while, the young lanchero pushed us off the bank, pulled hard on the motor cord, and pointed the bow north. The sun was knifing down from the open pan of the sky, and I dipped my hand into the opaque warm water, splashing my face and neck to palliate the burn. Alberto told me how, sometimes, without warning, there are periods when dozens and dozens of migrants come and need rides upriver, and then, also without warning, hardly any migrants will come for weeks at a time. The locals, he told me, can cross the border back and forth away from the official port of entry; nobody ever asks them for papers. We dropped the woman and her son off, and then I paid another twenty pesos for Alberto to take me downriver, back to Guatemala. After I disembarked, I took a few photos and sent them to Arnovis, asking if it looked like where he'd crossed.

Pretty much, he said.

One of the most notorious perils of traveling to the United States from Central America or southern Mexico is the Beast, the system of freight trains to which migrants cling to get a free but dangerous and sometimes deadly ride north. Arnovis rode the trains, by his count, at least four times. His coyote had found him again in Palenque, where he had also met a young woman, twenty-six, who was traveling with her sixteen-month-old daughter, Valeria. The way it worked, the coyote explained, was that he himself wasn't going to ride the trains but would meet his *pollos*, or chickens, in the destination cities, where they would pay him for places to sleep and for dealing with the cartels. Since Valeria was so young, however, and since Valeria's mom was so nervous, the coyote asked Arnovis if he would look after them, offering Arnovis a discount for doing so.

Once, the three of them had to jump on the train when it was already rolling. Arnovis had Valeria in his arms, and her backpack on his back. Valeria's mother climbed aboard first, and then Arnovis ran behind her, jumped up with one arm, and handed up Valeria.

How dangerous was it? I asked. What were the odds you could have dropped Valeria?

I wasn't going to drop Valeria.

Right, but it's a hard maneuver—to get on a moving train with only one hand while holding a child. It's possible you could have dropped her.

I wasn't going to drop her.

Arnovis told me about a few times when, heading north through Mexico, the coyotes got wasted. They'd pound cheap beers and gas station mezcal and then get high, and all the migrants would watch them nervously, not knowing where the ribaldry would lead. One night, in Mexico City, when there were only a couple other migrants in a safe house and they were waiting a few days to head north, the coyotes got so drunk they blacked out. They had weapons, food, a television, and probably some cash, as well as cell phones. Having made friends with them, they had let Arnovis out of the locked room the other migrants were confined to. He could have made off with the loot, but he didn't. They trusted me after that, he said.

And that was helpful for you?

Everything helps, he said. It's survival.

But why does an asylum seeker even need to crawl onto the top of a freight train, gain the trust of a coyote, swim across a swift river, walk through the jungle or the desert, and languish for days with little food in a cramped safe house run by murderous young men? Isn't there a more orderly and safer way to ask the United States for protection?

Journalist Danielle Mackey, in a 2017 article for *HuffPost*, wrote about the bureaucratic morass that was failing desperate Salvadorans, even after the United States had worked with the United Nations to supposedly make it easier for asylum seekers to apply for protected status. The program that emerged, the Protection Transfer Agreement (PTA), was intended to let asylum seekers from the Northern Triangle of Central America get "pre-screened," sent to safety in Costa Rica if they were found to be eligible, and then eventually shipped on to the United States or another receiving country. Six months after the launch of the program, Mackey reported, it had only assisted a single family. All the other applicants had been delayed or denied. The problem is that it takes too much wait time for an agency to process a claim, conduct the prescreening, and send info back and forth from Central America to the Department of Homeland Security. And time is what asylum seekers don't have. As Mackey puts it: "Death threats here have short grace periods."

In 2018 I spoke with an official in a small office in a Honduran city about the state of the PTA in Honduras, which had been initiated a year previously. (The official demanded complete anonymity before agreeing to speak with me, even asking that I not name the city we were in.) At the time of the interview, though an NGO partner had identified approximately eighty potential asylees, not a single Honduran had been granted protection. Twenty-five of them had been deemed inadmissible because of a prior deportation, a criminal conviction, or having been merely charged with some sort of gang affiliation. The rest of the nearly sixty cases were either stalled out or denied for unknown reasons, the official said. The whole program is choked by such secrecy that the actual applicants didn't even know to what country they were applying for asylum: the officials explain to claimants that there are multiple participating countries, though only the United States has signed on—ostensibly—to receive Honduran asylum seekers. "If everybody knew about the program, half of Honduras would show up at our office," the official told me. But it wasn't just fear of being overwhelmed with applicants. If the American taxpayers or American politicians —or Donald Trump, as the official quipped—knew about the program, it would probably get shut down.

This model—transporting potential asylees to temporary safe places—has precedent. In the United States, it's known as the "Guam option," after thousands of Vietnamese were transported to the US territory of Guam during the Vietnam War to await processing and resettlement in the mainland. In the 1990s, the United States also sent Iraqi Kurds to Guam for processing, and the United Nations currently has a similar emergency waiting room in Romania for hopeful refugees worldwide.

The danger and difficulty involved in staking an asylum claim is not exclusive to one particular region. The sea journeys tens of thousands of Africans and Middle Easterners take every year are, though extremely dangerous, effectively the only way for most people to make asylum claims in Europe after Hungary and other Balkan countries walled and fenced off entry to Central Europe, and the European Union offers few other avenues of relief. Melissa Fleming, the chief spokesperson for the UNHCR, expertly captures the extreme danger of making an asylum claim in Europe in her book *A Hope More Powerful Than the Sea*. She tells the true story of Doaa, a young Syrian woman hoping to find safety in Europe with her fiancé when their boat is sabotaged at sea—piratical smugglers had rammed their boat, and of the five hundred passengers, only a handful survived. The rest were chopped to pieces by the propeller, or drowned. Doaa watched as her fiancé weakened, slipped away, and sank into the sea. Incredibly, she survived for four more days, floating on a small inner tube with two young children— neither of whom were her own—balanced on her chest. The scene calls to mind a line from American poet Ocean Vuong, from "Immigrant Haibun": "That a woman on a sinking ship becomes a life raft—no matter how soft her skin."

Doaa said she was "outraged that the bottom of the sea was the only place five hundred refugees, including the man she loved, could find refuge."

"No person fleeing conflict or persecution should have to die trying to reach safety," Fleming writes, and yet, every year, thousands die drowning in the sea (in 2016, over five thousand migrants died just while crossing the Mediterranean) or dehydrating in the desert, falling under the wheels of the Beast, or getting kidnapped and buried in shallow graves as they look for safety.

The town of El Ceibo is a relatively easy spot to skirt immigration authorities and cross from Guatemala into Mexico. But it's still a two- or three-day walk from there to the first migrant shelter—which is maybe better termed a *refugee camp*—and only a short first stage of the extended journey through Mexico, which has long been an inferno for Central American migrants and refugees.

In continuing to trace Arnovis's journey, I caught a combi, a taxi van, to El Ceibo for fifty quetzales. The vehicle was parked in the hectic shade of the central market in Flores, Petén, right on Lake Petén Itzá. I asked the driver's assistant how close to the Mexican border they could drop me off and then— hesitantly—asked him if he knew how I could get across. I'd never queried a coyote before and was nervous, but it was just part of the job for him. He asked me if I needed a guide or just someone to explain how to go it alone. I told him I wasn't sure but probably wanted a guide. Okay, he said. He'd call a guy. I asked how much? Another fifty Qs.

And it's safe? I asked.

Of course it is.

We headed west and slightly north for about five hours, passing through a landscape of hillocks and humps, an infinite variety of green-on-green rolling hills occasionally cut by the gray of the sputtering road or the brown spill of a river. Bananas,

African palm, the occasional swollen ramrod of a ceiba trunk, vines and thick underbrush broken by small towns with open-air sundry stores, fried-chicken stalls, and the inevitable tire-patch shops—vulcanizadoras—at each end of town. The AC-less combi took a break halfway through the trip, and most of the passengers, myself included, assailed a vendor to buy Cokes and fried bananas. I was nervous the whole ride and, as if the details could somehow protect me, I tried to memorize faces, clothes, roads, and passing place names, taking multiple screenshots of my GPS location on my phone. I can still see the elegant line, like a chevron, shaved into the back of the driver's closely buzzed hairline, and the brightly colored threads on the ripped fake designer jeans of the driver's assistant, and his attached earlobes with little glimmering dots of fake diamonds. These are the specifics, I told myself, that could singularly identify someone. These are the details that convince a listener, a reader, or a judge. And I thought of Arnovis, on a similar bus, similarly nervous, and wondered how long your nerves can sustain that level of alertness, how long before you start to relax, or acclimatize, or fray. By the end of the fourth hour I had pulled out the novel I was reading, *The Unnameable*, and found Beckett's visions of anomie and solitary misery eerily relevant and still, somehow, supremely beautiful.

At the turnoff to El Naranjo, the driver's assistant eyed me and called back, *Mister!* The combi came to a quick stop and I was pointed to a van that would take me the rest of the way to El Ceibo. I boarded it and rode for another twenty minutes, until the young driver stopped to pass some cash to a woman at a roadside motel, and then pulled up close to the border-line. The few other passengers got out, and six tuk-tuk drivers crowded around me.

You don't have papers? they asked, seemingly gleeful to catch a gringo in such a predicament. Fredy, the man the assistant driver had called, and who had been waiting for me, shoved through the crowd and told me to come with him. I didn't move. It took some explaining, but I finally laid out that I was a journalist and wanted not just a clandestine crossing, but a clandestine crossing that went round-trip. He said it would be no problem, and we peeled away from the other drivers. The cost was fifty Qs, which is what everything cost that day. Fredy's friend, Gerónimo—another tuk-tuk driver—offered to tag along, and I accepted, wanting all the company I could get.

Is it safe? I asked again.

Of course.

Fredy and Gerónimo, both twenty-one, were thin and thinly mustached eager young men in sandals, shorts, ball caps, and T-shirts. Fredy led the way, insisting on wearing my larger backpack. Gerónimo went next, and I followed behind with my small pack as we stepped off the road and onto the narrow cowpath cut into the weeds and high grass.

I asked as many questions as I could think of. How many migrants a day? Where are the migrants from? What about Mexican authorities? What about narcos? Drugs? Locals crossing over? Gangs? Robberies? Snakes? US presence? Do people talk about building a wall? Their answers were short, and mostly some version of a little, un poco. There are poco narcos, poco robberies, poco crackdowns, poco locals, poco gangs, a wall is occasionally discussed, and they had heard of US officials sneaking around. Just un poco, though. Fredy and Gerónimo worked with a group of fifteen or so young coyotes/tuk-tuk drivers who guided, they estimated, between thirty and fifty migrants a day. It used to be a lot more. Before the migra got so strict, Fredy said, they used to guide over a hundred a day.

We broke into the woods and started climbing a steep, shadowed path. The shaded jungle seemed further shadowed by the clouds of mosquitoes. A pair of curraca birds squawked and bolted out of a bush. Breathing in the thickly humid air, trying to keep my wits, trying to keep up with my guides, I noticed about a dozen mosquitoes were riding on Gerónimo's back. I wanted to reach forward and swipe them off, and almost did, but wasn't sure how he would take the gesture. We had hardly met, and he was, un poco, my coyote—I didn't know the etiquette of the relationship. I thought, too, as we were walking, of La Arrocera, the notoriously dangerous path in the neighboring Mexican state of Chiapas that migrants take to skirt immigration checkpoints. Óscar Martínez described migrants he spoke with spotting a human skull in La Arrocera and recognizing that it was the site of a murder. "Bones here aren't a metaphor for what's past, but for what's coming," Martínez writes. I thought I had the advantage—if we, or just I, suddenly needed to run—of being in shoes, while Fredy and Gerónimo were both in sandals. I thought of the mosquito bites I was going to be scratching that night—they were sucking out blood right through my shirt. And then we broke back out onto the street, already in Mexico. My forty-minute journalistic jaunt, my tousled nerves, constituted, comparatively, an infinitesimally small portion of the long, impossible journey that migrants take.

I still had a day ahead of me—a return walk, which included spotting howler monkeys in the canopy above us, finding the water crossing that Arnovis took to get north of Tenosique, and hitching a ride to the next town—but, later, as I crossed the border for the third time that day, crossing legally into Mexico, all I had to do was flash my passport, open my bag, and, further north at the military checkpoint, smile and offer a quick explanation of my comings. And then I had a hotel to check in to, a torta to satisfy my hunger, a shower to rinse off the sweat, and a glass of rum to calm my nerves. The migrants taking that same mosquito-clouded "jaunt" were barely, *barely*, getting started. Most of them would have to continue the walk for another thirty miles north through the jungle bogs to the shelter in Tenosique. There were signs posted at bus stops throughout town, reminding people that if their lives were in danger in their home countries, they had the right to ask for asylum. In Mexican novelist Emiliano Monge's terrifying and moving *Las tierras arrasadas* (recently translated into English by Frank

Wynne as *Among the Lost*), a group of Central Americans cross at a similar—maybe the same—spot into southern Mexico and enter into a landscape of horrors. In the novel, Monge tells an *Inferno*-esque story that draws from both Dante and interviews he conducted with Central American migrants. One passage reads: "For those who have come from other lands comes *the gnashing of a thousand fearful teeth.*"

The howler monkeys, too, Fredy told me, crossed the border back and forth. Nobody, he said, making a joke, checks their papers.

In 2018, the United States tried to convince Mexico to join it in a "safe third country agreement," in which the two nations would regard one another as safe places for asylum seekers to make claims and, for those in need, receive protection. At its core, the agreement was really about the United States further foisting refugee protections onto Mexico, precluding any potential asylum seeker who passed through Mexico of making a claim for US protection. In 2004, the United States and Canada signed such an agreement, meaning that for the majority of Mexicans and Central Americans who cannot get to Canada without passing through the United States first (due to what are called "carrier sanctions"—heavy fines and penalties imposed on airlines for selling a ticket to someone who doesn't have a visa), their only option for asking for asylum was to do it in the United States. The problem, however, is that Mexico is not a safe country for asylum seekers. The horrific mass murder of migrants in San Fernando, Tamaulipas, in 2010, in which seventy-two migrants were slaughtered, is but a high-profile example of the country's systemic violence; many tens of thousands more migrants have been killed, kidnapped, tortured, enslaved, raped, robbed, or disappeared. And, despite facing systemic discrimination, if an asylum seeker does decide to make a claim in Mexico, they have to face bureaucratic obstacles nearly as formidable as the physical dangers. Aldo Vega, a Mexican human rights attorney working at La 72 migrant shelter in Tabasco, told me about a case of agents from the state attorney general's office who had actually kidnapped an entire family.

After the Trump administration made repeated threats and ultimatums in the summer of 2019 to embattled and outgoing Guatemalan president Jimmy Morales, Guatemalan officials agreed to sign a "safe third" agreement, despite the Guatemalan congress deeming its passage illegal. Next in line, with direct threats of the suspension of aid, were both El Salvador and Honduras. If Mexico isn't a safe country for asylum seekers, Guatemala is even less so: in 2019 the country only had twelve people working in its asylum office, and approved a total of only twenty claims the year before. Meanwhile, between 2017 and 2018, nearly fifty thousand Guatemalans fled their country to apply for asylum in the United States. El Salvador, meanwhile, had only a single official processing asylum claims. And, in 2019, calling Honduras a "safe country" for anybody is like calling a minefield a nice spot to have a picnic.

Two days after I crossed the border from Guatemala to Mexico, I spoke with Gerber Iván Lima Gomez, a thirty-year-old Guatemalan man who had fled Guatemala City after months of persecution, the firebombing of his house, and the discovery of a note left on his door promising his murder. Gerber was thin and back-hunched and wore a purple tank top when we sat down together in orange plastic-and-metal elementary school chairs near the outdoor kitchen in La 72. He had worked for ten years for a public health NGO, specializing in LGBTQ youth, and had to flee when a local gang tried to recruit him to start selling drugs to his own clients. He told me that he had fled immediately—after finding the note with the death threat—and wasn't even able to go to his house to pack clothes. He had taken the same path from El Ceibo I walked a couple days before, but he did it at night, and it took him much longer.

His guide made him pay two hundred quetzales up front, four times what they charged me. The coyote walked with a single flashlight, and Gerber had trouble seeing, slipping repeatedly on the muddy path. The mosquitoes were atrocious, he said, and when he tried to slap at them on his neck, face, and arms, he only slipped more. At one point, the guide stopped in the middle of the darkness, turned off the flashlight, and told him that if he didn't give him another two hundred quetzales right then, he was going to abandon him in the jungle. Gerber dug into his sock, fumbled with his cash, and forked over most of what he had left. A little while later they came out of the darkness and were only a few hundred yards away from the port of entry. His guide, who had completed his job, turned around and disappeared back into woods. He got lucky after that, snuck through the checkpoint on a bus, and then found his way to La 72 migrant shelter, where he would spend the next thirteen months fighting for asylum in Mexico.

The shelter, named in honor of the seventy-two migrants who were murdered in the San Fernando Massacre in 2010, feels like a small village: there's a women's building, a LGBTQ building, a family building, a kids' building, administrative offices, a medical office, a psychologist, a concrete soccer court, clusters of tables and chairs around which people mill and do laundry and line up for services and food, or lie on the concrete to catch up on sleep. La 72's chapel—the cross on the wall has a mass grave painted on it—is for overflow, with about fifty thin mats stacked along the wall. Some nights, well over one hundred migrants and refugees sleep in La 72.

Gerber's case was approved in February of 2018, but he wasn't informed that it had been approved until two months later, in April. When we spoke in early September of the same year, he was still waiting for his final residency card and work permit so he could travel freely to support himself. In the last thirteen months he had lost significant weight, gotten seriously ill from eating undercooked meat, felt consistently stressed, anxious, and sleepless, and claimed he had to deal almost constantly with discrimination and incompetence from UN officials, Red Cross officials, public health officials, Mexican immigration officials, and fellow migrants in the shelter who tried to help him or said they were trying to help him. He told me he still feared for his life, and, if he ever actually received his papers, he was hoping to make it to Mexico City.

I don't think I've ever come across someone so visibly exasperated by bureaucratic runaround, deteriorated physical health, and a perilously nagging fear of death. After he finished his story, Gerber's jaw dropped and he sank further into his hunch. At one point he seemed to be about to laugh at his predicament, but, instead, a sob gulped out of his throat. He told me about a doctor he visited who, when Gerber presented with symptoms of salmonellosis (from the undercooked meat), told him—noting to him that he was gay—that he had HIV, probably even AIDS, and he should start treatment right away. Having worked for ten years in sexual health, Gerber knew he didn't have HIV or AIDS and, stricken by the display of vile ignorance, thanked the doctor and left. He later filed a complaint. Given the limbo that such discrimination had placed him in, I asked him why he wouldn't just head north himself, take the train, go to the United States.

The train, no. Just no, he told me. It's not for everyone.

Considering the dangers of riding on top of a cargo train, it *should be* for no one. No one can say how many lives the Beast has claimed over the years. There aren't statistics for how many people fall off and are mutilated or killed by the metal scream of the wheels. One of the Honduran men Óscar Martínez profiled in his book *The Beast*, Jaime Arriaga, barely survived getting bucked off, and was able to tell his story only thanks to his almost superhuman will to drag himself and his barely attached leg to the next town to ask for help. Jaime had fallen asleep, briefly, and was then rattled off the train. He was run over, thrown into the air, and run over again.

And the wheels aren't the only danger: bandits, immigration authorities, police, and even train operators are also a threat. It's disturbingly unclear which institution poses a bigger danger to migrants riding the Beast: Los Zetas or the Mexican police. Or maybe the correct answer is the one I heard from another migrant I spoke with, who said, of the police and gangs in Honduras, They're the same thing.

A few years before I met Gerber, after hearing so much about the train and reporting about incidents occurring on the train, as well as translating *The Beast* with Daniela Ugaz, I decided to ride it. I boarded one night and took the train from Ixtepec, Oaxaca, in southern Mexico, to Medias Aguas, Veracruz, close to where, a few months later, about a dozen cars would derail. But that night I feared the humans aboard much more than the prospect of the train skipping the tracks. And I was, in a few ways, much more prepared than most of the migrants riding with me—I had a couple layers, a hoodie, good shoes. Plus, a very solicitous cook, Cayetano, at the migrant shelter/refugee camp Hermanos en el Camino, had insisted I take a rope he had found for me, to tie myself in so I wouldn't be shaken off or slip off if I fell asleep. Still, some of the migrants, assuming—correctly—my feebleness and naiveté, took it upon themselves to look after me, even making sure I had a piece of cardboard to absorb the cold of the steel.

I watched and occasionally got smacked as the many tree branches occasionally flashed darkly and clocked unsuspecting riders in the head or foot or flank, the rushing air working its way down our collars and up our sleeves. After the initial nervous thrill of departure, the cold and the anxiety settled in. There was also a long moment of lingering, building fear: maybe a half an hour outside Ixtepec, after the train suddenly slowed and came to a halt. There were zero lights or signs of civilization around—the stars were brilliant, but there was no moon—and the surrounding blackness and absolute quiet after the rough clacking of the train made it seem like we had been deposited into outer space. I had heard and read about attacks and ambushes that occur on these trains: the engineers will coordinate with the cartels to extort or kidnap migrants riding on the back of the Beast. No one said a word—if they had, I would have heard it in that absolute silence—or barely even seemed to move for the twenty or thirty minutes that we were stopped there in that unpeopled, sky-startled jungle. And then suddenly the train lurched again—the domino noise of the cars thudding against their couplings coming *thud-thud-thud-thud-thud* from the front—and, slowly, powerfully, it started crawling forward.

On top of the train that night, one of the long-term shelter volunteers who was also riding told me that the vivacious, quick-smiling, often-dancing fourteen-year-old Salvadoran refugee, Lupita, who had been staying at the shelter and had charmed the entire place as she waited the months-long wait for a Mexican humanitarian visa, was eligible for that visa because, slightly further south on her journey, in Chiapas, she had been gang raped.

Mexico is not a safe country for migrants. And the dangers of the journey in Mexico are not happenstance. Just as the United States instituted a policy of Prevention Through Deterrence in the southwestern US borderlands, pushing migrants to the outermost desert and the most dangerous crossing corridors, so has it outsourced the immigration enforcement gauntlet structure by the funding and training of the notoriously abusive and deadly immigration and police forces in Mexico that regularly violate human rights. With increasing insolence and repudiation of international protocol, the US government is purposefully making it harder for all migrants, asylum seekers included, to make any petition—for human rights, asylum protection, or residence—to the US government, a deliberate deterrence strategy that flies in the face of the 1951 Convention.

Thomas Gammeltoft-Hansen and Nikolas F. Tan, writing in the *Journal on Migration and Human Security* about the deterrence paradigm, describe how "restrictive migration control policies are today the primary, some might say only, response of the developed world to rising numbers of asylum seekers and refugees." Gammeltoft-Hansen and Tan explain how in the past thirty years the world has seen a dramatic increase in the introduction of measures to stymie, deter, and deny asylum seekers, by laying out three deterrence strategies: one, the "procedural door," which includes the introduction of time limits for making an asylum claim, as well as safe third country agreements; two, the physical blocking of potential asylum seekers by building or expanding walls and fences and even interdicting arriving asylum seekers en route; and three, the cooperation with transit or origin states, as demonstrated by the European Union working with Libya to stop migrants, Australia working with Indonesia, and the United States with Mexico.

So: a Central American asylum seeker cannot take a boat or a plane because of carrier sanctions; travel by bus in Mexico is increasingly restricted by checkpoints (during a four-hour bus ride from the Guatemala-Mexico border to the airport in Villahermosa, I hit five checkpoints); and prescreening programs such as the Protection Transfer Agreement are pathetically ineffectual. All of which means, if asylum seekers from Central America are going to make a claim, they have no real option but to pass through Mexico "illegally," forcing them into dangerous and deadly terrain and an increasing reliance on smugglers who often work in concert with paramilitary criminal organizations. Itamar Mann, in his book *Humanity at Sea*, calls deterrence "a polite term for the idea that some migrants must suffer to prevent other migrants from seeking remedies."

Deterrence, too, was the idea behind the Trump administration's "zero tolerance" and family separation policies: make migrants suffer so much, the logic goes, that other migrants will hear about it and not want to come. I asked a number of migrant aid workers in Central America if they thought that the family separations were having a chilling effect on adults who were thinking of traveling with their children. Most recognized that the conditions on the migrant trails have long been dangerous, and parents don't even consider subjecting their children to such conditions without recognizing that the alternative could be even worse. Family separations do nothing to mitigate the push factors. All they do is amplify the human misery. Some of the migrants I spoke with hadn't even heard about the separations. Those who had—like the parents who took advantage of the Kindertransports in the 1930s—were trying to save their children's lives.

Draconian deterrence policies push asylum seekers onto the horns of a horrible dilemma, but it is the immediate fear of death that typically overrides the fear of flight. If you are on a burning boat, you're probably going to jump into the water even if you don't want to get wet, even if the water is cold, and even if there are sharks swimming beneath. If you make it into the water, at least you have a chance.

In 2018, the Canadian Council for Refugees, along with other groups, challenged in Canadian federal court the designation that the United States could reasonably be party to the safe third country agreement. Alex Neve, secretary general of Amnesty International Canada, succinctly captured the concern: "Canadians have watched with mounting anguish as the cruel assault on the rights of refugees and migrants, including babies and children, has deepened rapidly in the United States." At face value, it seems clear that the United States, like Mexico, is *not* a safe country for asylum seekers.

Despite multiple layers, a skullcap, and a patch of cardboard, despite the fact that it was summer in southern Mexico, I was still cold on top of the Beast. Arnovis took the train in central Mexico, at a much higher elevation, in November, and with nothing but a T-shirt and thin button-down collared shirt, and he had Valeria in his arms. He was also running for his life, not engaged in a privileged gallivant borne out of journalistic solidarity, or whatever it was I had been doing. To keep warm, Arnovis turned a black plastic bag into a vest, but the metal of the train, he told me, was still so cold it burned. They rode, and they waited, they froze, and they starved. Finally, after the last leg to Monterrey, Arnovis and Valeria and her mother took a bus to Piedras Negras, where they met El Suri. Since Valeria's mother had already paid in full, El Suri took the woman and Valeria right to the border to cross. Arnovis was still waiting for the last payment from his brother. He called—the money, his brother assured him, would come in a few days.

During that wait at the safe house, Arnovis got another call, this one from Florida. It was Valeria's father, calling to tell him that his wife and daughter had safely arrived. Arnovis told me that he felt a special pride when he heard that news. He had helped bring Valeria to safety. Now, if only he could get there himself. A few days later he got the call from his brother: the money was sent. He went and told El Suri. About an hour later, they realized that there was a problem. El Suri hadn't received anything. Arnovis's brother's friend had wired the money to the wrong coyote.

6

The force of the fall buckled Arnovis's legs. After he hit the ground he pitched forward, slamming his knees, hands, and then face into the cement of the schoolyard. His pants ripped, and he felt the skin split on his palms, but instead of pain he felt a rushed shock. He looked up and saw students in white and navy uniforms staring at him—in a shock of their own.

And then he took off running.

He ran hard, passed through one of the school's open hallways, skittered across the street, broke over the sidewalk, and took off into a field. He stumbled, panted, and ran. He heard commotion behind him but didn't turn to see if it was his pursuers, if they were catching up or taking aim. If a bullet stung him, it would sting him. Si me matan, me matan. He was aware enough to realize these could be his last few moments, his future coming at him hard—that rush of a train. His chest tolled and he ran into a brake of trees, smashing through the underbrush and still pumping his legs and heaving his lungs, a lactic burn aching in his thighs. Not until he had covered a half mile, or maybe a whole mile, or more—gasping in the dry November air, tears in his eyes, mind blanked by fear—did he slow down.

And then he ran again, ran until he broke back out of the trees and lost himself into a neighborhood of narrow streets and small houses.

It was the kindness of a stranger that finally gave him some relief. For kindness it is, that ever calls forth kindness, Sophocles wrote. Or fear that calls forth fear. Arnovis saw an old man in a wheelchair, posted out on a sidewalk. He needed to ask for help but didn't want to scare anybody, and he knew he looked like hell. After trying to catch his breath, he approached and explained to the old man that he was from El Salvador, and that he had been kidnapped. They looked at each other for a few moments, paused in an unlikely connection. I can help, the man said.

He had escaped, but to escape a safe house on the migrant trails is, too often, to trade one sort of captivity for another.

The old man called his son. The son came and drove Arnovis to another part of town and bought Arnovis a refresco and a couple tacos, let him use his phone. Did it help to eat something? I asked Arnovis. Pues, sí, he said. The person Arnovis called—and this surprised me—was Gustavo, the wrong coyote, the coyote whom his brother's friend had accidentally wired seven hundred dollars to and who hadn't given it back. Was calling Gustavo a gamble, an astute reading of humanity, or was it merely desperation? Arnovis had never met him before, but they'd spoken on the phone and, despite pocketing money that accidentally fell into his hands and refusing to return it, even though it meant almost certain death for Arnovis, Gustavo was straight with him when he warned him he better escape if he wanted to live. Arnovis appealed to that glimmer of concern and asked Gustavo to earn that seven hundred dollars. If I make it to Reynosa, will you take me across?

No, Gustavo said. But he would pass him off to another coyote who was leaving from Ciudad Acuña, the other direction from Piedras Negras.

To get to Ciudad Acuña, Arnovis had to rely, again, on charity. He borrowed bus fare from the man who had already given him a ride and bought him tacos, and then ditched Piedras Negras as soon as he could. In Ciudad Acuña he joined a group of twelve other migrants guarded over by a troop of coyotes in a room that felt a lot like the room he had just escaped. For the next three days the new coyotes dicked around, made promises, and got hammered. They tried to corner some of the women in the group, but the women wouldn't be wooed, and Arnovis and some of the other men stood up for them.

I asked Arnovis why he didn't just go and present himself at the border. Though there were already accounts in 2016 of asylum seekers getting turned away at official border crossings —the phenomenon had come to brief national attention in 2014 with the arrival of Haitians in Tijuana and Nogales—the illegal turnbacks weren't nearly as widespread then as they became in 2018. He explained to me that the coyotes had tight control over where and how you cross, and you can't just do as you please. Also, Mexican police and other federal agents sometimes congregate around the bridges and ports of entry. Further, the cartel-controlled trafficking and smuggling organizations—for whom the militarization of the US border has boosted profits—need to justify the high crossing fees they charge migrants. If a smuggling organization were charging seven hundred to drop someone at the port of entry, migrants would just take the cheaper option of a bus or a taxi. By 2019, for an asylum seeker to present themselves at a port of entry got even trickier, with cartels and other smugglers beginning to charge exorbitant fees for help to even get close to official border crossings. One Nicaraguan told me that someone tried to charge him three hundred just to approach the bridge between Juárez and El Paso.

There's also a difference in US law between an arriving alien (a migrant who presents at the port of entry without a visa) and an EWI (entry without inspection—a migrant who fords the river or hikes through the desert). Despite the obvious dangers and the de facto provocation to break the law, US immigration regulations push migrants to skirt the ports of entry and take to the water or the wilderness. If a border crosser survives the trek, they're actually in a better position than if they "followed the law" and presented themselves at a port of entry. "Arriving

aliens" are not statutorily eligible for parole—they typically have
to fight their asylum cases behind bars. EWIs, meanwhile, *are*
eligible for bond, and, if they can pay, they can stake their asylum
claim from outside the gulags—where they stand a significantly
better chance of winning their case. I've asked multiple attorneys
about the logic of the US government effectively incentivizing
migrants to take the less orderly and more dangerous route
across the desert or river, and I've heard plenty of speculation,
some of it probably correct, about deterrence: if you could just
knock on the door and get bonded out, more people would try
for asylum. That might be true, but it doesn't erase the fact that
government policy is intentionally forcing "bona fide" asylum
seekers to make a dangerous border crossing just to ask for relief.
By the end of 2019, the US-Mexico border had been effectively
closed to asylum seekers, and anyone in search of safety had
few other options other than setting out into the wilderness.

In the safe house Arnovis worked to make friends with the
caminador, Pedro—the coyote who would actually walk the
migrants across the border. Pedro shared cigarettes with Arnovis
and told him that by Sunday (it was Friday) they'd all be in
Houston. By the following Wednesday—five days in the safe
house during which they endured languishing hunger, a hard
floor, fitful sleep, and the constant checking and charging of
phones—they still hadn't moved. Arnovis spent most of that
time with two Honduran women, Xiomara and Jamileth, griping
with them as the coyotes daily promised the crossing would
happen that night, but by the afternoon they would be cracking
beers, hustling in and out of the safe house, often yelling into
their phones.

One night there was a commotion outside, and one of the
guides yelled *Cates!* and took off running. *Cates* is a nickname
for Mexican marines, known to be especially violent in the
region. The migrants jumped up and followed the guide out
the back door, and then took off running. A gunshot blasted

into the night, and then another. Arnovis made it around the side of the next building, and then the fear nailed his heels to the ground. After a moment, knowing he wasn't in the clear, he booked it to the street and, desperate to find cover, slid to the ground and shimmied under a car.

I pulled myself up by the front tires and hugged the asphalt, he told me. Some people, the cates, I think, walked right by, and I just held my breath, shaking. I stayed under there for like three hours.

Bugs were crawling over him, but he couldn't move as someone from the adjacent house had come outside and was standing right next to the car. At one point, Arnovis told me, I thought someone was going to get in the car and turn it on. What was I going to do? If I just appeared out of nowhere, they would have screamed. I thought of yelling for help, but I was too scared. So I just stayed there. After a long time, the person went back inside the house, and the street went quiet.

The asphalt slowly sucked out his warmth, his arms went numb, a bug crawled under his collar, and he breathed in the oily fumes of the pavement. Hours later, he finally wiggled himself out from under the car. Dazed and shivering, he didn't know where to go but back to the safe house. He poked in the back door and saw a couple coyotes sitting around with beers. All the migrants' backpacks, he could see, had been rifled through.

Later that night, the marines came by again, but this time the coyotes' boss was there. He talked with the soldiers like they were old friends, and then they left. Arnovis wondered if it was all staged—the coyotes working with the marines to get the migrants running in order to rob them. One of the migrants had 5,000 pesos hidden in his backpack, around $260, which had been taken. Maybe another migrant had even more. Arnovis had nothing.

The day after the raid, the thirteen migrants and two coyotes finally left the safe house, rode in a van down a remote dirt road—which stopped in the middle of the desert—and started walking. Pedro wouldn't explain anything; all he did was give orders. Still on the Mexican side, they were within a half hour of the border on a creosote flat, though they wouldn't cross the river and enter the United States for another eight days, during which they barely ate, drank from muddy puddles, and slept on the ground—they spent the drawn and nervous days waiting and sickly cold. The grama grass and saltweed tufting up from the dirt made it hard to find a smooth spot to lie down, and everything felt sharp and cold. He never got used to the hunger.

Each day the guides told them that this was going to be the day they were to cross, but they didn't move. Nights, the thirteen of them slept in a human huddle on the ground, everybody wearing all the clothes they had to try to stay warm. It was so uncomfortable, Arnovis said, struggling to describe the experience to me. It was … you never think you can be in a situation like that. When you stood up, you couldn't feel anything. Even your ears hurt.

After days of waiting in the middle of nowhere, *en la nada*, as he put it, he borrowed the one working phone and called his brother in Kansas, asking him to pressure the coyotes.

I asked his brother if he remembered that phone call, and he told me that the family hadn't heard from Arnovis in five days and were all terrified that he had gotten lost in the desert or killed along the way. He said he wrote to one of the coyotes via Facebook Messenger, trying to figure out what was going on.

You have no idea, Arnovis's mother told me, about the fear she was feeling. She added a *ha!* and snapped her fingers. *N'ombe*, she said. No, man.

We sort of went on strike, Arnovis explained. The migrants told the coyote that if they didn't cross the next day they were all leaving, turning around. And it worked: the coyotes said it was time to go. The migrants said a prayer before they left, and then Arnovis told a joke to try to lift everybody's spirits. It was about a coyote having a crush on a Guatemalan man with a nice ass. He wanted to lighten the mood, he said.

That lightened the mood?

Yeah, people laughed.

He told the joke again to his mother and me, his mother laughing from the first word and me forcing out encouraging chuckles. A coyote, Arnovis said, tricks a handsome Guatemalan man into bending over by telling him a vulture is coming to try to peck his eyes out and the only way to defend himself is to bury his head in the sand. When the coyote comes from behind and starts, *you know*, he asks the Guatemalan if the bird is getting his eyes. No, the Guatemalan answers, but he's pecking me from behind. The Spanish version has a little more wordplay, although the joke, I'd say, heavily depends upon the verve of the teller.

That didn't make people more scared, or confused? I asked. No, he said, and he and his mother burst out laughing again.

As they were hiking through the brush to the cold, muddy river, Xiomara, one of the Honduran women he had befriended, told Arnovis she didn't know how to swim. It's okay, he told her, I'll watch out for you.

At the riverbank, the thirteen of them undressed, linked arms, and waded into the cold water. The current was slow, but at the deepest point the water reached up to Arnovis's chest. Because it was December, and they would need dry clothes to put on once they crossed, they were in their underwear, some of them completely naked. On the other side they dressed quickly, leaning on each other, shivering, trying to get socks on over wet, sandy feet, punching arms through their shirts, and tripping into their pants. The coyotes were hurrying them. Ándale, cabrones! Hurry, hurry! And then, trembling and numb, they scrambled through the chaparral and up the bank.

Though less familiar with the Texas deserts, I know the Arizona migrant crossing corridors from my work as a volunteer with No More Deaths—on and off since 2008—and when I hear someone tell me about a group setting out into the desert, it's impossible not to think of the harrowing stories of disorientation, desperation, and death: people drinking from putrid cow tanks, going days or weeks without food, turning ankles, crawling through thorns, chased by Border Patrol helicopters, ATVs, and horses, falling off cliffs, or getting lost in canyons they never come out of. Excruciating death is the fate of at least hundreds of people annually who attempt the crossing. Since the turn of the century, over eight thousand people are known to have died. (The actual number is likely significantly higher.) Many more have disappeared, lost into the desert, their remains scattered by scavengers and the elements. The correct term is *remains* because entire bodies hardly last in the desert, where the chain of causation is short—a day without rain, two days, and your bones are scattered across the malpaís.

Shivering, hungry, damp, and sleepless, Arnovis and his group didn't get far before the coyote spotted a Border Patrol truck and told them to turn back. If they catch me, the coyote told them, they're going to give me twenty years.

The group rushed back to the bank, scratching and stumbling through the mesquite and salt cedar, undressed, waded south across the cold river, and clawed back on their wet clothes. They spent another night shivering in a huddled mass and praying in the darkness. The next morning they hiked to the river again. After taking off their clothes and crossing the river and putting their clothes back on, they walked north for an hour and saw another Border Patrol truck in the distance. Again, the coyote wanted to turn back.

There was a standoff this time. Xiomara, one other man, and Arnovis decided they had had enough and were going to turn themselves in. They split from the group and climbed a hummock to get a coign of vantage, and then followed signs for the road.

Xiomara and the man hung back as Arnovis approached the Border Patrol truck from the front, so as not to startle the agent. He raised his hands above his head, walking forward slowly. The female agent stepped out of her truck and yelled at Arnovis to stop. Where are you from? she called. She put a hand on her gun.

I'm from El Salvador. Soy migrante. I want to turn myself in.

The agent told him not to move and put in a radio call.

They treated us well, Arnovis said. No problems. Everything was calm. They loaded us into the truck without handcuffing us. And they took us to the station. Overall, they treated us well. I told them that I wanted to ask for asylum.

What did they say in response? I asked him.

Pues, nada.

It's hard to imagine a more dangerous or disorderly method of appealing to the United States for protection. Arnovis hadn't been trying to sneak into the country; he was asking for asylum, and yet he had no other viable way to do so but to dart across the Mexican border, board a deadly train, submit himself to the riotous whims of human smugglers, and then wade across a river and trek through the desert. His story resembles tens of thousands of other stories that take place every year: men, women, and children escaping a safe house an hour before they'll be hacked into pieces, dodging sometimes sanguinary border guards, trekking for a week across a barren desert, stepping over bones of those who have gone before them, or sleeping on bare concrete outside an official port of entry—this is how you appeal to the United States government. This is how you ask for help, for relief, for asylum.

Beginning in the summer of 2018 there were widespread reports of Customs and Border Protection (CBP) officers turning away potential asylum seekers from ports of entry. After so many had been refused a chance to stake their claim in Tijuana, asylum seekers self-organized and started logging names into what they called "the notebook," in which they listed whose turn it would be to make their asylum claim. "The notebook is supposed to be impartial," Cindy Carcamo of the *Los Angeles Times* wrote. "But there are doubts about that. Some immigrants believe that it is colored by prejudices, favoritism and sometimes corruption. Whoever holds it wields power. Their position is temporary. They"—the one who holds the notebook—"are eager to cross, too."

In late 2018 I spoke with one woman, Elizabeth, from Michoacán, Mexico, who by that point had been managing the notebook for a couple weeks outside the Chaparral border crossing in Tijuana, just an infielder's toss from the United States. The notebook itself is a thick accounting ledger, with its fore-edge colorfully shaded with a rainbow of highlighter ink. Elizabeth had been elected by a show of hands after another man left his post—his number was called and he was swallowed into the immigration detention system on the other side of the border. Elizabeth told me that after assuming her post, she felt she had a lot of responsibility to make sure the process was fair. I watched one couple with a young baby in the woman's arms walk up, talk to Elizabeth for a few moments, and then receive from her a square, scissor-cut slip of manila folder with a number on it: 1756. The family probably had two months to wait before they could make an asylum claim. That morning they called only two numbers: 1252 and 1253 (each number represents ten people).

When extremely vulnerable people come, Elizabeth explained to me, the committee can decide to give them a lower number. I asked who was on the committee. She gestured to a cluster of people behind her, refugees like her. This is the make-do orderliness that asylum seekers submit themselves to if they don't want to cross the border "illegally."

According to Anne Chandler, executive director of the Tahirih Justice Center's Houston office, told the *Texas Monthly* in June of 2018:

> Border Patrol is saying the bridge is closed. When I was last out in McAllen, people were stacked on the bridge, sleeping there for three, four, ten nights. They've now cleared those individuals

from sleeping on the bridge, but there are hundreds of accounts of asylum seekers, when they go to the bridge, who are told, "I'm sorry, we're full today. We can't process your case." So the families go illegally on a raft—I don't want to say illegally; they cross without a visa on a raft. Many of them then look for Border Patrol to turn themselves in, because they know they're going to ask for asylum.

A 2018 report by the Department of Homeland Security's (DHS) Office of Inspector General noted: "Two aliens recently apprehended by the Border Patrol corroborated this observation … that they crossed the border illegally after initially being turned away at ports of entry. One woman said she had been turned away three times by an officer on the bridge before deciding to take her chances on illegal entry." To *take her chances*, we know, meant to risk her life, or even to lose it. That was what happened to Óscar Alberto Martínez Ramírez and his twenty-three-month-old daughter, Angie Valeria, who drowned in the summer of 2019 while crossing the Rio Grande in an attempt to reach the US shore. In a widely shared photo of them, their dead bodies appear facedown in the turbid water, their faces tangled in the reeds. Óscar had tucked his daughter's body into his T-shirt to try to keep her safe. In the photo, Angie Valeria's little arm was still clinging around her dad's neck.

By the summer of 2019, the practice of turning away asylum seekers, or "metering" them, had become the standard, and it was paired with another turnback policy—the wildly euphemistic Migrant Protection Protocols, otherwise known as Remain in Mexico. MPPs, which were initiated in January of that year, were a means by which immigration officers pushed asylum seekers back into Mexico to wait in notoriously dangerous border towns as their claims proceeded through the courts. Over the span of roughly ten months, nearly sixty thousand asylum seekers had been forced back into Mexico, and critics took to calling the policy the "Migrant *Persecution* Protocols."

One Guatemalan asylum seeker told the *Los Angeles Times* of the conditions at the shelter where he was waiting, "They don't secure us, we can't bathe, they don't have food, they treat us like dogs." By August, not a single person who had been forced into the program had been granted asylum, and Mexican authorities were busing MPP asylum seekers hours away from the border, sometimes as far south as Tapachula, on Mexico's southern border. After being initially "metered"—restricted from the ports of entry—for months, asylum seekers would be given the opportunity to present to CBP, get processed, initiate their asylum claim, and then be given a court date months later and dumped back into Mexico. That court date wouldn't even be an individual hearing, in which they could testify to their fear before the judge, but simply a master calendar hearing in which their *actual court date* was set, months in advance, at which point they would be dumped back across the border again. The waits for the migrants—on edge, unsafe, and unable to legally work in Mexico—were extending past the year mark.

That summer, one of the pastors in charge of Love Migrant House, a migrant shelter in Nuevo Laredo that had become home to hundreds of migrants turned away through MPP, was kidnapped and disappeared. Just a few weeks later, Border Patrol agents apprehended one woman who was eight and a half months pregnant and had just crossed the border, brought her to the hospital, where she was given medicine to halt her contractions, and then sent her back across the border. By October of 2019, according to a Human Rights First report, there were over 340 confirmed cases of rape, kidnapping, torture, and other violent attacks against asylum seekers returned to Mexico under the program.

The pervasiveness of the deterrence paradigm is obvious not only in the forms of physical and regulatory obstruction the United States employs to stop asylum seekers from reaching the border. It also inheres in how immigration officers and agents treat them once they make it onto US territory. Asylum seekers are placed in "expedited removal" proceedings—a means by which Border Patrol and CBP officers can rapidly deport noncitizens without letting them see an asylum officer or immigration judge. Though not introduced into law until 1996, expedited removal echoes another bureaucratic deterrent policy from the Immigration Act of 1891, which created the principle of what is known as "entry fiction."

According to the new law, noncitizens arriving to the United States by sea would not be considered having actually landed until they were examined by an inspection officer, who was permitted to "order a temporary removal of such aliens for examination ... and then and there detain them until a thorough inspection is made." Daniel Wilsher writes in *Immigration Detention: Law, History, Politics* that the concept of entry fiction was a "critical legal (and constitutional) innovation because it meant that those incarcerated must be treated as if they were not there ... It suggested a type of limbo—with the detention center constituting perhaps an extralegal space—putting immigrants beyond the reach of constitutional norms." In a 1953 Supreme Court case, *Shaughnessy v. Mezei*, the court not only upheld the indefinite detention of the "arriving alien" but, in the words of legal scholar Zainab A. Cheema, "also withheld any constitutional entitlement to due process protections." The Orwellian term *arriving alien* calls to mind another dehumanizing one—there are plenty—used in immigration law: asylum seekers, when finally given a court date for a hearing in front of a judge, are issued an NTA, or Notice to Appear. In the government's view, the persecuted are invisible until they can formally detail their fear and ask for protection; only then do they "appear" in the eyes of the law.

The entry fiction doctrine was meant to carve out a legal no-man's-land, now constituted in the archipelago of over two hundred detention centers throughout the United States, as well as in the hundred-mile "constitution-free zone" that runs along all international borders, including maritime borders. These exceptional zones—where approximately one-third of the entire US population lives—is where the Constitution doesn't fully apply, where searches can be performed on a whim, where racial profiling is protected by the law.

In their book *Boats, Borders, and Bases*, Jenna M. Loyd and Alison Mountz trace how the maritime anti-immigrant enforcement regime, including the entry fiction doctrine, has been subsequently applied on the US-Mexico border. The treatment of Haitian migrants in the 1980s, for example, led to the "invention of the 'criminal alien'" as well as the "permanent temporariness" that immigrants are subjected to today. Coast Guard cutters chased down the boats Haitians were fleeing in and Immigration Naturalization Service officers summarily denied them asylum and warehoused them, before their deportation, at the newly established detention center on the Guantánamo Bay Naval Base. The "decidedly racialized asylum policies," according to Loyd and Mountz, set a new precedent for criminalizing and detaining asylum seekers entering through the US-Mexico border.

You're in, but you're not really in. You're on land, but you're really still at sea. Your entry is a fiction. Your very being is unmoored. Anytime you leave the protection of your home state, or step out from under the roof, or the roof crumbles above your head, you enter that limbo, that floating, still-at-sea purgatory of statelessness.

Arnovis was transferred by the officer from that remote spot in southern Texas to the Del Rio Border Patrol station. He was locked in a temporary holding facility with a dozen other men. He was still wearing his secondhand Adod church shoes, but agents had removed his shoelaces. His socks were cracked from dried sweat, his dress shirt was filthy, and he hadn't showered in almost ten days. An agent gave him a juice box and some crackers, a small polyethylene blanket that barely cut the cold of the holding cell. Nobody explained anything. He was afforded no lawyer. He had no idea how long he was going to be held. He ached, shivered, and hoped. He had arrived, or so he thought. He was here, or so he thought. He was under the wing of the leviathan. He could ask for protection, but that didn't mean anybody would listen.

7

You shall also love the stranger, for you were strangers in the land of Egypt.

—Deuteronomy 10:19

For hundreds of millennia humans have left their homes in search of refuge—Lucy, one of the earliest hominin specimens, was thought to have died while migrating. But not until the twentieth century—the century of the refugee, it's been called—did the numbers of people fleeing soar into the millions, or did states collaborate to contend with, welcome, or refuse them. Large-scale war and the dissolution of empires, as well as technology catching up to the politics of hate, spurred violence at unprecedented levels in the last century, pushing entire populations to choose between slaughter and the high seas, between starvation and squalid camps, or between political oppression and desolate deserts. Russian poet Anna Akhmatova called the fear and terror felt by those millions *the real twentieth century*. Today, there are 70.8 million forcibly displaced people throughout the world, living what may turn out to be part of *the real twenty-first century*—though there are decades left in this century for a new and yet-to-be-imagined set of horrors, for this century's reality, to set in.

Numerically, those forcibly displaced today roughly match the population of the entire West Coast of the United States (California, Oregon, and Washington) plus the neighboring states of Arizona, Nevada, Idaho, and Utah—what would be

the whole western quarter of the country on the run and searching for safety. If we were to extend this hypothetical scenario
to the historical trend, the next line of states—New Mexico,
Colorado, Wyoming, and Montana—would militarize their
state borders, erect walls, build prisons, and develop a massive
deportation regime and persecutory institutions, all while letting
in a scant few of their neighbors and harassing, humiliating, and
driving into the shadows those who risked their lives in search
for safety.

Before the twentieth century's mass movements of people,
for all of human history individuals, families, and communities
or tribes have needed to abandon their homes to seek refuge,
a richer alluvium, or more teeming forests. It wasn't always
fear that drove us: the first bipedal protohumans ambled out
of Africa and reached as far as Indonesia, and we continued
the junket, too, following seasons and prey, pushed by scar-
city and violence, pulled and chased by the horizon, rains,
riches, curiosity, and all else that pulls and pushes us, arriving
to Australia and the Americas, always shuttling and mobile.
As most humans settled into cities, empires, and nation-states,
we started trying to control and block these inborn migrations,
though some people were blocked more consistently than others.
Daniel Trilling writes in *Lights in the Distance*: "The history
of migration is a history of controls on the movement of all
but a wealthy elite." And today, still, it is almost exclusively the
poor who are blocked by borders. The rich have the pull, the
money, and the passports to travel, move, and settle at their
will and leisure.

Humans remain the farthest-reaching of all animal species,
and it's certainly possible that our migrations will not be limited
to this planet, though only for the last squeak of human history
has migration been regulated by laws rather than impulse—
whether laws of comity or of cruelty.

And even while we spread humanity to the farthest crusts
to fulfill our anthropocentric narratives, the custom of offering

afeard neighbors welcome is not limited to the human species. Primates offer something akin to asylum to females seeking to escape their priapic brothers and fathers. As Linda Rabben notes, "Female primates are more averse to incest than males and therefore more likely to leave home to avoid it." Rival primate troops, which typically repel and attack individuals from other troops, are known to provide safe harbor to fleeing females.

While etymologically the word *politics* is related to *policing* —derived from a word denoting the walls of a fortress—at the root of both terms is the ancient Greek city-state, the *polis*, which demarcates the organizing rules guiding how we live with and next to the other. And though the "the iconic founding act of establishing a Sumerian polity was the building of a city wall," as James C. Scott explains in *Against the Grain*, early walls, including the Great Wall of China, were meant to keep people inside as much as repel invaders. Furthermore, though the idea of a political "safety valve"—expertly analyzed by Greg Grandin as a key concept in America's genocidal westward expansion—wasn't conceived for a few millennia, early wall engineers, as well as state founders, recognized that letting some foreigners in, as well as some insiders out, would relieve political pressure. In other words, the strongest walls have the widest gates.

Asylum—the practice of asylum, developed initially as a detente against retributive or political violence—has a "long and sacred history," Hannah Arendt writes, dating "back to the very beginnings of regulated political life." "Since ancient times," she continues, asylum "has protected both the refugee and the land of refuge from situations in which people were forced to become outlaws through circumstances beyond their control."

Before the Greeks named the practice, the patriarch Abraham set an enduring example to the Semetic-originated religions by receiving three strangers who, unbeknownst to him, happened to be angels. In their honor he offered them shade and water to wash their feet, as well as gave them bread that they might "refresh their hearts." The Greeks have a similar myth, with Zeus showing up, disguised as a poor man, to the home the impious sons of Lycaon.

Later, the Levites were charged, by Pentateuchal decree, with establishing cities of refuge for accidental killers—those who killed someone not out of murderous intent but by mistake. The cities of Bezer, Ramoth-Gilead, Golan, Kedesh, Shechem, and Hebron were set aside so people who were responsible for an unintentional killing could find refuge from a surviving relative or friend enacting blood revenge. It was likely the first codification of any form of refuge or asylum policy.

The exhortation to offer hospitality wasn't only for accidental murderers; it was a fundamental precept that Hebraic lawmakers were encoding into the culture. The destruction of Sodom and Gomorrah, for example, was not a homophobic hate crime, as some contend, but punishment for Lot's breach of hospitality laws. Ezekiel chides "sister Sodom" for not strengthening "the hand of the poor and needy," as well as for being proud and full of bread—not for being gay. Yet another case is found in Leviticus: in the year of the Jubilee (the word comes from a ram's horn or trumpet, and is described in the Septuagint, or Greek Old Testament, as "a trumpet's blast of liberty"), held every fifty years, slaves were released, debt was forgiven—even the land was given a rest. Thus the origins of asylum may not even be exclusively spatiobiological but may also contain an agricultural pulse, a rhythm. Even land, the earth itself, needs reprieve.

According to Thomas Lewis's 1724 book *Origines Hebrææ: The Antiquities of the Hebrew Republick*, the six Levitican Cities of Refuge offered safety "to every Perfon who dwelt in them, whether he reforted thither for that Purpofe or not." The "manslayer," according to Lewis, was even given a free house in these cities. And the benefits of protection were also available to "Strangers and Sojourners," according to Numbers 35:15. The asylum seeker had "the Privilege to fly infantly to one of thefe facred Afylums, to fecure himfelf from the violent Profecution of the Avenger." But the welcome extended even beyond the gates of the cities: to afford the asylum seeker "all poffible Advantage in his Flight," the Sanhedrin rabbis made the roads approaching the Cities of Refuge as convenient and easy to travel on as possible "by enlarging them, and removing every Obfruction that might hurt his Foot, or hinder his Speed. No Hillock or River was allowed, over which there was not a Bridge." At every turning point there were signs with the inscription "Refuge, Refuge," and "two Students in the Law were appointed to accompany" each asylum seeker.

Aeschylus imagined a similar form of state-funded hospitality in ancient Greece. In his play *The Suppliants*, King Pelasgus offers the fifty daughters of Danaus fleeing their incestuous cousins not only asylum but free public housing: "In Argos you may choose to live with others in large houses or, if you prefer, alone in single dwellings; pick out, free of cost, what suits and pleases best."

It's hard to imagine a more antipodal stance from today's refugee policy: the United States, for example, turns people away at ports of entry, pushes them into the desert, encourages Mexico to arm a gauntlet, refuses petitions from abroad, imprisons asylum seekers—sometimes indefinitely—affords them no legal representation, and, instead of hiring "two Students in the Law" to accompany asylum seekers as they make their way through the bureaucratic thickets, in 2018, the US Justice Department halted a legal orientation program that provided a cursory overview of the legal process. The program led to shorter legal proceedings and saved the federal government millions of dollars a year.

Islamic culture also established varying asylum traditions. Religious scholar Tahir Zaman explains that the phrase *haraka baraka*, or "there is blessing in movement," sums up the traditional stance toward the welcoming of the stranger. Muddathir

Abd al-Rahim suggests that asylum was a "moral and legal right" in early Islamic thought, and Zaman notes that the Islamic calendar begins not with the birth of Muhammad but with the act of *hijrah*—migrants following in the footsteps of the Prophet who himself fled a death threat. Mona Siddiqui likewise notes that "Islam holds hospitality as a virtue that lies at the very basis of the Islamic ethical system, a concept rooted in the pre-Islamic Bedouin virtues of welcome and generosity in the harsh desert environment." As the Prophet said: "There is no good in the one who is not hospitable."

In the pre-Islamic Arab tradition, too, hospitality was a critical component. Tenth-century poet Ibn 'Abd Rabbih writes of an ancient poet ordering—paradoxically—his slave on a cold night to kindle a fire on a hill in case it might be seen by a passerby and serve to bring them to warmth and safety. And though we are left with relatively scant documentation, tribes and early settlements all over the world had cultural codes importuning their communities to welcome the stranger. As Christine Pohl writes in *Making Room*, "In a number of ancient civilizations, hospitality was viewed as a pillar on which all morality rested." Linda Rabben similarly notes that sanctuary and asylum "are ancient, perhaps primordial, institutions, part of the foundation of our species."

And yet there is, always, a tension when offering refuge, as evident in the shared etymology of the words *host*, *hostile*, and *guest*. The shared root, *hostis*, comes from the Indo-European *ghosti*, or "someone with whom one has reciprocal duties of hospitality." These duties, in ancient Greece, forged intergenerational bonds. In the *Iliad*, for instance, Glaucus and Diomedes decide not to brawl because Glaucus's grandfather had once invited Diomedes's grandfather over for some mead. Nestor, too, in Shakespeare's *Troilus and Cressida*, harks back to the same tradition when he receives Hector: "I knew thy grandsire, and once fought with him … Welcome to our tents."

Today, in the logic of the nation-state, that "bond" between citizen and stranger is more a demarcation of hostility than an incentive to share the roof: anyone crossing the borderline is a potential enemy to be surveilled, scrutinized, and suspected. "Hospitality," philosopher Jacques Derrida notes, "carries within it the concept of hostility. When the host opens the door to the guest, she is introducing vulnerability. She becomes the hostage of the guest." You are beholden to your boarder, or, in Derrida's dialectical phrasing, "The guest becomes the host's host."

Homer's *Odyssey* is a tale rooted in the traditions of the guest-host relationship. As Emily Wilson writes in an introduction to her recent and illuminating translation of the epic, "Travelers, in an era before money, hotels, or public transportation, had to rely on the munificence of strangers to find food and lodging and aid with their onward journey. *The Odyssey* suggests that it was the responsibility of male householders to offer hospitality of this kind to any visitor, even uninvited guests, strangers, and homeless beggars." One telling example is when Princess Nausicaa instructs her slaves to look after Odysseus: "All foreigners and beggars come from Zeus, and any act of kindness is a blessing. So give the stranger food and drink, and wash him down the river, sheltered from the wind." Over the centuries, these traditions of familial hospitality expanded into a political expectation. But Odysseus wasn't just a peripatetic traveloguer. More *hostis* than *ghosti*, he was a pirate who, marauding with his band of Achaeans, happened to get lost and pine for the comforts of his home. Pirates—integral in the development of asylum protocols—later became known in international maritime law as *hostis humani generis*. The enemy of mankind.

In Book Six of his *History*, Herodotus writes that the Persians, having conquered Eritrea, set out to "commit sylan," or piracy —a growing regional problem in the millennium before the common era. The formation of the early city-states was predicated on the fraught relationship of host and increasingly mobile strangers. As maritime technology advanced, the Greek islands became increasingly interconnected, but swifter ships didn't lead just to trade and cultural exchange. As hostilities heightened, city-states began to mark off sacred spaces that would be off-limits to *sylia*, or plundering. And yet, to return to philosopher Daniel Heller-Roazen: "the very delimitation of one region free of pillaging necessarily confirmed the practice to which it marked an exception: by definition *sylia* remained licit in all those spaces not expressly protected by statutes of asylum."

The core principle of these early antipiracy laws was closer to today's concept of sanctuary than political asylum, according to authors Louise Bruit Zaidman and Pauline Schmitt Pantel, who explain that *asylia* was "terrain that was deemed to be sacred [and] was delimited as a *temenos* or 'cut-off' space, separated, that is, from its non-sacred surroundings." These carved-out spaces—altars and groves—became places not just where it wasn't acceptable to loot but also spaces of refuge "for runaway slaves, ousted politicians on the run, and other individuals who were being pursued." Zaidman and Pantel emphasize, "To assassinate someone who had taken refuge in a sanctuary was considered a heinous enough crime for the gods to inflict a scourge (a plague, for instance) on the whole city as a punishment."

The early Greek Olympics, too, offered not only the spectacle of athletic prowess but a sort of temporary political easement. "The sacred truce was announced throughout the Greek world by the *spondophoroi* [olive branch-crowned heralds] so that competitors and other intending participants ... free or slave, Greek or non-Greek, might take advantage of the temporary *asulia*," according to Zaidman and Pantel.

Refuge, sanctuary, truce, political pardon—these were elemental concepts woven into the fabric of the earliest democracies. In Sophocles's *Oedipus at Colonus*, a 2,400-year-old play that stands as a remarkable allegory for our present-day asylum struggle, Oedipus asks his daughter, Antigone,

> if you see somewhere
> to rest—on public land, or in a grove
> set aside for the gods—
> guide me to it, sit me down there.

Father and daughter eventually find their relief in the Eumenides' sacred grove near Athens, an official place of asylia. Elders from the nearby village of Colonus, however, irate to discover the incestuous patricide in their park, yell at him and Antigone to "get out of here! ... Leave this land as fast as you can walk, so you won't burden our city with your deadly contagion." Oedipus counters:

> Men call Athens the most god-fearing city,
> a safe haven for persecuted strangers,
> their best hope when they need a helping hand.
> ... I am
> a suppliant to whom you promised
> safety.

The village elders eventually relent, somewhat, proceeding to interrogate Oedipus, even asking him, "What is your worst fear?" They are acting in the role of the contemporary asylum officer: demanding Oedipus legitimate his fear and need for refuge.

"Athens' reputation as a haven for exiles in distress was prominent in myth and the dramas derived from it," translator Robert Bragg notes. "Athens sheltered Orestes when he was pursued by the Furies; both the children of Herakles, who were persecuted by King Eurystheus; and the crazed Herakles himself after he had murdered his wife and children. Athens maintained that reputation in Sophocles's era by welcoming and granting legal status to immigrants as *metics* [noncitizens permitted to reside in a Greek city], allowing them to work and take part in some civic activities." According to Thomas John De' Mazzinghi, writing in his 1887 book *Sanctuaries*, "The wisdom of the Athenians soon brought them to the conviction that the kernel of the institute lay in the protection of the wretched." By *institute*, he meant democracy itself.

Though Greek laws didn't recognize all sacred places as asylia, Thucydides, in his *History of the Peloponnesian War*, conceives of asylum much as we think of the concept today: "The leading men of Hellas, when driven out of their own country by war or revolution, sought an asylum at Athens; and from the very earliest times, being admitted to rights of citizenship, so greatly increased the number of inhabitants that Attica became incapable of containing them, and was at last obliged to send out colonies to Ionia." It's a neat parallel to contemporary policies: let some asylum seekers in, worry that the natives are getting cramped, and then send incoming claimants to detention centers or Ionic colonies.

As part of its founding myth, it is important for a polis or a nation to demonstrate that through its power and equanimity, it can serve as a place of refuge—think of the mythos of melting-pot America—but, as the state matures, the spirit of welcome often turns cold. A few thousand years after establishing the world's first asylum laws, Greece today is less a place of refuge than a hurdle in a longer flight: asylum seekers in modern Greece are confined to squalid detention centers, go hungry on the streets, and are attacked by xenophobes and neo-Nazis. Italy, too, the other nation that had a fundamental role in bringing the lexicon and practice of asylum to the world—Romulus and Remus found safety in the Lupercal, above Rome, where they were suckled by a wolf—has, in recent years, turned away boats of refugees from its shores, consigning the intrepid asylum seekers to find, to use the words of Doaa, the Syrian woman chronicled in *A Hope More Powerful Than the Sea,* no refuge but "at the bottom of the sea."

It's certainly tempting to analogize the plight of Greeks and Romans to today's refugee crises, as Patrick Kingsley does in

The New Odyssey. Movingly describing the successful voyage of Syrian asylum seeker Hashem al-Souki, Kingsley relates the struggles of modern-day refugees to Aeneas and Odysseus: "Just as both those ancient men fled a conflict in the Middle East and sailed across the Aegean, so too will many migrants today." But equating refugees or asylum seekers with piratical heroes—such as Odysseus and Aeneas—isn't a helpful framing. If anything, the Syrians (among other groups around the world) fleeing today more resemble the unnamed Trojans uprooted by nine years of imperial conquest by the likes of Agamemnon and his mercenaries, Achilles and Odysseus among them. And though Aeneas himself fled ransacked Troy, he went on to become a colonizer and violent avenger.

A more apt Greek lens, along with Sophocles's *Oedipus at Colonus*, is Aeschylus's *The Suppliants*. Aeschylus wrote the drama in the fifth century BCE when, after over a hundred years of increased migration to Athens, the Persian Wars ended in victory for the Athenians, and "the flow of immigrants became a flood," as Geoffrey Bakewell explains in his exegetical study, *Aeschylus's Suppliant Women*. To handle the increased numbers of foreign-born living in their city, Athenians created a new legal category to designate the free noncitizens: *metics*, literally, "livers with." By mid-fifth century BCE, some estimates place the metic population at around 50 percent of the population. And though, at first, Athenians did offer their city as refuge, as more and more foreigners arrived, tensions rose. This was the fraught political backdrop in which Aeschylus wrote his tragedy about fifty Danaid "suppliant maidens" seeking to "escape from the lust of men"—their libidinous Egyptian cousins, also referred to as the "numerous, wanton male swarm." The Danaid women fled to the Peloponnesian city of Argos, where they appealed to the mythical King Pelasgus for asylum from the foreign men. In considering their application, he asks them to respond to his questions—essentially a credible fear interview—"as newcomers should, with words to move tears and compassion for your need." "Say clearly why you have fled here," he demands, even making sure that they haven't committed a crime and that their "hands are innocent of blood." But as the king hesitates to grant them relief, the suppliants insist,

> I will not be
> Man's chattel won by violence.
> I'll stretch my flight from this cruel arrogant rape
> Far as the stars stretch over earth.

The suppliants go on to enumerate the reasons why they have fled, insisting that their "heart is darkened and trembling" and that they are "dead with fear." After consulting with his citizens, the king grants them asylum, and though the remaining installments of Aeschylus's tetralogy have been lost, we know that the king later goes to war to defend the asylees.

As the suppliants remind us, early in the play, making one of the world's first literary references to refugees:

> Even for distressed fugitives from war
> an altar is a defence against harm,
> that gods respect.

You could read *The Suppliants* today and think about the women fleeing domestic violence in Central America and seeking protection in the United States. Guatemala, for example, has one of the highest rates of femicide in the world, and all three countries in the Northern Triangle suffer from epidemic levels of domestic violence, even as former attorney general Jeff Sessions—countering the example of the Argive king—did all he could to disqualify them, barring "exceptional circumstances."

In Greek tradition, suppliants such as the Danaids carried *eiresione*, laurel branches decked with wool, in their left hands, which meant they were seeking asylum. Such symbolic traditions carried over to Europe through the millennia, with suppliants banging on special door knockers outside churches—such as the sanctuary ring on the door of the Notre-Dame cathedral—

ringing special bells, or sitting on "frith stools." *Frith* is Old English for "freedom."

Asylum was an integral part of a democracy's political power. It is what, in part, politics is, or can be: mutual protection, a collective roof extending over our heads. And yet it is also a challenge to that power: the baggage and hazards of the newcomer. The asylum story of *The Suppliants*, indeed, contains the earliest evidence of the word *democracy*—the people's sovereign vote (*demou kratousa keir*)—as Alan Sommerstein notes in his translation. Another fossil of early democracy, with reference to asylum and calling to mind the challenges it brings, is found in another line of the play: "And may the people [*damion*], which rules [*kratunei*] the city, protect well the citizens' privileges, a government acting with craft and foresight for the common good; and to foreigners may they offer painless justice under fair agreements before arming the god of war."

As people began to live in tighter proximity—as they toiled, organized, and eventually ruled together—they began to establish the rule of the *demos*, the people. And they not only recognized the need to extend the franchise (though it only extended so far) but to extend welcome. That is what ruling together is—possessing together, building a common roof. Hobbes argued that it is fear of each other that draws us into politics, and though that may be true, one of the reactions to that fear is to establish refuge. This is what a state, in theory, can offer. Asylum, that is, is at the heart of democracy. The wing of the leviathan is a roof.

And yet the roof can leak, sag, begin to crumble. About ten years after the first performance of *The Suppliants*, in 451 BCE, Athenians enacted Pericles's Citizenship Law, which limited citizenship to children with two Athenian parents, and further distinguished between metics and citizens by barring the former from owning property, as well as prohibiting them from voting or holding office. If they "illegally assumed the privileges of a citizen, metics were degraded to the condition of slaves," Julia Kristeva writes.

Greek notions of mutual aid, hospitality, and asylum are rooted in the concept of *xenia*, which Emily Wilson defines as "hospitality," "friendship," or "guest-friendship." The word is the base for *xenophobia*, as well as the more recondite *xenodochial* —literally "stranger's banquet"—or someone who is friendly to strangers. In the Middle Ages, *xenodochia* were hospitals or hostels, and *xenodochium pestiferorum* were hospitals specifically for victims of the plague. That the root *xenos* can be pulled to such extremes again points to Derrida's reflection on the inherent dialectic of giving welcome: "So it is indeed the master, the one who invites, the inviting host, who becomes the hostage—and who really always has been."

But, like Circe turning her guests into pigs, or the beautiful Calypso conniving to make Odysseus stay on her island in a sort of administratively romantic indefinite detention, it is usually the "guest," or in modern politics, the stranger, who is actually taken hostage. For the Greeks and their shape-shifting deities —as well as for Abraham and Sarah—the stranger at the door could always be a god.

It was the Romans who served as a bridge into the modern era for the cultural and political attitudes toward asylum, as they did for many other ancient Greek traditions. Second-century senator and historian Tacitus summed up for the Romans the moral and political import of welcoming the stranger: "It is accounted a sin to turn any man away from your door. The host welcomes his guest with the best meal that his means allow. When supplies run out, the host takes on a fresh role; he directs and escorts his guest to a new hostelry. The two go on, uninvited, to the nearest house. It makes no difference; they are welcomed just as warmly. No distinction is ever made between acquaintance and stranger as far as the right to hospitality is concerned … There is a pleasant courtesy in the relations between host and guest."

In the centuries that followed, the Christian church was next to bridge the asylum traditions of its predecessors—in this case the Greeks and Romans—into its own practices. And, as early as 344 CE, the Council of Sardia officially recognized sanctuary in churches. Rabben explains that "to maintain the sanctity of church premises (and the power of the church as an institution), it was necessary to protect everything and everyone, even fugitives, within them." Early versions of passports, *litterae communicatoriae*, were given to Christian pilgrims, signaling to distant churches that they should offer hospitality to the foreigner. In the Egyptian city of Oxyrhynchus, the magistrates sent men to the city gates "to intercept foreigners and offer them the necessary care according to the principles of Christian hospitality," Kristeva writes. John Chrysostom, fourth-century archbishop of Constantinople, suggested an almost identical practice, writing that "one should act on one's own, go sit at the gates of the town, and spontaneously welcome the new-comers." The "principles of Christian hospitality," however, were circumscribed: non-Christians were pointedly not offered litterae communicatoriae, and were rarely afforded welcome.

In 785 Charlemagne decreed, "If anyone seeks refuge in a church, no one should attempt to expel him by force." In his biography of the king, Johannes Fried complicates the idea of the Charlemagnetic magnanimity: when an accused foreigner hid himself away in a church in Tours, Charlemagne ordered him pulled out of the church and sent back to Orléans. According to Fried, "the crucial thing was to arbitrate between the ecclesias-tical right of asylum and the proper jurisdiction of the diocesan bishop. Charlemagne came down in favor of the Church hier-archy; order took precedence over asylum." And yet, notions of hospitality were still important to the early church, as Christine Pohl observes in a pronouncement given by the seventh-century bishop Isidore of Seville: "A layman has fulfilled the duty of hospitality by receiving one or two [guests]; a bishop, however, unless he shall receive everyone … is inhuman." This policy of protection was extended to England in the ninth century, when Henry VIII "established eight cities of refuge based on the Old

Testament model," Rabben writes. The church would stand as both a sanctified space and a sanctuary for the following centuries. Meanwhile, both Ottoman sultans and Polish kings took in Jews fleeing spates of anti-Semitic massacres in the Rhineland in the fourteenth century.

"The man who wishes to exempt himself from providing for his neighbors should deface himself and declare that he no longer wishes to be a man," John Calvin warned in the sixteenth century. "For as long as we are human creatures we must contemplate as in a mirror our face in those who are poor, despised, exhausted, who groan under their burdens." Pohl notes, however, that Calvin was also wary of welcoming every stranger, thinking that in some earlier heyday "there was greater honesty than is, at present, to be found among the prevailing perfidy of mankind; that the right of hospitality might be exercised with less danger." Calvin was reacting to his home city, Geneva, struggling to take in thousands of fleeing Protestants, which was stretching Genoan generosity thin. Martin Luther, similarly skeptical, recommended that hosts "get references for strangers from persons who were trusted." That practice would carry over into the twenty-first century in the form of asylum sponsorship letters and affidavits of community support.

In *The Use and Abuse of Political Asylum in Britain and Germany*, Liza Schuster explains that the extralegal sanctity of the church (as a site of exception) was pointedly attacked by Martin Luther and his philosophy of Reformation. The church, Luther claimed, is not jurisdictionally distinct from anywhere else; and "the spirit is not unique to church grounds," therefore nullifying its special protection as a sanctuary. Despite the Reformation's undercutting of church sanctity, however, Luther wrote that when the persecuted were received, "God Himself is in our home, is being fed at our house, is lying down and resting." And yet, despite Luther's rhetorical philanthropy, the idea of spreading asylum beyond the confines of the church diluted the strength of the concept, and official church-wide sanctuary policy didn't last much longer. As Kristeva puts it, "The fate of the foreigner in the Middle Ages—and in many respects also today—depended on a subtle, sometimes brutal, play between *caritas* and the political jurisdiction." By 1624, the English Parliament had officially ended the church sanctuary policy.

Perhaps the repeal owed, in part, to weariness over increasing numbers of refugees—a parallel to fifth-century BCE Athens or contemporary United States. In Middle Ages Europe and North Africa there had been a series of events and decrees that sent an unprecedented number of people fleeing their homes: in 1492, Jews and Muslims were expelled from Spain, and Portuguese Jews were exiled five years later. In the following years, Protestants fled slaughter and ditched continental Europe; the Huguenots escaped France; the Hutterites fled Moravia; and oppressed Puritans and Quakers soon began leaving Great Britain for the Americas. By the nineteenth century the flights of refugees had reached unprecedented numbers, with estimates of half a million Circassians, Abkhazians, Chechens, and Tatar Muslims fleeing the Russian Caucasus and, later, the Crimean Peninsula, as Philipp Ther details in his splendid compendium of European refugee movements, *The Outsiders.*

Some of these asylum seekers would find refuge; many would not. As Schuster explains, "Fortunately for the Huguenots, while church asylum was dying out, the conditions necessary for territorial asylum were in place." The 1648 Treaty of Westphalia ended the Thirty Years' War and established the concept of equality between sovereign states, linking statehood to territory for the first time and giving rise to the modern nation-state. Now it was the state itself—not a church "asserting its separateness from the state"—offering protection from neighboring enemies.

Around the same time, in 1685, the word *refugee* made its first appearance in the English language, in reference to those fleeing France after the revocation of the Edict of Nantes, which withdrew substantive rights for Protestants. And it was five years later, in 1690, when Sir Thomas Browne, in his *Letter to a Friend*, coined the term *migrant*, even tying its first mention to the idea of asylum: "Death hath not only particular stars in heaven, but malevolent places on earth, which single out our infirmities, and strike at our weaker parts; in which concern, passager and migrant birds have the great advantages, who are naturally constituted for distant habitations, whom no seas nor places limit ..."

Two hundred and fifty years later, Hannah Arendt notes that asylum "was the only modern remnant of the medieval principle that *quid quid est in territorio est de territorio*," or "what is in the territory is of the territory": you are where you are, a sort of locational citizenship law. Rabben pushes the history of sanctuary law's import even further, claiming that "secular procedures such as habeas corpus (which appeared in England in the twelfth century) and the concept that one is innocent until proven guilty may have evolved from royal laws protecting sanctuary seekers."

France was the first country, in its 1793 Constitution, to recognize an actual right to asylum, affirming as much in the 1958 Constitution, and guaranteeing asylum to "anyone persecuted because of his action for freedom" who was unable to seek protection in their home countries. Asylum law in France, however, now adheres to the much more limiting guidelines set by the European Union, and, today, nowhere in the world does anyone have a right to asylum, only a right to apply for it.

After World War II, Germany also extended asylum protections well beyond the 1951 Convention and its 1967 Protocol—the international standards for today's asylum agreements—enshrining in German Basic Law a person's *right* to asylum, not just a state's right to grant it. After a series of state crises in the late 1980s and '90s, however, including a large influx of guest workers after the collapse of communism in Eastern Europe (which led to the emigration of millions of Eastern Europeans, many of whom were ethnically German), as well as an economic downturn, asylum became a point of high political tension in Germany. Matthew Gibney notes, "Nowhere was this hostility [toward asylum seekers] more in evidence than in the economically depressed five new *Länder* [states] in East Germany," where "economic hardship and high rates of unemployment fueled immense antipathy towards the asylum seekers they had to accommodate." It's hard not to think of struggling counties and states in the United States and *their* antipathy toward migrants today. By 1993—after hundreds of attacks from anti-immigrant hardliners, including neo-Nazis—Germany amended its constitution, rescinding its protection of the right to asylum and establishing that asylum seekers who had passed through a "safe third country" in the European Union could be refused welcome.

The political history of asylum is a history of, as Aeschylus wrote, "hearts leaping green with fear," and then politicians or judges deciding if the hearts are leaping high enough. Over the millennia, humankind has met the fear of neighbors and strangers with welcome and succor as well as a turned back and a shut door. Today, it remains primarily the state through which we navigate political sanctuary practices, but the culture and tradition of hospitality still lives in many homes, churches, temples, and hearts.

Besides the Greek tragedies, the early Romans' politicking, and the Middle Ages' upheavals, nineteenth-century United States is another lens by which we can understand today's refugee crises. As Andrew Delbanco writes in his book *The War before the War*, on the dehiscent ramifications of the Fugitive Slave Act, that just as "fugitive slaves ripped open the screen" of a unified country of liberty to expose Northerners to the horrors their complacency and economy were wreaking, refugees and asylum seekers today unveil the imposed misery our modern comforts would otherwise conceal. Just as cotton became king on the scarred backs of slaves, our cheap T-shirts, smartphones, tech support, and year-round bananas and fresh lettuce today all depend upon a workforce subjugated and marginalized by border militarization and the global immigration enforcement regime. And the migrant aid activists of today—like Scott Warren of No More Deaths, who faced prosecution for providing water and humanitarian aid to border crossers—stand in the tradition of the abolitionists of the nineteenth century who struggled against the laws of the land. Rather than reporting runaways to the slave catchers or sitting idly by as men, women, and children were hunted down and sent back to danger, abolitionists saw assisting runaway slaves as a higher moral, religious, or ethical calling. "But the strongest 'rhyme' between fugitive slaves in the 19th century and illegal immigrants today is their shared anguish—the 'degenerating sense of nobodiness,' in the Rev. Dr. Martin Luther King Jr.'s devastating phrase—inflicted by a society that treats them as non-persons," Delbanco writes in a *New York Times* op-ed. "People demeaned in this way forced Americans then, and force us now, to confront the central question of our history: Who is—or isn't—recognized as fully human?"

8

I asked Arnovis about the first time he'd heard of the concept of asylum. He told me that some people who worked with his brother in Kansas had mentioned it, and that his brother had then explained it to him: in the United States there's this law that says if you're fleeing your country, they protect you. So, in my case, Arnovis said, they told me I had to have a lot of proof, and I did have proof. I had the number of the person who called and threatened me. And the boss, the brother of the guy on the soccer field, I had his name. And the name of the gang.

Before 2005, asylum seekers in the United States didn't need to show proof or corroborating evidence of their persecution. Some judges may have pressed on specific points, and attorneys often provided records or affidavits attesting to the truth of the applicant's claim, but decisions were made based on the asylum seeker's testimony, country condition reports, and, as always, on politics. That changed with the 2005 REAL ID Act, which was passed with little initial notice as a rider on a military funding and tsunami relief bill. The REAL ID Act also waived thirty-seven federal laws that could interfere with the construction of a border wall, including the Endangered Species Act, the Clean Water Act, the Clean Air Act, the Archaeological and Historic Preservation Act, the Antiquities Act, the Historic Sites Act, the Wild and Scenic River Act, the Bald and Golden Eagle Protection Act, and the American Indian Religious Freedom Act. What seemed like two distinct issues ten years ago, the continued funding of the wars in Iraq and Afghanistan and a change in the evidentiary burden for asylum claims, have since become closely interconnected: the wars sparking one of the largest refugee crises in history and, simultaneously, the regulatory change making it harder for those refugees to find protection. Pushing people overboard and pulling up the ladders in one bill.

The REAL ID Act, according to Andrew Schoenholtz, Philip Schrag, and Jaya Ramji-Nogales, codified adjudicators' "authority to require corroborating evidence beyond the testimony of the asylum seeker and make credibility findings on the basis of immaterial inconsistencies." In other words, not only would Arnovis need to corroborate his testimony with evidence beyond just providing the names of his persecutors, but if he were to mix up a name during his testimony, if he confused a date or misremembered the weather on such and such a date, or betrayed any other "immaterial inconsistency," he could be denied asylum. Not every judge would discredit an entire case because Arnovis said Peluca's shirt was cobalt at his first hearing and cerulean at the next, but requiring proof is a high burden for someone who had to flee in a hurry and is a few thousand miles from the scene of the threat. An attorney I met in El Paso, Eduardo Beckett, explained the difficulty in obtaining evidence for asylum claims. "Hey, MS-13," Beckett joked, "will you write a nice letter for me to give to the judge? I'm seeking asylum, and the judge wants evidence you want to kill me, so put the threat in writing for me, would you?" Meeth Soni, an attorney for Immigrant Defenders Law Center in Los Angeles, told me about the case of a woman who was gang-raped, set on fire, and had burn marks on her face. During the credible fear interview, she supposedly said she was attacked at a certain time of the day, and then during the hearing in front of the judge she said it happened at a different time. The judge ruled her not credible and denied her asylum.

~

140

As a belated response to the 9/11 attacks, the REAL ID Act was ostensibly aimed at terrorists. And, indeed, two of the major asylum policy changes (before the Trump era) came about after attacks on the World Trade Center—without doubt the building that has most influenced US asylum policy. The first change was the Illegal Immigration Reform and Immigrant Responsibility Act (IIRIRA), the 1996 immigration reform bill passed in response to the 1993 World Trade Center bombing, which introduced expedited removal proceedings to allow Border Patrol agents to deport people without a judge's order, established the system of credible fear interviews, and the one-year filing deadline for asylum—because of which at least one judge consigned one Senegalese woman to a probable clitoridectomy —along with a host of other less significant changes. The 2005 response to the 9/11 attacks further raised the bar for asylum seekers: it required evidence and allowed judges to dismiss claims on the basis of immaterial inconsistencies. It's telling that security concerns emerging from attacks on the World Trade Center, in particular—a beacon of global capital—have so affected asylum policy. And yet, across both strikes, only one of the perpetrators, Ramzi Yousef, had applied for asylum, though his case was still pending at the time of the attack.

While some immigration judges seem intent on finding any reason to deny asylum claims, and have leaned on inconsistencies in testimony to issue denials for decades, those denials may be more a matter of politics than personal animus or even objective juridical appraisals: immigration judges are subject to the executive branch's Department of Justice, and, unlike other courts, are not an independent part of the judicial branch.

"If a person's story had even a small inconsistency," historian Jonathan Hansen quoted a witness saying in his book, *Guantánamo*, "he is told 'you are lying' and sent back to Haiti." One judge, in a hearing I attended in New York City in 2018, referenced the REAL ID Act, which, besides raising the evidentiary burden, grants authority to issue a ruling on the basis of the "demeanor, candor, or responsiveness" of the asylum seeker. He told the asylum applicant that he was sorry: though he may have believed her, she had provided no medical records to prove that she had undergone a forced abortion, and she was ordered deported.

Retired immigration judge Paul Grussendorf, who wrote a self-published memoir about his life as an immigration attorney, law school professor, and immigration judge, explained that it's not only hard-hearted judges who seek to deny asylum claims. Some prosecutors, whom Grussendorf calls "arrogant, proto-fascist bureaucrats" dreaming of working at the US attorney's office, "treated the immigrants who came into my courtroom as criminals who had to be broken down on cross-examination" so they would expose an inconsistency in their testimony.

Grussendorf recounted one anecdote of a judge who was about to grant asylum to an Egyptian man who had an obviously meritorious claim; his wife, also in the United States without papers, stood to benefit from the asylum grant. The DHS prosecutor, knowing he was going to lose the case, and that the man and his wife were going to be granted asylum, asked for permission to leave the courtroom so he could quickly track down an ICE officer to arrest the man's wife. She had been waiting, with an infant in her arms, outside the courtroom.

And if a judge is willing to dismiss an entire case because of an immaterial inconsistency, how can you, an asylum seeker, hope that your story will be exactly straight? How to recall the exact circumstances of the state agent picking you up to drive you to your abortion operation? What are the details by which a judge in the United States will weigh the veracity of your claim? What to recall of the moment you saw the gang member sprint around the corner? Or what detail of the day Peluca told you you had to pretend he had put a pistol in your mouth? Was it Friday or Saturday? Was it before your brother-in-law got the gun barrel to his temple, or after? The system wants to see not only fear but narrative. They want a good story. And yet memory, trauma, and narrative all have a complicated relationship; the hormones that help trigger survival responses also interfere with how memory is formed. To quote Ennius again: "Fear drove out all intelligence from my mind." Joan Didion, recalling a moment of terror she experienced while reporting on the Salvadoran civil war, said that she was "in a single instant demoralized, undone, humiliated by fear."

One woman I met at the New Sanctuary Coalition asylum clinic in Manhattan, where I volunteer as an interpreter, told me that she didn't remember the moment she crossed the border with her one-year-old daughter. She knows she got to the river, and she obviously knows she's now across the river, but the moment of crossing is blank in her mind. The trip through Mexico, she explained, was ugly, so ugly—she saw a young boy, by her estimate just eleven or twelve, robbing migrants with an AK-47—and she remembers the trip afterward, and has no other memory problems. But she simply can't remember anything at all about crossing the border. It's just blank, she said. A hole, a caesura, in her story. When I mentioned this episode to neuroscientist Joseph LeDoux, he said it makes perfect sense. "Cortisol"—a hormone released in response to stress —"is toxic in high doses to the hippocampus," which is where long-term memory is processed. "Stress," he told me, "disrupts memory formation."

That blankness in another asylum seeker might present as a memory warp rather than a memory hole, and yet the "confusion" —imperfect human memory—can be grounds for asylum denial. Denial and then deportation, and then fear, hiding, renewed persecution, and possible death.

After a few hours inside the freezing cold, unhygienic human warehouse—the hielera—it was time for an agent to *roll* Arnovis (Border Patrol lingo for processing apprehended migrants). *Processing* itself is a common euphemism: in 2018 DHS secretary Kirstjen Nielsen claimed that the United States didn't detain children, it only "processed" them. The first immigration detention centers in the country were initially called "processing centers," and some of them still bear that name.

When I spoke, in 2018, to a former Border Patrol agent and the first frontline whistle-blower he described to me the "processing" of asylum seekers: Once you get them to the station, you start rolling them. You bring them all in. They're all handcuffed. You take all their property. You give them a property tag. Hey, don't lose this or you'll lose your bag. Put a property tag on their bag, give them the other copy, kind of like valet. And then, after that, put them in a cell by groups. If it was all one group, put them all together if you can. If there's females or minors, separate them. There's tinier cells for them.

I asked him if agents asked migrants if they wanted to make asylum claims. Border Patrol agents are legally obligated to ask migrants if they fear being returned to their home countries. Specifically, according to Customs and Border Protection protocol, "to ensure that an alien who may have a genuine fear of return to his or her country" is not deported, "you should determine, in each case, whether the alien has any concern about being returned to his or her country. Further, you should explore any statement or indications, verbal or non-verbal, that the alien actually may have a fear of persecution or torture or return to his or her country. You must fully advise the alien of the process ... and of the opportunity to express any fears."

We never ask that, the ex-agent bluntly told me. We were just, What's your name? Is this your real name? What country they're from. This was where a lot of people would lie.

When I pointed out to the agent that they were supposed to ask about fear of return, he told me, Yeah, you are. But it's kind of like ... and he went on to describe their "processing"—the opening of cells, the prodding of bodies, and the capture of biometrics. You're kind of thrown in, he said. Like baptism under fire. They don't give you a class in processing aliens. The guy that you're relieving tells you, "Hey, this is what you're going to do, this is how I do it."

"So-called 'asylum fraud,'" German author Jenny Erpenbeck writes in her novel *Go, Went, Gone*, "is nothing more than telling a true story in a country where no one's legally obligated to listen, much less do anything in response."

After a months-long investigation in 2019, I found that Border Patrol agents were consistently putting false or fabricated information on their arrest reports, called I-213s. The consequences, especially when asylum seekers were later grilled by judges or government attorneys, who often found that their statements didn't accord with what Border Patrol officers recorded on their forms, could be an "adverse credibility determination." In one case I profiled for the *Intercept*, I spoke with a Nicaraguan man who had fled his country after he was beaten, tortured, and threatened to be killed by government goons. He told the Border Patrol officer who "rolled" him all about it, explaining that he was scared to be returned to Nicaragua. Yet the agent wrote on his form that the man "does not indicate any claim fear [*sic*] of persecution if returned to their native country of Nicaragua." The judge later cited that alleged statement in court, ruled the man not credible, and ordered him deported. He was arrested before he could even leave the airport in Nicaragua. Police officers took him into a back room where he suffered "hours of torture—psychological, physical, and verbal."

Arnovis told one of the Border Patrol officers, without being asked, that he wanted to ask for asylum.

The agent said okay, Arnovis told me. But then nothing happened.

They tried to pull a trick, Arnovis said. They tried to confuse me. I told them I was scared to go back to El Salvador, but the officer told me just to sign, that I had to sign. Whether you sign or not, he said, we're going to send you back to your country.

Arnovis refused to sign, and he thinks they punished him for it. For three days, he said, I was in that freezing cold room. Everybody else came and went, but they never called my name. I tried to talk to the boss, the director, or whoever was in charge, but nothing. Eventually, they sent me to Corpus Christi.

He spent three more days in Corpus Christi, and then was transferred, again, to Karnes County Correctional Center, in Karnes City, Texas. He estimated that there were about one hundred inmates in Karnes. Of those hundred, only eight didn't pass their credible fear interview.

The credible fear interview, or CFI, another "process" initiated with the 1996 IIRIRA reforms—the response to the World Trade Center bombing—was purportedly designed to ensure that migrants who are placed in expedited removal proceedings have a chance to ask for asylum. Instead of summarily deporting all apprehended border crossers, those expressing a fear of returning to their home countries—if the Border Patrol doesn't ignore those expressions—are screened by an asylum officer who weighs the *credibility* of that fear. If their fear is deemed "credible" and the asylum officer determines that the claimant has a "significant possibility" of demonstrating eligibility for asylum, they are referred to regular removal proceedings (instead of expedited removal proceedings) and are allowed to present their asylum claim before a judge.

The outcome of a CFI depends, however, on which asylum officer is hearing the claim, according to Schoenholtz, Schrag, and Ramji-Nogales, who closely studied asylum adjudication in their book *Lives in the Balance*. As an example of the subjective influence of the asylum officer, they cite the drop-off in positive CFI determinations given to Muslim applicants in New York immediately after 9/11, when asylum officers seemed to succumb to the anti-Muslim hysteria and the grant rate plunged 55 percent.

Finding state protection is, in large part, the luck of the draw, or amounts to, as the same authors memorably put it in a previous book, "refugee roulette." The variation in grant rates for asylum in the Newark office ranges from 2.5 percent to 90 percent, depending on nothing more than which asylum officer the applicant is randomly assigned to.

In 2015 I was able to sit in on a CFI in the family detention center, often referred to as a "baby jail," in Dilley, Texas. The for-profit facility run by CoreCivic was a hellish place, not because of its oppressive conditions or gross mistreatment—though conditions of confinement were bad, and there were instances of, for example, medical negligence and forcing double vaccines on women and children—but because of the slow-boiling existential heat applied to the people inside: they were denied freedom and denied credibility, their family members and friends were made to pay tens of thousands of dollars in bond to get them released, and they were held up as a spectacle, effectively turned into billboards for the deterrence of other potential asylum seekers. Many of the children consigned to this baby jail developmentally regressed, started to wet their beds, wet their pants, lose speech capability, lose weight, and cry for excessive periods, as well as exhibit other signs of childhood depression.

As a volunteer with the CARA Family Detention Project, helping do intake interviews for attorneys or paralegals and giving basic know-your-rights presentations, I was asked to sit in on a CFI for Carolina, a Honduran circus performer. The CFI guidelines stipulated that I was only allowed to witness the interview and make a conclusory statement. After prepping with Carolina twice, helping her walk through the story of her persecution, we met one morning in a mobile trailer-cum-courtroom inside the detention center and waited, chatting nervously, until the asylum officer called us in. Before the interview, Carolina's two-year-old daughter was plopped down in the adjacent room to "play" with the handful of toys that were strewn in the corner. At one point, about halfway through the hour-long session, her daughter started crying, and for about ten minutes you could hear her slowly sobbing through the thin wall. Carolina started crying, too, as she tried to explain to the asylum officer how an MS gang member had stabbed her twice in the leg after she stopped being able to pay her circus troupe's extortion fee. Her story was long and complicated, and amid the tears and the sounds of her daughter next door, she tried to explain it via speakerphone to the telephonic interpreter who translated for the asylum officer sitting behind her desk. Though I was expressly told I wasn't allowed to interrupt or speak until after the interview, I spoke up, once, to ask the asylum officer if she had any tissues to give Carolina.

Some of Carolina's story got confusing—there were multiple tax collectors, multiple threats, years of living in fear, a dramatic chase through a market, an attempted internal relocation, and discord within the circus troupe. Some pieces of the story seemed irrelevant, some seemed like they could have been exaggerated —the emotion blurring it all together.

But even if Carolina had been able to remember every detail of her ordeal, and her daughter's cries hadn't been distracting her, the asylum officer still might not have been able to understand her. The telephonic interpreter simply wasn't very good, or maybe just didn't understand Carolina's Honduran accent. At one point, I almost breached protocol again to correct a mistranslation: the interpreter was erroneously translating a critical turn of the story. As Carolina's past devolved into mayhem and violence, as she represented it, and as she strained to invoke the painful details, her voice softened, and the interpreter had trouble hearing her. The asylum officer repositioned the phone, and this time offered her a tissue without my prompting. After an exhausting sixty minutes, the asylum officer deemed Carolina's fear as *not credible*.

The set-up-to-fail tech translation wasn't nearly as bad as the tele-hearing I sat in on the following day, still in the Dilley baby jail, in the adjacent trailer/courtroom, in which an indigenous Mam speaker from Guatemala sat before a flat-screen television to appeal her own negative CFI decision. The judge, via videoconference, was in Miami, and spoke neither Mam nor Spanish, so when he (in Miami) asked a question in English, the Spanish interpreter (also in Miami with the judge) spoke in Spanish into a phone to a Mam interpreter (in an undisclosed location), who translated it into Mam for the Guatemalan asylum seeker (back in Texas) to understand the question and respond in Mam so the response could cycle back through and eventually pop out to the judge (in Miami) in English. This game of trilingual, multilocation telephone went from English to Spanish to Mam to Mam to Spanish to English. Not surprisingly, it was a total bungle, but this time ending in a positive result for the woman. The judge, visibly frustrated, vacated the asylum officer's decision, allowing the woman's asylum plea to move forward.

Only after you receive a positive credible fear hearing are you eligible for bond and thus able to make your case outside the detention system. The bond price typically ranges from a few thousand dollars to over $20,000, with the minimum price set at $1,500. One Cameroonian asylum seeker I was in contact with had his bond set at $75,000. An attorney once joked to me that the US government and Los Zetas are both in the migrant kidnapping business, demanding ransom fees for migrants' liberty. Another analogy also comes to mind: as these asylum seekers are detained, as they tell their stories again and again—to Border Patrol officers, asylum officers, attorneys, immigration judges, appeals judges, circuit court judges, and journalists—the asylum seekers begin to resemble Scheherazade, telling stories to save their lives, trying to keep the listener captivated so the storyteller can live another night.

The asylum officer ruled that Arnovis did not have credible fear. He was not eligible for bond. I asked him how long his CFI was. About a half an hour, he estimated. I just explained myself, he said. Told him what happened.

But I didn't understand anything, he continued. The only information I had was, fifteen days after the interview, they started calling people, and only eight of us didn't pass. They called me again, and they started asking for my name, and asking if I said this and this and this, and I was like, yes, yes, yes. And they said, *We're sorry to tell you that your case has not been approved. That you can be deported to El Salvador, or if you want to appeal, you can see a judge to rule on your case.* And since I knew what I was going through in my country, I said that I did want to appeal.

Arnovis spent another thirty days waiting for the chance to appeal before they took him to San Antonio to see a judge. Not having money for a lawyer, he represented himself. He told me that the judge didn't ask him for any proof, but he was confused about the process, and tried to give the judge the names and phone numbers of his persecutors. Instead, the judge gave him another court date, and said he was going to have to come back. A few weeks later, he met with the judge again, thinking, Since it was true what I was saying, I was going to be able to stay. And then the judge started reading my case and asking questions. I remember that the judge told me, Look, everything you told me, I believe you. But I have to rule this case according to the laws of the United States. But he still didn't tell me if he was going to deport me or if he was going to give me asylum. So my case was ongoing. And at that point I didn't feel bad, because I wasn't being deported. And I told myself, okay, I'm going to stay in the US, I'm going to fight my case, god willing. And so I remember I was in for three months, and they sent me back to southern Texas, and then I was sent from there to Louisiana. And when I got to Louisiana, they asked me if I was going to keep fighting my case, or if I was going to sign for my deportation.

After another three months in detention, it still wasn't clear to Arnovis where his case stood.

His deportation officer told him that if he were to be released on bond, which wouldn't be certain for another six months, he would need to front at least twelve thousand dollars. These decisions, however, are not made by deportation officers, and it's unclear if the officer purposefully misinformed Arnovis, if Arnovis was misremembering, or if something got lost in translation. Immigration law is extremely complex, and it's no surprise that Arnovis, lacking an attorney and facing an antagonistic government actively trying to deport him while he was locked up in a remote prison and repeatedly frog-marched from one processing center to another after a traumatizing journey—one that included a kidnapping, a narrow escape, being chased and maybe shot at by Mexican marines, and multiple death threats—would be unsure of how to insist on his rights and win his case. The same can be said of tens of thousands like him.

I thought that maybe, Arnovis said, I could last the six months, but a twelve-thousand-dollar bond I just didn't have. So, I asked the deportation officer for advice. And he told me, *If I was you, I'll be honest, everybody wants to be in the United States, but the United States isn't for everybody. I don't think the United States is for you. You've fought so hard. And you've been in detention, but you don't have anybody to help you outside. And so you're not going to be able to stay here.*

And a few days later—I think it was a Wednesday—I remember the officer came and pulled everybody out that was going to be deported to El Salvador. I had been in for five months at that point. And so he took out all the Salvadorans. I remember the officer closed the door, but, through the glass, he was looking at me, and he opened the door again and said, *I'm going to give you a chance—do you want to go back to your country today? This chance I'm not going to give you again for another month. But if you want to save yourself that month, you can go today.* So, I said to myself, Don't keep on fighting. You don't have anybody to pay for you in the US. *Are you staying or going?* he asked me. I told him, Okay, I'll go. When I signed, Arnovis said, the deportation officer started laughing.

He was laughing like he had tricked me. That he had got what he wanted.

9

Tunc tua res agitur paries cum proximus ardet.
Your own property is in peril when your neighbor's house burns.

—Horace

Every minute that passes, twenty new people around the world are displaced. In the time it takes you to read this paragraph, twenty people have permanently left their homes. Most of them, 51 percent, are children. And though Europe is seeing the bulk of today's asylum seekers, hundreds of thousands are also heading to different parts of Asia and the Americas. Despite these alarming figures and the havoc cried by nativists—or the soapboxer at the rally—the percentage of the global population that's displaced had remained steady over the last seventy years until recently. According to sociologist and migration researcher Hein de Haas, refugees make up roughly 0.3 percent of the total world population, while migrants in general make up roughly 3 percent—both numbers had gone slightly down since 1960. That has changed since 2010, with an increase in the percentage of refugees and migrants: as of 2019, they now make up 3.5 percent of the total global population. In terms of gross numbers, there are by far more migrants, more refugees, and more asylum seekers today than ever before in history.

And while, before 2010, the percentage of refugees had been holding steady for decades, in the first half of the twentieth century the total number of international refugees rose sharply. The first precipitating event was the dissolution of the Ottoman

Empire and the sprawling conflict in the early Soviet Union that drove millions to flee. At least 2 million people fled the Soviet Union in the late 1910s and early 1920s. As there was no international organizing body to react or receive them, the League of Nations convened a conference in 1921 and established the Office of the High Commissioner for Refugees, appointing a Norwegian polar explorer and wonderfully mustachioed scientist, Fridtjof Nansen, as its first high commissioner.

One of the high commissioner's initial moves, besides some political leveraging to push countries into accepting more refugees, was offering the recently expelled and stateless people IDs—identification papers that became known as Nansen passports, letting their carriers legally cross international boundaries and look for work. The passports cost five gold francs apiece—a prohibitive cost for some. Michael Marrus, writing in *The Unwanted: European Refugees in the Twentieth Century*, explains that "for the first time [the Nansen passports] permitted determination of the juridical status of stateless persons through a specific international agreement."

Initially, the Nansen passports were specifically intended for the Russians, Poles, and Germans fleeing the Soviet Union after, as Arendt put it, "the Soviet regime had disowned one and a half million Russians." In the following years, the mandate of the high commissioner was extended to include Armenians, Assyrians, Assyro-Chaldeans, Syrians, Kurds, and Turks. In sum, nearly half a million Nansen passports were issued, and fifty-two countries recognized the document. Both Vladimir Nabokov and Igor Stravinsky carried the passport, which Nabokov once referred to as the "Nonsense Passport."

Over the next decades, millions more people would continue to be driven by fear to cross international boundaries in search of safety: Italians fleeing Fascist Italy and Spaniards fleeing Francoist Spain, as well as Poles, Finns, Kosovars, Serbs, Croats, Estonians, Hungarians, and Jews fleeing the hate and slaughter campaigns of the Nazis or Nazi-collaborating governments.

In Asia, too, Japanese aggression forced Koreans and Chinese to take flight. After World War II, the Japanese were expelled from Taiwan and Korea, and almost three-quarters of a million Palestinians were displaced in the 1948 Palestinian exodus.

Surely, I'm missing entire populations, skipping over millions of people. The enormous numbers reach abstraction, which is, perhaps, part of the problem. Quantity and empathy have an inverse relationship, and the sheer numbers of people crossing a border in search of safety so often provoke not empathy but its opposite—a hardening of the heart.

"In the long memory of history," Arendt wrote, "forced migrations of individuals or whole groups of people for political or economic reasons look like everyday occurrences." In the twentieth century, "suddenly, there was no place on earth where migrants could go without the severest restrictions, no country where they would be assimilated, no territory where they could found a new community of their own."

In her groundbreaking work, *The Origins of Totalitarianism*, which traces the rise of imperialism, racism, and anti-Semitism and the unprecedented uprooting of people that resulted from these evils, Arendt notes that protections and human rights were afforded by the state and only by the state, leaving millions of stateless and refugees to existential uncertainty. With no state to protect them, refugees were left without, in Arendt's famous phrase, "the right to have rights." Nansen passports, and a series of international agreements, sought to fill that gap of rightlessness, but they fell short. As author Lyndsey Stonebridge, in her illuminating book *Placeless People*, writes, "For German and Austrian Jews access to the passports was minimal and haphazard."

In 1933 the high commissioner for refugees drafted the Convention Relating to the International Status of Refugees, recognizing the urgent need to protect persecuted Jews. The 1933 Convention, though only ratified by nine states (the United States was not among them), laid out the legal arguments and language that would be adopted by the 1951 Convention. Importantly, the 1933 Convention established, for the first time, the principle of non-refoulement, the crux of today's asylum law: the right not to be returned to a country where you face grave danger. As the drafters of the Convention put it, "Each of the Contracting Parties undertakes not to remove or keep from its territory by application of police measures, such as expulsions or non-admittance at the frontier (*refoulement*), refugees who have been authorized to reside there regularly, unless the said measures are dictated by reasons of national security or public order. It undertakes in any case not to refuse entry to refugees at the frontier of their countries of origin."

The 1933 Convention was followed by a flurry of assemblages and convergences relating to the persecution and status of Jewish refugees leaving Germany, culminating in the Évian Conference of 1938 (in the spa town of Évian, France), where representatives met to find a way to protect Jews stripped of their citizenship by the 1935 Nuremberg Laws. Specifically, the conference was provoked by Hitler's annexation of Austria and, just days later, the young SS officer Adolf Eichmann's arrival in Vienna on a mission, as Michael R. Marrus and Robert O. Paxton write in *Vichy France and the Jews*, "to terrorize the Jews of Austria into flight." Despite the thousands of Jews storming the American embassy in Vienna and pleading for visas, Marrus and Paxton write, President Roosevelt remained "determined not to enlarge the modest American quota for [immigrants from] Germany and Austria." Hearing of the conference, Hitler wrote, "I can only hope that the other world, which has such deep sympathy for these criminals, will at least be generous enough to convert the sympathy into practical aid." An obvious provocation, he wanted the global community to help rid Germany of its Jewish population.

Despite grandiose posturing, very few Jewish refugees were settled after Évian. Although he was the one who called for the conference, President Roosevelt, rather than sending an actual government official as his emissary, instead sent his pal and envelope manufacturer Myron Taylor. The bars on resettlement into the United States that Roosevelt refused to lift at the conference—highlighting how pointless international posturing could be when coupled with domestic abulia—were set by the eugenicist-inspired 1924 US Immigration Act, which limited the number of future immigrants based on the population from that country already present in the United States according to the 1890 census, thereby greatly disfavoring southern and eastern Europeans and rendering immigration from Africa practically zero. Without changing the 1924 cap, no promise of protection could possibly be met. The Dominican Republic's Rafael Trujillo, in what Lyndsey Stonebridge notes was an unapologetic attempt to make his nation more white, was the only national leader to make a concrete offer to take in Jewish refugees. Other conference emissaries, meanwhile, considered sending European Jews to Madagascar. Famed American journalist Dorothy Thompson called the failure of the Évian Conference "the most cataclysmic event in modern history." At that point, and if by *event* Thompson meant *conference*, the comment may not have been hyperbole.

A few months later, the sound of shattering glass rang throughout Germany, Austria, and Sudetenland, as Hitler's youth and Nazi soldiers destroyed synagogues and rounded up thousands of Jews on Kristallnacht.

Writing an op-ed in the *New York Times* in 1979, Vice President Walter Mondale pointed out that if each of the thirty-two countries attending the conference had taken in a mere seventeen thousand Jews, every Jew in the Reich (just over a half a million) would have been saved. Mondale was technically correct, but 1938 was still early in the Nazi Lebensraum—before they conquered territory where millions more Jews were living, and the thirty-two "nations of asylum" hardly lived up to the sobriquet.

Despite the gestural, milquetoast stance of the Évian delegates, another important precedent was set: for the first time, as Gilbert Jaeger, former director of protection of the UNHCR, writes, "protection was extended to would-be refugees inside the country of potential departure." That is to say, the conference established the modern political notion of the refugee, someone who *needs flight* as much as someone who has already taken it.

Given the lack of governmental response and unwillingness to ease immigration restrictions in the late 1930s, private organizations, mostly British, organized the Kindertransport, shuttling about ten thousand young Jewish children from Nazi-occupied Europe into the United Kingdom. In 1940, the Vichy government of France sought to transport over one hundred thousand anti-Franco Spanish refugees to Mexico, but Mexico refused.

In their defense, countries pled a lack of capacity, which seems a poor excuse when, for instance, landlocked Bolivia—having just been browbeaten in a war with neighboring Paraguay—acted the friendly outlier (and without the execrable ulterior motives of Trujillo) to the persecuted Jews and admitted over twenty thousand refugees between 1938 and 1941. Another outlier was Muslim-majority Albania, where various towns and villages hid refugees after the Nazis invaded in 1939. The Albanians were adhering to *besa*, a traditional honor code that includes, as Linda Rabben describes, "a moral imperative to offer one's home to protect and shelter any guest in need." Photographer Norman H. Gershman cites an Albanian proverb that also may have inspired the villagers: "Our home is first God's house, second our guest's house, and third our family's house."

The world's refusal to offer refuge to critically endangered Jews came to dramatic climax when a ship, the *St. Louis*, departed Hamburg, Germany, for Cuba in May of 1939 with 937 passengers on board. Almost all of them were fleeing Jews; some of whom had already experienced the horrors of the camps. After a relatively placid, three-week journey—there was a band on board, the passengers dined on linen tablecloths, and the weather was calm—the Cuban government denied the ship

harbor in Havana. A few passengers with connections were able
to disembark, but the rest were left floating. One man threw
himself into the water to try to swim to shore—he made it—
and urgent appeals were sent out to the Cuban president
Federico Laredo Brú, as well as US president Roosevelt. Both
of the presidents dithered, deflected, and eventually refused to
let the ship dock. After days of waiting, the *St. Louis* sailed from
Havana to Miami, hoping to pressure the US government to
give in. As Roger Daniels writes in *Guarding the Golden Door*,
"For a time [the *St. Louis*] was so close to Miami Beach that the
passengers could hear dance music being played at the resort's
luxury hotels." They may have heard Glenn Miller's "Moonlight
Serenade," one of the top hits in 1939: "I stand at your gate
and the song that I sing is of moonlight." The melody seems
to come into its own if you imagine the *St. Louis* passengers
listening to it—the lapping, mournful, opening bars not fit for
dancing as much as witnessing a distant dance, harmonizing
with the underlying power of a dark sea, and then, the trill of
the clarinet as you steam back to the land you just escaped from.
Rich Miami locals sailed their yachts close to the ship to take
photographs of the waving Jews. At the same time, "suicide
patrols," Stonebridge writes, "monitored the decks at night to
prevent passengers from throwing themselves overboard or
trying to swim to shore."

When the passengers learned they were sailing back to Europe,
as Gordon Thomas and Max Morgan-Witts write in *Voyage
of the Damned*, some of them "were shouting, a number were
crying, a few prayed aloud. In the babble of sounds, a theme
gradually emerged—a monotonous, frightening chant: 'We
must not sail. We must not die. We must not sail.'" They set sail.

The exact number is unknown, but at least two hundred
of the passengers on the *St. Louis* were later killed in Europe,
some of them gassed in Theresienstadt.

The legal shield the United States used to deflect the passengers back into the camps was, again, the 1924 Immigration

Act. It established the quota for German immigrants at 27,370, which had been met by the time the *St. Louis* was within sight of Miami. Between 1929, with the onset of the Great Depression, and 1939, however, the quota for Germans was rarely filled, as US authorities relied on a strict interpretation of the "likely to become a public charge" rule to keep out immigrants. These were the "paper walls" that consigned people to their death. (Roosevelt's refugee policy adviser, Isaiah Bowman, was also an avowed racist and eugenicist.) Admitting the *St. Louis* passengers would have been a politically precarious move for Roosevelt, given, according to Sarah A. Ogilvie and Scott Miller, the "powerful anti-immigrant lobby that was reaching the height of its influence." A 1938 Gallup poll, as Tara Zahra reports in *The Great Departure*, found that 77 percent of Americans "opposed allowing substantial numbers of refugees into the United States."

Another bar to entry—on top of the national origin quota—was the "public charge" rule, which was signed into law by President Herbert Hoover in the 1930s and whose spirit was recently invoked by the Trump administration as a way to prohibit low-income immigrants from entering the country. In the 1930s the rule's cruelty was particularly evident in that most Jews who were able to leave Germany were dispossessed of their assets by the Nazis before escaping. The Nazis thus rendered them likely to become public charges and were basically giving the US government an easy excuse—which they took —to deny protections to refugees.

In his moving YA novel *Refugee*, Alan Gratz retells the saga of the *St. Louis* to compare the experience of the Jewish refugees fleeing Europe in 1939 with the Syrian child refugees of today and with Cuban refugees in 1994. In a story arc that parallels actual US policy, only one of the novel's three young protagonists—the Cuban girl, Isabel—is allowed into the United States. Because she was fleeing a Communist-run country, merely touching a US shore was enough to permit her to remain. But while Isabel is allowed to stay, Josef, the Jewish boy, despite being in the same waters, isn't allowed off the *St. Louis* and is returned to Europe where, in the novel, he is murdered in a concentration camp.

Another fictionalized voyage, involving what Hungarian author Arthur Koestler called "little death boats," takes place in George Orwell's *Nineteen Eighty-Four*. Winston, the protagonist of the frighteningly prescient novel, goes to the movies and watches a war film, one of which, a "very good one," showed a ship full of refugees that was bombed in the Mediterranean. The audience in the cinema is "much amused" by shots of a fat man sinking, the water around him turning pink with blood. A "Jewess," clinging to the sinking prow, holds on to her young son until a helicopter bombs the boat "to matchwood," and the audience applauds. Stonebridge points out that at the same time Orwell was writing *Nineteen Eighty-Four*, in 1941–42, there was the famous case of the *Struma*, a small ship fleeing Europe with 769 passengers crammed onto its decks. British authorities denied the refugees visas, and then Turkey denied the boat harbor and towed it back to sea, where it was believed to have been torpedoed by a Russian submarine.

A few years earlier, the same forbidding year as the moral catastrophe of the *St. Louis*, New York senator Robert Wagner introduced a bill for the United States to receive an additional twenty thousand refugee children from Europe. Republican opponents in the Senate bitterly fought the bill, and, along with many of the millions clambering to get out of Europe, it died before passage.

It wasn't all refusal, however. Albert Einstein was offered asylum—and we understand the universe better because of it. But there are few Einsteins in the universe. As Arendt writes: "The chances of the famous refugee are improved just as a dog with a name has a better chance to survive than a stray dog who is just a dog in general."

At one point in my stay with the family, Arnovis's mother

told me, referring to Corral de Mulas, They kill people like dogs here. She might have said, Like *dogs in general.*

In the United States, immigration judges use the word *relief* to refer to what they grant or refuse asylum seekers. When I first heard the term I thought it sounded minimizing, without enough gravitas to capture the burden of fear an asylum seeker carries. But in light of what they are most desperate for, their basic human need for comfort and security, it makes sense. I remember watching a woman in court wait for a judge's decision on her asylum case—she sat rigidly in her chair, eyes fixed, hardly even breathing, it seemed. When the judge said, *For those reasons I am denying you relief,* she tensed further, her spine arching backward, her breath snagging like the snap of a rope catching its weight. Another woman I watched, at the moment she heard that the judge *was* granting her relief, burst immediately into tears. Thank you, sir, thank you, thank you, she said, switching from Spanish to English. Thank you, sir Judge. It was as if she were, finally—after more than a year fighting her case—coming up to the surface for air.

The first major international postbellum effort to protect refugees was the 1946 establishment of the International Refugee Organization (IRO), which was given a mandate to settle all the refugees. Unsurprisingly, it failed to fulfill its charge, and the organization was subsumed into what would become the United Nations High Commissioner for Refugees, which would draft the international legal framework for the protection of refugees and asylum seekers and grow into an institution present today in 128 countries.

Two years after the creation of the IRO, the 1948 Universal Declaration of Human Rights proclaimed in its first article, "All human beings are born free ... and should act towards one another in a spirit of brotherhood." In thirty subsequent articles, equally broad promises, as well as specific protections, were made against, in sum, the concentration camp—the death and terror camps that symbolized and actualized the political reduction of human beings to "bare life," to again quote philosopher Giorgio Agamben. Arendt called a similar state "the abstract nakedness of being human." Being divorced from citizenship, Arendt explained, "it seems that a man who is nothing but a man has lost the very qualities which make it possible for other people to treat him as a fellow-man." The 1948 Declaration is, in effect, politics protecting human beings from politics.

"The inclusion of bare life in the political realm," in Agamben's words, is how quality of life descended into the sheer biological fact of life—human beings relegated to disposable statistics or means. This led to the state of exception: the protracted crisis, life on the unending knife-edge, on which torture, indefinite detention, extrajudicial rendition, and murder are the daily bread. This is the essence of the camp, where "bare life and juridical rule enter into a threshold of indistinction," and it's from that indistinction that the 1948 Declaration sought to protect humanity.

The Declaration lays out not only the proscription of the camp but prescribes what life outside the camp could (or even should) entail: liberty; the recognition of a person as a person; freedom from torture; freedom of movement (with restrictions); the right to own property; the right to assemble and associate; the right to work; and even the right to rest, leisure, and paid holidays. And yet, these rights protecting us from the politics of exception, where bare life and law are indistinguishable, are only guaranteed *through* politics, a critical point considering that some humans—the stateless, refugees, and asylum seekers—are effectively abandoned by state protection. And the Declaration seems to—almost—recognize as much: "Everyone is entitled to a social and international order in which the rights and freedoms set forth in this Declaration can be fully realized." All human beings, in other words, are not only free to be free, but free not to be restricted from being free. Under the current system of *state and guaranteed-only-by-the-state* rights, the right to asylum is the only entrance through which those abandoned by the state can enter and gain access to *any rights*. Sir John Hope Simpson, in his 1939 book *The Refugee Problem*, writes, "All refugees are for practical purposes stateless."

International treaties like the 1948 Declaration, as Arendt notes, ironically made it harder for states to offer asylum—as they and the treaties they signed affirmed as sacrosanct the reciprocal sovereignty of other nations. The 1951 Refugee Convention, building off the 1948 Declaration, was meant to undercut this supreme deference to reciprocal sovereignty—that in certain circumstances, such as when a state persecutes, refuses to protect, or is unable to protect its citizens, other states *may* offer avenues of relief, which is understood as an admonishment, or an acknowledgment of another state's lack of capacity—and yet still relied on the state to be the exclusive defender of refugees, which leaves the stateless and denied asylum seekers floating off the coast of protection. We see lasting evidence of the primacy of reciprocal sovereignty with today's extradition laws—nations' willingness to extradite, or threaten to extradite, someone for political points—and nations' unwillingness to grant asylum to those fleeing their allies. As I detailed earlier, the United States succumbs to this logic in its extreme reluctance to grant asylum to Mexicans. If Canada were to offer asylum to a US citizen fleeing police brutality, for example, it would be raising an international alarm. This is the gamesmanship Russia has been playing by offering protection to Edward Snowden. "Sovereignty is," Agamben writes, "this law beyond the law to which we are abandoned."

The 1948 Universal Declaration of Human Rights also promised, in Article 13, that "everyone has the right to leave any country." But, of course, in a world carved into nation-states, if you leave one country, you have to enter another: there's no interstitial "elsewhere" or "alter parts" between the political walls of nations, as China Miéville imagines in his novel *The City & the City*. Neither the Universal Declaration of Human Rights nor any universal international treaty would move to grant, explicitly, the right to *enter* into any other country. The purgatory brought on by the "entry fiction" doctrine seems to have predestined this demi-liberty.

Furthermore, while Article 14 of the Declaration states that "everyone has the right to seek and to enjoy in other countries asylum from persecution," to *enjoy* something is to already have it, and that is not the case for asylum *seekers*; and very few states have actually codified the right to enjoy, not to mention *receive*, asylum in their own domestic law—with the short-lived exceptions of Germany and France. Hersch Lauterpacht, a judge at the International Court of Justice, wrote soon after the Declaration that the paragraph about asylum was "couched in language which is calculated to mislead and which is vividly reminiscent of international instruments in which an ingenious and deceptive form of words serves the purpose of concealing the determination of states to retain full freedom of action."

In 1948, the same year as the Declaration, the United States passed the Displaced Persons Act, which permitted the entry of two hundred thousand persons in two years. The racial origin quotas, however, remained on the books until 1964.

In the original charter of the 1951 Refugee Convention—the culmination of decades of compacts and negotiation—protections were geographically and temporally limited, and the United States, despite being fundamental in drafting the convention, didn't sign it. Though it remains uncertain why the United States didn't commit, nationalists at the time were wary of the country falling beholden to international agreements and treaties, and the Bricker Amendments—a series of constitutional amendments proposed by conservative Ohio senator John Bricker aiming to limit foreign influence on domestic US politics—built enough public pressure to keep President Truman from uncapping his pen. Even the American Bar Association—highlighting the contention over international treaties at the time—came out against the Universal Declaration of Human Rights, calling it a "blueprint for socialism" and worrying that it promises "a lot of the other nice things ... that add up to totalitarianism."

Today the United States maintains the stance adopted during the 1969 Vienna Convention on the Law of Treaties, that international treaties to which the United States is a party are domestically binding and part of the "supreme Law of the Land." But treaties, like all laws, are only as binding as they are respected or enforced, and the United States often holds itself aloof from international agreements. As Trump's former national security advisor, John Bolton, wrote in 1997, dismissing the Vienna Convention as breezily—and as dangerously—as gassing through a red light, "treaties are simply 'political' and not legally binding."

Eisenhower and subsequent presidents similarly skirted around the Refugee Convention, refusing to sign but promising that they would abide. As the civil rights movement of the sixties pushed the United States closer toward actual democracy, it also had effect on immigration law—in 1965, with the Hart-Celler Immigration and Naturalization Act, the racist national origin quotas set in 1924 were finally removed. The INA is typically seen as a liberal reform, although the law kept in place a ceiling on overall immigration, with a cap, for one example, of 20,000 entries a year on Mexicans. The termination of the Bracero program the year earlier also canceled the allotment of 450,000 temporary visas for Mexicans. Mae Ngai points out that, at the time of the INA's signing, "legal" migration from Mexico was as high as 200,000 temporary workers and 35,000 annual admissions for permanent residency, more than eleven times the INA cap. She also notes that the act "naturalized the construction of 'illegal aliens'" as a concept, wedding the term to Mexicans and setting the legal and rhetorical groundwork for the militarization of the US-Mexico border. Officials, of course, were aware that Mexicans were migrating north—sometimes only temporarily—and illegalizing that movement for the first time became justification for a massive "security" buildup. The move was, in effect, building a fence around where somebody was living and then arresting them for trespassing. Though the 1965 INA expanded the number of refugees who could be admitted, refugees were only allocated 6 percent of the Eastern Hemisphere quotas of 170,000 immigrants, or a little over 10,000 people a year. During the heightening anti-communist climate of the Cold War, asylum policy remained staunchly political. According to Gibney, asylum seekers' "very desire for asylum provided much-needed ideological evidence of the superiority of Western liberal democracy." This political bracketing of asylum protections came from both sides of the iron curtain. Otto Kirchheimer, in writing of the Soviet refugee admission policy, explains: "Far from benefitting all persecuted toilers, admission of exiles has been determined solely by the political and economic needs of the Soviet government."

Though the 1951 Refugee Convention was meant to protect only those who had been uprooted or rendered stateless because of the recent war, the US delegate, Louis Henkin, spoke in much broader terms: "Whether it was a question of closing the frontier to a refugee who asked admittance, or of turning him back after he had crossed the frontier, or even of expelling him after he had been admitted to residence in the territory, the problem was more or less the same. Whatever the case might be, he must not be turned back to a country where his life or freedom could be threatened. No consideration of public order should be allowed to overrule that guarantee."

And yet, public order and fear-politicking continued to justify refusing hospitality to millions. "No country knit together its definition of a refugee with escape from communism as tightly as the US," Gibney explains. Authors Alexander Betts and Paul Collier echo Gibney in their book, *Refuge*: "The US was primarily motivated by a desire to control and discredit

Communism." The very definition of refugees on the basis of individualized "fear and persecution," they argue, emerged because of the United States' "vehement rejection of repatriation" of asylees who had been displaced from Eastern Europe back to communist countries. Before 1980, refugees from noncommunist countries, unless they were from the Middle East, had no means to gain protection under US law.

The United States wasn't unique in circumventing its obligations to accept refugees. Betts and Collier show how other signatories to the Refugee Convention adapted the same stance: soon after signing, states almost immediately started searching for "ever more elaborate ways to disregard or bypass the principle of non-refoulement, adopting a suite of deterrence or *non-entrée* policies that make it difficult and dangerous for refugees to access their territory: carrier sanctions, razor wire fences, interception en route." As Agamben put it, "the figure that should have embodied human rights more than any other—namely, the refugee—marked instead the radical crisis of the concept."

Not only were there temporal and geographic limitations for who could be protected, according to the Refugee Convention, the uprooted were only protected if they were persecuted *on account of* their "race, religion, nationality, membership in a particular social group or political opinion." If you suffered economic warfare or financial terrorism, if you were dispossessed of your home or your property, or if your house was destroyed by a hurricane or earthquake, even if you were caught in the crossfire of a civil war, you were and are not necessarily considered a refugee, and you may have no legal claim to asylum. You are just another dog in general, another human ground into the dirt.

The tens of thousands fleeing the massive US bombing campaign in Korea in the early 1950s, for one potent example, did not qualify as refugees under the Refugee Convention's guidelines: they were persecuted after January 1951. Koreans were also still barred by the Asian Exclusion Act of 1924. Some Korean orphans, however—largely children of mixed-race descent (around forty thousand children were fathered by American service members)—were permitted visas under the 1953 Refugee Relief Act.

Despite the refusal to sign the Refugee Convention it was integral in drafting, the United States still let in asylum seekers and refugees through an administrative end run. In 1957, President Eisenhower issued an executive order authorizing the attorney general to parole in up to fifteen thousand Hungarians who had risen up against their Soviet-controlled government. Eisenhower explained: "Last October the people of Hungary, spontaneously and against tremendous odds, rose in revolt against communist domination. When it became apparent that they would be faced with ruthless deportation or extinction, a mass exodus into Austria began. Fleeing for their lives, tens of thousands crossed the border into Austria seeking asylum. Austria, despite its own substantial economic problems, unselfishly and without hesitation received these destitute refugees."

The statement, absent its anti-communism, could have applied to dozens of contemporary situations throughout the world, including the millions of Muslims fleeing post-partition India, hundreds of thousands displaced Palestinians, or even the Guatemalans beginning to flee the CIA-led overthrow of its democratically elected president, Jacobo Árbenz. Spaniards, too, continued to seek safety from fascist Generalissimo Francisco Franco, and, soon, hundreds of thousands more would begin fleeing violence erupting from decolonization fights in Africa. In following decades, millions of Mozambicans, South Africans, Rwandans, and Burundians would flee across recently imposed borders. But none of these millions of refugees fit into the anti-communist paradigm, and extremely few of them found protection.

Offering refuge to those fleeing your rivals has been used as a political jab for millennia. Hellenic scholar William Smith writes,

"Those slaves who took refuge at the statue of an emperor were considered to inflict disgrace on their master ... as it was reasonably supposed that no slave would take such a step, unless he had received very bad usage from his master." Demosthenes, in *On the Peace*, notes, "The Thebans are, as people admit, hostile and likely to be even more so, because we offer an asylum to their exiles."

"Offering refuge to the slave of one's rivals became a common practice in imperial relations," Eric Foner likewise writes in *Gateway to Freedom*, his book on the Underground Railroad. During the War of 1812, Vice Admiral Sir Alexander Cochrane proclaimed that American slaves who made it to British naval encampments would be further relocated to British Canada, in either Nova Scotia or New Brunswick, or Trinidad. Writing about escaped slaves seeking refuge in his moving and relevant book *Blacks on the Border*, Harvey Amani Whitfield undercuts any ideas that the policy was motivated by anti-slavery sentiment: "This military policy had been designed to create economic problems and a climate of fear in which white Americans would imagine blacks roaming throughout the countryside to murder them in their homes and churches"—an attitude eerily resembling today's anti-immigrant and anti-refugee arguments. The freed slaves, some of whom were conscripted into the Merikins division of the British army and fought against the United States, were known as "Black Refugees" or "American Refugees." The exodus continued beyond the War of 1812, too. After the passage of the 1850 Fugitive Slave Act, up to 20 percent of the free Black population fled the United States for Canada, Haiti, Britain, and Africa. As Abraham Lincoln said: "People of any color seldom run unless there be something to run from."

In 1967, after sixteen years of impromptu paroles and political pretext, the international community convened to expand the 1951 Convention, doing away with the geographic and temporal limitations of the definition of refugees and asylum seekers, and expanding protection globally. The next year, in 1968, the United States finally signed the 1967 Protocol Relating to the Status of Refugees, which made the country party to the 1951 Convention.

In that same year that the United States finally agreed to officially acknowledge and protect refugees, it doubled down on the mass slaughter campaign in Vietnam, launching the Tet offensive and killing, in just one instance, hundreds of innocent villagers in the My Lai massacre. Throughout the war, American and American-led forces killed well over 1 million people, rendering much of Vietnam and parts of Laos and Cambodia uninhabitable, as well as forcing over 3 million people to flee. The war also prompted what is perhaps the most lauded US refugee policy of the last century, though still a relatively meager expiatory move—the acceptance of around a quarter million fleeing Vietnamese, Cambodians, and Laotians. The refugees, to their benefit, fit neatly into the ideology of the US refugee policy: they were fleeing a communist state.

The "boat people," as they disparagingly came to be known—a term that "smacks of anthropological condescension," as Viet Thanh Nguyen notes in his novel *The Sympathizer*—were also resettled in parts of Europe, Canada, and Australia. At a perfunctory glance, the admission of the Southeast Asian refugees seemed to symbolize the promise of the 1951 Convention. To rescue some of the dispossessed and to save some sort of face amid the ongoing moral calamity of the war, President Jimmy Carter ordered the US Navy's Seventh Fleet to conduct search and rescue operations. At the same time, Carter would send boats to push back asylum seekers from non-communist countries, and subsequent administrations would do the same. Notably, Carter's rescue operations weren't even popular—62 percent of Americans were against increasing the number of accepted refugees, according to a 1979 poll. Nonetheless, the United States spent about a billion dollars on resettlement programs, while the total cost of the Vietnam War, from 1961 to 1975, was $141 billion (with some estimates putting the amount significantly higher). In 1979 Carter doubled the refugee ceiling, from 7,000 to 14,000 a month, or about 168,000 a year.

The United Nations–led Orderly Departure Program attempted to promise fleeing Vietnamese a means of travel that didn't require boarding unseaworthy boats, and the program assisted over 600,000 people to depart Vietnam. Still, according to most estimates, somewhere between 200,000 and 400,000 fleeing Vietnamese and Laotians drowned at sea.

Hung Truong, in a narrative compiled in Mary Terrell Cargill and Jade Quang Huynh's *Voices of Vietnamese Boat People*, recounts that after setting off from Vietnam in a small boat, they were ignored by two merchant ships unwilling to rescue him and his fellow passengers. In order to force what Itamar Mann calls a "human rights encounter," Truong and another passenger decided to pound a hole into their own boat as they came within sight of another ship—provoking the international duty to rescue ships in distress, a long-established maritime practice codified in 1910's Convention for the Unification of Certain Rules of Law Relating to Assistance and Salvage at Sea. "I took my big hammer," Truong said, "and I hammered out the floor. As I hammered, I cried. I told the boat: 'That's my friend. That's my heart.' Because that boat had helped me escape from Vietnam. It had helped me get away from pirates and get away from the thunderstorm." Truong and the other passengers were rescued, and Truong eventually resettled to Arkansas.

In Border Patrol parlance, Truong would be considered a "give-up"—a border crosser who submits themselves to apprehension in order to survive. Though many of those locked up in the archipelago of US detention centers suffer enough that they want to give up their cases—or even give up their lives, as the dozens of nooses found in cells in the Adelanto ICE Processing Center in California (to cite just one of many examples of detained immigrants' suicide or threatened suicide) make clear—sometimes, after leaving detention, they find themselves once again in such fear they would gladly turn themselves back in rather than face their persecution. Take Ernesto, for instance, the nineteen-year-old Salvadoran orphan from Sonsonate who grew up hounded both by gangs and the police. After making it to the United States and being detained in Stewart Detention Center in Georgia for a year and a half, he told me he'd lost hope and wanted to go back to El Salvador: I couldn't stand being locked up anymore. It was so cold, too cold inside. The cops harass you too much. They get on your back if you're taking a shower, if you don't keep your cell clean, if you don't want to go to lunch.

After being deported and falling prey, again, to the gangs and to the police they collaborated with, he wanted back in detention. A life sentence up there, he told me, would be better than staying here.

The ongoing departure of refugees from Southeast Asia pushed lawmakers to write the 1980 Refugee Act, which was unanimously passed by the House (a miracle in light of today's state of immigration politics) and signed by President Carter on March 17, 1980. The move meant to bring order to the refugee system, though the implementation of the law brings to mind Michel Foucault's insight: "Just as people say milk or lemon, we should say law or order." While establishing regulations by which anyone who fears returning to their country could apply for asylum, in subsequent years, the 1980 law granted asylum to Salvadorans and Guatemalans less than 3 percent of the time, deporting hundreds (at least) back to their deaths.

The 1980 act officially amended the Immigration and Nationality Act of 1952 and the Migration and Refugee Assistance Act of 1962, officially raising the annual ceiling for refugees from 17,400 to 50,000, creating a process for adjusting the refugee ceiling (which was actually set, through a grab bag of emergency provisions, at over 231,000 in 1980, and has averaged around 100,000 people per year since) and requiring annual dialogue on the ceiling between Congress and the president. The act also articulated for the first time, under US law, the definition of an asylum seeker, complying with the 1967 Protocol, and paving the way for the establishment of the Asylum Office and the corps of asylum officers to screen claims, and, in some cases, approve them. Though these changes would take years to implement, "if one thing is clear from the legislative history of the new definition of 'refugee,' and indeed the entire 1980 Act," Justice John Paul Stevens wrote in the 1987 majority opinion in *INS v. Cardoza-Fonseca*, "it is that one of Congress' primary purposes was to bring United States refugee law into conformance with the 1967 United Nations Protocol Relating to the Status of Refugees."

In 1982, Deborah Anker, director of Harvard Immigration and Refugee Clinic, wrote that the 1980 Act was "a clear statement" contesting refugee and asylum policy that for forty years had "discriminated on the basis of ideology, geography, and even national origin," and amending it "to one that was rooted in principles of humanitarianism and objectivity." And yet, while the United States has granted asylum to over half a million refugees since 1980, a year after the passage of the Refugee Act, the US Coast Guard began intercepting boats and rafts Haitians were using to come to the United States to stake asylum claims. Over the next two decades, the United States would continue to interdict Haitians at sea, either caging them in Guantánamo Bay or refouling them right back to Haiti—hardly a humanitarian or objective interpretation of the Refugee Convention. In 2015, there was another influx of Haitians arriving overland to ports of entry at the US-Mexico border. Despite wanting to ask for asylum, they were "metered," forced to wait weeks and even months—a practice that was replicated and expanded in 2018 with the arrival of the Central American caravans to the border. I remember seeing Haitians slumped on the ground outside the port of entry in Nogales, Sonora, where I often, and easily, crossed the border; some of them, as they waited to make their claims, had been sleeping in the cemetery.

Asylum seekers, then and now, are not merely politely denied and gamely deported—they are detained, punished, humiliated, and shackled in an elaborate show of force meant to deter other potential asylum seekers from staking their own claim. They are also accused of using their children to gain access to the United States, of lying about their fear, and of taking advantage of "lax" laws and loopholes. Or, as Matthew Gibney writes in his powerful essay "A Thousand Little Guantanamos"—a nightmarish title if there ever was one—"asylum-seekers are widely characterized as welfare cheats, competitors for jobs, security threats, abusers of host state generosity, and even as the killers of swans." This is a reference to Eastern European asylum seekers in London who had been falsely accused of capturing and roasting swans—also donkeys—in public parks.

Guantánamo is indeed the most apposite metaphor for the denial of refugees, and it's far from merely a metaphor. The origins of Guantánamo Bay as a prison camp trace back to one ship, the *St. Joseph*. In 1977, 101 passengers were fleeing by sea from Haiti to the Bahamas when the *St. Joseph* started taking on water, and the ship sailed toward the US Naval Base in Guantánamo Bay for assistance. They were given harbor, but then, instead of helping them repair their boat, US Navy personnel repossessed it. When American officers next tried to bus the Haitians to the airfield to fly them back to Haiti, the Haitians refused, explaining that they were refugees, and they couldn't go back. After asking for asylum, US State Department officials flew onto the island to assess their claims, granting asylum to only 4 of the 101 passengers. The brief detention of the passengers of the *St. Joseph* established precedent, and as Haitians continued to take to the sea to try to make it to Miami, INS officials scrambled to keep them away. In 1978, deputy INS commissioner Mario T. Noto, as Jonathan Hansen describes in *Guantánamo*, sent a memo to his boss, Leonel J.

Castillo, with a potential solution to the "Haitian problem"—detaining intercepted Haitians at Guantánamo Bay where, Hansen explains, they "would have few if any constitutional protections and no access to lawyers."

The United States was guarding its shores not so much from the Haitians themselves but from their *claims*, using the remote detention of asylum seekers to, as Gibney put it, "obviate the need to grant them the constitutional protections"—such as due process or the freedom from cruel and unusual punishment. If the Haitians couldn't even ask for protection, the United States wouldn't need to betray its own domestic and international laws by refusing it to them.

In one instance in the 1980s, when Haitian refugees refused to disembark a deportation boat, US soldiers threatened, according to Hansen, "to blast them off the ship with fire hoses." In 1986, after the passage of a law prohibiting the admission into the United States of people with HIV, guards isolated HIV-positive Haitians interned in Guantánamo Bay (Gitmo) behind barbed wire. According to Brandt Goldstein, quoting Yolande Jean, who was locked into the HIV/AIDS section of Gitmo, "There was no place to move. The latrines were brimming over. There was never any cool water to drink, to wet our lips. There was only water in a cistern, boiling in the hot sun. When you drank it, it gave you diarrhea." When the abused detainees revolted, over three hundred marines were dispatched in Operation Take Charge.

In 2015 I reported on an uprising in a Criminal Alien Requirement prison in Raymondville, Texas. CAR facilities lock up nearly forty thousand people at a time, sometimes for years, often for nothing but immigration violations, including "illegal reentry" after a prior deportation, which is considered a felony. The prison in Raymondville was commonly referred to as "Ritmo," as it resembled the awful conditions—overspilling sewage, weeks spent in solitary confinement, violent explosions from the guards—of Gitmo. The inmates rose up in defense of their humanity—with guards trying to quell the rising tension by setting off a "hornet's nest," a BB-filled grenade, inside one of the bunk rooms. Eventually, the inmates chased the guards out and burned down parts of the facility. The inmates maintained control over Ritmo for days, but, lacking food and facing the threat of the surrounding officers, they eventually relented and were transferred.

The island-like remoteness of many immigrant detention centers makes access to counsel and oversight of abuses extremely difficult—non-detained asylum seekers have a 68 percent better chance of not being deported, and even previously detained and released applicants have a harder time receiving asylum, evidence of the lasting negative effects of detention. Los Angeles–based immigration attorney Meeth Soni referred to FCI Victorville—one of the federal prisons that in 2018 began taking overflows of detained immigrants and is a two-plus-hour tramontane haul from Los Angeles—as "Guantánamo Bay for asylum seekers." The prison, Soni said, "may as well be on a Caribbean island as far as access to representation goes."

Throughout the 1980s, State Department officials were dispatched onto the Coast Guard cutters to hold asylum screenings. Out of twenty-five thousand intercepted Haitian "boat people," only twenty-eight were granted asylum. Ten years later, in 1992, Bush signed Executive Order 12807, also known as the "Kennebunkport Order," authorizing the Coast Guard to return all fleeing Haitians back to their country with no screening process at all. Many of them were sent to Guantánamo Bay.

Of course, this was before the Gitmo-orange jumpsuits, the rape, and the waterboarding of detainees that eventually brought the prison its notoriety, but perhaps this account could provide a warning about the potential future uses of immigration detention centers—there are currently over two hundred throughout the United States. Nearly one hundred thousand Haitians, including some Cubans, were detained in Guantánamo Bay detention centers in the 1980s and '90s, long before the first "enemy combatant" was ever detained on the island. According to the indefinite "lease" signed by United States and Cuba in 1934, the US government annually cuts a check of $4,085 to Cuba, which, since the 1959 Revolution, the Cuban government declines to cash.

There was another US-run "safe haven"—which is how US officials referred to Guantánamo Bay—established to detain Cuban asylum seekers in Panama, the country the United States invaded in 1989 in the absurdly euphemistic Operation Just Cause. (The official justification for the invasion was to protect a handful of Americans in Panama City and depose the formerly CIA-funded President Manuel Noriega. Critics, however, point to Noriega's calling George H. W. Bush "an incompetent wimp" as the final straw that invoked the wrath of the imperium.) A few years later, by 1994, when conditions in Guantánamo Bay were so hellishly crowded with Haitians and, increasingly, Cubans, the United States started sending the Cubans south to Panama—calling the move "Operation Safe Haven and Safe Passage"—where they were housed, once again, in crowded conditions without clarity as to when they would be resettled. After the Cubans rose up in protest, the US military filed an emergency order to an ax handle company to provide the soldiers with extra batons to beat the Cubans into submission. Some of the detainees tried to commit suicide, as later reported in the *Washington Post*, by cutting themselves with barbed wire and drinking shampoo.

As the US government refused to protect, tortured, and threatened to fire-hose Haitians back to Haiti, its stance toward Cuban asylum seekers, meanwhile, was generally welcoming (with the exception of the Panamanian fiasco)—extending protections first to Cuba's bourgeoisie hightailing it out of there, and then to practically any Cuban who asked for it. The United States saw the Cuban refugees as a means of delegitimizing President Fidel Castro—draining the country of its people—even going so far as to institute in 1960 Operation Peter Pan, in which private Catholic organizations and US government agents seeded the lie that Castro was going to send children to Soviet reeducation camps, and subsequently flew more than fourteen thousand Cuban kids to the United States. After the floundered Bay of Pigs invasion, in 1961, the United States staged numerous "boatlifts" to bring thousands more Cubans to Florida, as well as airlifts, or "Freedom Flights"—the twice-a-day, five-times-a-week, US-funded flights between Havana and Miami that shuttled over a quarter million Cubans onto a path to permanent residency after the Cuban Adjustment Act of 1966. That act was a precursor to the famed 1995 reinterpretation, which became known as the "wet foot, dry foot" policy—if fleeing Cubans could reach dry land, they would, after a year, be allowed to apply for residency.

In 1991, a coup brought down Jean-Bertrand Aristide, the first democratically elected president in Haiti's history (the long absence of democratic rule in large part due to successive interventions and the US backing of dictators). The post-coup conditions were dire enough for the United States to temporarily stop the Coast Guard's pushback efforts. After a short hiatus, however, it resumed the practice, and Florida's Haitian Refugee Center filed a lawsuit, which would work its way up to the Supreme Court and become a critical litmus test of US obligations under the 1980 Refugee Act.

In *Sale v. Haitian Centers Council*, lawyers representing the Haitian Refugee Center claimed that interdicting and refouling Haitians on the high seas violated Article 33 of the 1951 Convention and Section 243(h)(1) of the 1980 Refugee Act. The court ruled otherwise, voting eight to one in favor of the government: they could continue the pushbacks. Justice John Paul Stevens, writing the majority opinion, exonerated the United States of all responsibility toward asylum seekers who were still outside US territory, even if the Coast Guard cutters were blocking them from entering in the first place. The Bush administration would later make a similar argument—that the Constitution had a limited geographical reach—when claiming that, with respect to its operations in Guantánamo Bay, it didn't need to abide by the international treaty against torture.

Writing an op-ed about the *Sale v. Haitian Centers Council* decision in the *New York Times*, Deborah Sontag asked, "If the United States, with the imprimatur of its highest court, appears to put the protection of its borders above its responsibilities under international law, will others be enticed to follow suit?" The answer is yes. Australian, Thai, and Italian governments—among others—would all, in the following years, engage in nearly identical pushbacks, guarding their shores against pleas for protection. While historically, the United States took in more refugees than all other resettlement countries combined, that changed in 2017 when Trump took office, and the US anti-refugee stance began to influence other nations. We are looking at a "domino effect that is reverberating backwards," as researchers Molly Fee and Rawan Arar put it, with countries backing out of refugee resettlement agreements and denying hospitality. According to Hans van de Weerd, of the International Rescue Committee, "American humanitarian leadership has previously spurred a race to the top in meeting humanitarian obligations; today it leads a race to the bottom. Cruelty has replaced compassion." In 2018, the United States was one of only two countries to vote against the UN Global Compact on Refugees, a nonbinding agreement to bolster global refugee responsibility-sharing. The other country, led by the anti-democratic, anti-immigrant, and anti-Semitic homophobe Viktor Orbán, was Hungary.

Defending the *Sale v. Haitian Centers Council* decision, Justice Stevens claimed that "general humanitarian intent cannot impose uncontemplated obligations on treaty signatories." Article 33 of the Refugee Convention, however, was written not with "general humanitarian intent" but in direct response to the hardheartedness of the United States and other countries in refusing to accept fleeing Jews who were later tortured and slaughtered in concentration camps. The article itself was inspired directly from the 1933 Convention, in which countries were forbidden from restricting asylum seekers from entering their territory "by application of police measures, such as expulsions or non-admittance at the frontier (*refoulement*)." Fourteen years after the Supreme Court decision, in 2007, the UN issued an advisory opinion clarifying that the principle of non-refoulement doesn't depend on whether the asylum seeker is physically "on the State's national territory ... but rather whether or not he or she is subject to that State's effective authority and control." The same opinion specified that non-refoulement also applies not just in returning an asylum seeker to their country of origin "but also to any other place where a person has reason to fear threats to his or her life or freedom"—which would designate the Migrant Protection Protocols as a clear violation of the 1951 Convention.

Though Justice Blackmun would, in his dissent, call the decision "extraordinary ... in disregard of the law ... and that the Court would strain to sanction that conduct," the United States would go on to take even more extreme measures. In the same years it was justifying refouling Haitians, the INS was deporting Salvadorans and Guatemalans into war zones. Article 45 of the 1949 Geneva Convention, another critical predecessor to the 1951 Refugee Convention, states that in wartime, "in no circumstances shall a protected person be transferred to a country where he or she may have reason to fear persecution for his or her political opinions or religious beliefs." Further, Article 147 specifies that deporting such people back to a state of war would be considered a "grave breach" of the Convention, which "shall be regarded as war crimes." In 1981, only two Salvadorans were granted asylum in the United States. By 1984, the number went up to 328, while 13,045 were denied—a 2 percent grant rate. Meanwhile, 5,017 of those fleeing a state considered a foreign enemy, Iran, were granted asylum, and only 3,216 were denied—a 61 percent grant rate.

As Robert S. Kahn reports in *Other People's Blood*,

immigration officials in California "had arrested a Salvadoran woman who had seen her daughter raped by Salvadoran soldiers after they forced her to watch them execute her husband. To prevent her from applying for asylum, US immigration agents pushed Valium down her throat, then guided her hand to force her signature on form I-274, waiving her right to seek asylum." Under Article 147, this conduct constitutes a war crime.

El Salvador is not officially at war today, but, for many, it may as well be. As we stood in the shade and watched a family preparing for a funeral in the Mejicanos neighborhood of San Salvador, Beto told me: Nobody wants to accept that we're a country at war, just because there aren't helicopters flying overhead, or rifles in the streets. But it's true, we're at war.

He would know—he lived through the civil war as a teenager. He was there on November 12, 1989, when Air Force helicopters strafed the Mejicanos neighborhood, killing at least 339 people. Mejicanos residents who made it to the United States, as Kahn describes, "arrived with stories of troops and death squads who had strangled with barbed wire and burned alive young men found out of uniform." It was bad, Beto told me, of his childhood. It was everywhere.

Today, it's still bad. An armored vehicle is often stationed just around the corner from Beto's home. And, in the gas station where we met for coffee, a plainclothes security guard loitered by the door, a shotgun resting in the crook of his arm. He would occasionally open the door for customers and smile. It was everyday life. Violence, the potential for violence, was never far. In 2010, Barrio 18 gang members fired machine guns at a Route 47 bus in the neighborhood. They then doused the bus with gasoline and set it on fire. As frantic passengers tried to escape out the windows, gang members shot at them, killing fourteen people. One of the convicted murderers lived a few houses down from Beto. The man's son, Jeremy, was left an orphan, and Beto and his wife have since adopted him. After

THE DISPOSSESSED

lunch at his house one day, I again asked Beto about what he termed today's *war*: Who's going to win? he asked himself. Nobody. I'm not going to win. I'm going to end up poor or shot.

After receiving death threats at one point in 2018, he and his family recently had to flee Mejicanos. His wife and kids went to her mother's house, but Beto, worried he was putting them in danger, kept his distance for a few weeks, sometimes having nowhere to sleep but on the street. He texted me one morning: he had spent the night in a small alcove, and a scorpion had stung him. During the war, he told me, it was actually better, because you hoped it would end. Now, this is just life, he said. This is just how things are.

The extraterritorial denial, the pushbacks, the fingers-in the-ears response to asylum claims in the 1980s and '90s set a pattern for the future handling of influxes of asylum seekers. In 2014, the United States armed and funded Mexico (as well as Guatemala, and then El Salvador—with the creation of its own Border Patrol in 2019) to act as its extraterritorial border guards to prevent potential refugees from making claims of protection. Beyond maintaining a singular line of physical-barrier defense, the idea was to create a "layered" border, shifting control of it both inside and outside the actual geographic boundary: inside the border, there would be increased enforcement in the interior of the United States; outside it, there would be funding for and training of other countries to block immigrants potentially on their way to the United States. Such foreign subcontracting of border enforcement undermines a simplistic nationalist appeal: that a country doesn't exist without a border, that the perimeter is sacrosanct and a breach is a violation of sovereignty. Borders, however, are mercurial concepts more than they are hard lines, and their scarring reaches both into the interior of the nation and outward, into neighboring nations and beyond.

Former Border Patrol chief Mike Fisher called the US-Mexico border, in 2014, the "last line of defense," a strikingly martial approach to thinking of the nation's boundaries in terms of immigration. As author Todd Miller reported, "In 2014 alone, the United States designated $112 million to help modernize and make more efficient Mexico's border policing and militarization" as part of the Plan Frontera Sur, or the Southern Border Plan, initiated after the so-called unaccompanied minor crisis at the US-Mexico border. The same year, and only a week after the announcement of the Southern Border Plan, Mexican interior minister Miguel Ángel Osorio Chong sounded like a Border Patrol spokesperson when he said, "Who doesn't have the necessary documents to enter into our territory and enter the United States, we can't allow them to be in our territory."

Two years earlier, in 2012, to lean again on reporting from Miller, US Department of Homeland Security official and former border czar Alan Bersin claimed that "the Guatemalan border with Chiapas, Mexico, is now our southern border." The Trump administration would double down on such exportation of border defense beginning in 2018, threatening Mexican and Central American governments to block refugees, or even to stop their own citizens from leaving their territory, which is a clear breach of international law.

In an even more striking example of a nation redefining its borders to keep out asylum seekers, Australia excised part of its national territory to deny Iraqis and Afghanis the ability to stake asylum claims. A 2001 law territorially amputated Christmas Island, Ashmore Reef, and the Cocos Islands from Australia's migration zone, so that asylum seekers in these territories could not appeal to Australia's legal obligations to offer protection.

One hundred years earlier, one of the first acts of the newly established Australian government was the Immigration Restriction Act of 1901—that telling stamp of national self-proclamation: denying entrance to the other. But not just any other—specifically the black or brown other—as the 1901 Act marked the beginning of the official "White Australia" policy prioritizing white Brits over Pacific Islanders and Chinese immigrants. The official White Australia policies began to be dismantled in the 1950s, but later policy changes reveal the outrageous efforts Australia still takes to deny safe harbor and imperil the lives of non-white immigrants.

Australia's "Pacific Solution" to asylum seekers asking for safe harbor—including the $330-million fleet of ships to patrol for and interdict asylum seekers—was inspired directly by US policy, as journalist Ben Doherty has pointed out. In the midst of Australia's "*Tampa* affair," when 433 asylum seekers were rescued at sea by a Norwegian freighter—and then subsequently refused entry into Australian waters—the government sought guidance from the country that led the world in immigration restriction. Daniel Ghezelbash reveals that "a senior US policy maker provided Australian policy makers extensive advice relating to the US experience with interdiction and extraterritorial processing in the immediate lead-up to the introduction of the Pacific Solution." They quickly implemented hard-line US-inspired policies, including the mandatory detention of asylum seekers and their offshore "processing"—which the United States had been subjecting Haitians to for years. "We've entered what some have referred to as a deterrence paradigm," Ghezelbash notes, "where states are continuing to pay lip service to their obligations under the refugee convention, but are bending over backwards to come up with new and innovative ways of keeping asylum seekers from accessing these protections."

But Australia wasn't only refusing entry and detaining asylum seekers, it was doing so by putting individuals in horrifying, Guantánamo-like conditions. Nobel Prize–winning author J. M. Coetzee described Australia's approach as one of "spectacular heartlessness." Part of the Pacific Solution was the establishment of the Nauru Regional Processing Centre on the South Pacific Island nation of Nauru, one of the smallest countries in the world: an eight-square-mile island with a population of ten thousand. The detention center, under lease by the Australian government, has a capacity of twelve hundred people, and came under fire almost as soon as it opened for its inhumane living conditions, though it's been difficult to get a clear understanding of what the detainees have suffered on Nauru as journalists are consistently denied access.

From leaks and direct testimony—including that provided in the stunning memoir *No Friend but the Mountains*, by Behrouz Boochani, an Iranian journalist confined on the island since 2013 who smuggled out his book via text message on a clandestine cell phone—we know that imprisoned asylum seekers lived in small tents where indoor temperatures sometimes reached 115 degrees, the toilets were filthy, and they suffered gross medical neglect. According to a 2016 Human Rights Watch report, the detainee hospital lacked basics such as bandages and sterile gloves. "Refugees and asylum seekers interviewed said they have developed severe anxiety, inability to sleep, mood swings, prolonged depression, and short-term memory loss on the island," the report described. Children started wetting their beds and suffering from nightmares—a similar reaction children in the United States have to being jailed in family detention centers. According to a 2016 UN study, 83 percent of asylum seekers on Nauru suffered from PTSD or depression, or both, and both adults and children spoke openly of wanting to kill themselves. An eight-year-old girl, Sajeenthana, who has been detained on Nauru since she was three, told the *New York Times* in 2018, "One day I will kill myself. Wait and see, when I find the knife. I don't care about my body." She and her family had been hoping to resettle in the United States after a previous agreement between the two countries, but the Trump administration reneged on some of the resettlements, and detention for children like Sajeenthana seems indefinite. Kids in Nauru also expressed symptoms of what is known as *resignation syndrome*, which includes "extreme withdrawal from reality" and the refusal to eat, drink, or talk. According to the *Times*, "Children now allude to suicide as if it were just another thunderstorm," and there are a lot of thunderstorms on the island.

It's not always clear who learned how to inflict this brutality from whom, but the United States, Mexico, Australia, and Greece, among other countries, all consign asylum seekers to prolonged or indefinite detention, solitary confinement, physical abuse, unsanitary conditions, death threats, racist, homophobic, and gender-based hate from guards, and deadly medical neglect.

Ghezelbash warns, "If Europe goes down the same path as the United States and Australia, it will be inflicting a mortal wound on the universal principle of asylum." In 2018, the European Union piloted its "regional disembarkation platforms," apprehending migrants crossing the Mediterranean and, instead of fielding their claims, shipping them back to "processing centers" in Morocco or Turkey. Researcher Stephanie Schwartz saw it as an attempt for EU countries to "fob off their obligations by shifting the physical duties of refugee protection and non-refoulement to less powerful countries." Banks Miller, Linda Camp Keith, and Jennifer S. Holmes refer to states converging toward the "lowest common denominator in terms of generosity." The slow-burn bouleversement of asylum policy—efforts to protect giving way to scrambles to deny—is often referred to as a "race to the bottom"—a race that the United States is winning.

An outlier to this charge to the depths of inhospitality was the 1984 Cartagena Declaration, in which Latin American countries, in response to the US-backed wars in Central American and the US-backed repressive regimes in South America, amplified the 1951 Convention in an unprecedented way, recognizing as refugees those fleeing "generalized violence." The Cartagena Declaration is the most encompassing and generous refugee standard to date, but remains, in large part, unimplemented—yet another example of high promise and scarce fulfillment.

Philosopher Adam Knowles compares Article 33, the provision against refoulement, with the Kantian notion of hospitality. In his philosophical sketch "To Perpetual Peace," Kant writes,

"We are dealing here with right and not with philanthropy, and within right, hospitality (hospitable reception) means the right of a stranger to not be treated with hostility upon arriving in the territory of another. The other can turn him away, but not if it leads to his downfall." Downfall, or *Untergang* in the original German, is sometimes translated as "death" or "destruction." But Knowles posits a more capacious understanding: *Untergang* should be read "as the very opposite of what philosophers fondly call 'human flourishing' or 'the good life.'" He goes on to define *Untergang* as "perdition, downfall, doom, extinction, and ruin." We must open our doors hospitably, Knowles argues, and not return anyone to their Untergang, not consign them to whatever would oppose human flourishing. Knowles here echoes exiled former member of the Black Liberation Army Assata Shakur, who fled the United States and found asylum in Cuba. Shakur's vision of freedom, as she explains it—quoted by rapper Common in "A Song for Assata"—is not the lack of privation, enslavement, or incarceration, but "the right to grow, the right to blossom."

Political philosopher David Miller calls the question of refugees and asylum seekers "morally excruciating." And while he may be right—that it is morally excruciating for the politicians, judges, and sometimes the citizens deciding between offering asylum protection or protecting the "integrity of the state"— the uprootedness, homelessness, statelessness, persecution, and lack of protection are—more than *morally* excruciating for the asylum seeker—exacting tolls that are both mentally and physically excruciating. The dispossessed, that is, are denied the right to grow and blossom. They are denied freedom and denied life. They are consigned to Untergang.

Third Attempt

10

Arnovis returned to El Salvador in chains.

Along with about another hundred men and a few women, private security guards chained Arnovis ankle, waist, and wrist, loaded him onto a charter plane, and flew him to Central America as one among the many millions of people deported from the United States in the last decade, part of what Daniel Kanstroom calls "the new American diaspora." Transfer and deportation days are discombobulating and awful for deportees. It's common to be transferred multiple times in the days leading up to deportation, given little food, woken up at three in the morning, left to wait for hours on buses and airplanes, and sometimes chained for twenty-four or more hours straight. In fact, ICE's guidelines for transferring a detainee stipulate that they are only to be notified "immediately prior" to the transfer, and once they are finally notified they are not allowed any phone calls, neither to their family nor, if they have one, to their attorney. More than one deportee told me about urinating in his pants after not being allowed to use a bathroom during the long deportation process, or, if they were let into the bathroom, the guards wouldn't take off the chains, leaving them to struggle with a fly zipper while handcuffed. One older deportee, a grandfather, cried while telling me how humiliated he felt.

In 1954, during Operation Wetback, as the Eisenhower administration worked to deport over a million Mexicans and Mexican Americans, the government converted cargo ships to use for mass deportations. The ships would transport bananas and other cargo north, and unwanted people or extraneous labor south. On one of the voyages of the *Mercurio*, as it was carrying over five hundred migrants in a space meant for around ninety, the deportees rose up and mutinied. As the crew fought to take back the ship, at least forty of the "passengers" jumped into the sea to escape; seven of them drowned. One congressman, Joseph Kilgore, probably accurately described the boatlift as a "penal hellship," and you can almost hear the deportees chanting, as did the Jews who were sent back on the *St. Louis*, We must not sail! We must not sail! We must not sail!

After touchdown, Arnovis and the other deportees were transferred to a bus and driven to La Chacra, a sprawling migrant reception campus in San Salvador that receives around thirteen thousand people a year.

The day I first got inside La Chacra—I'd spent a few days waiting outside and trying—seventy-four men and eleven women had been deported. I spoke for an hour with the director, Ana Solórzano, who was very friendly, and pretty vague, and pointed me repeatedly to a six-step "modelo de atención." She told me, at one point—seeming to refer to the whole process of forced displacement, detention, removal, vulnerability, and dismissal of valid asylum claims—"their condition, it's not dignified." Solórzano also took me on a hurried tour of the facility, which felt like a small campus. In the clothes stockroom, there were stacks of Super Bowl XLVIII Denver Broncos Super Bowl Champions T-shirts, though the Broncos had lost that year.

I asked one man sitting in the back of the La Chacra waiting room how the flight was. Bad, he said, and that was all he wanted to say about it.

Most of that waiting room was raptly watching a European Champions League match: Real Madrid vs. Juventus. A couple psychologists, along with a handful of psych students from a local college, were doing interviews at a bank of desks behind a half wall. Occasionally, a woman would come out from a back room with a few Styrofoam to-go boxes of food and call out, Who's hungry?! Everybody was hungry, and most of the men raised their hands. The woman closed her eyes—so as not to be biased, she said—and, seeming to be acting out a disturbing allegory, blindly handed away the food only to those nearest her. As I left, a tropical downpour was pounding down from the sky, turning the parking lot into a soup of mud and gravel. A fifty-something deportee—who I had spoken with earlier, and who told me he had lived almost three decades in the United States—was waiting to get picked up by his family. In unaccented English, he said to me, "How you doing, brother?" and gave me a fist bump.

When, about a year before, Arnovis walked into that same parking lot outside of which I first bothered the guards to let me pass, his father was waiting for him under a brilliantly spilling magenta bougainvillea by the tall front gates. Arnovis was scared to be home again, even if he had heard that a few of the gangsters who had been threatening him had had to attempt their own escape. Maybe if he lay low, found work in another village, he would be okay. Or maybe he wouldn't. He didn't have the money, or the spirit, to head north again—at least not yet.

He had been gone five months. It was hard for Mirna, especially as Meybelín often cried for her father, but Mirna also admitted that she had felt relieved after he had left. In the weeks leading up to Arnovis's departure, she had lived with the constant fear of men with machetes, pistols, or AK-47s storming through her door. That fear had then lapsed, lapsed into a sort of numb history. But now with the target—Arnovis—back home, she worried that the hunter might be stringing his bow again.

Look, Mirna said to him one of the first nights he was back in Corral, I don't want to lie to you, but it was better when you were gone. We were okay, we weren't scared. Now that you're here again, she said, the nightmare is back.

Arnovis proposed that they all leave together. That the three of them migrate north, but that wasn't the life Mirna wanted. I don't want to live like this, she told him. Within a couple days, she had gone to stay with her family in San Salvador.

She left, Arnovis told me, and she took my daughter with her. I was suffering so much. I couldn't eat. I got sick. It was so bad that I begged her to come back, or to let me raise our daughter.

After a fraught few days, they agreed they were done, separated, and that Arnovis would take Meybelín.

Back in Corral, now a single father, Arnovis knew he needed to adjust—to start living and working—but he was hardly leaving the family property. Not only was he depressed, he was still scared. For the same reason that I fled to the United States, he told me, I ended up losing so much. I lost my family. I know it's hard on Meybelín, not seeing her mother. It's something that doesn't give me any peace. But I have to go on, I have to keep fighting for her.

But being a single parent in Corral de Mulas doesn't mean you are completely on your own. Both Arnovis and Ale, his sister, who gave birth to Pedrito in 2017, are raising their children without a second parent. But they live communally, with six adults in the house and five more on the adjacent property, plus a gaggle of children and almost constant visitors—extended family, neighbors, and friends.

After about a month, Arnovis, who had been helping around the house, started to venture out, harvesting corn and gathering coconuts and cashews on the family's land, as he had done before—but he was still scared to be on the street. That fear is not uncommon or unsubstantiated. Researcher Amelia Frank-Vitale explained a similar circumstance in Honduras: "Many young people in the San Pedro Sula area have told me that the only way to stay safe in their neighborhoods is to leave the house as infrequently as possible, only during the day, and never alone. Hector, a young man who has been deported four times, described his life in his neighborhood as *encuevado*—encaved."

Meybelín, though, was beginning kindergarten, and she needed a uniform and school supplies. Having grown up in poverty himself, Arnovis wanted to give his daughter a life without the same sting of lack and hunger. He told me of the single bike that he and his seven brothers and sisters shared when they were young. That bike, he said, never got to rest. Somebody was always, *always* on it. Arnovis wanted to buy Meybelín a bicycle of her own, a bike that got its rest.

Finally, he found a solution. A cattle ranch in Isla de Mendez—a village about ten miles up the peninsula—was hiring ranch hands. Arnovis could work there, stay in a hut on the ranch, and come home every couple weeks to share his earnings and spend time with his daughter. He'd only be making seven dollars a day, and he'd be doing grueling work under a bone-hot sun, but he'd be able to send home a hundred dollars or so a month and would, so he thought, be avoiding his persecutors.

Because you were still scared, after almost a year? I asked him. He nodded. You have no idea what it was like, he said. Why, though, I asked, did the gang care so much?

It's like they have a mission, he said. When they say they're going to do something, they have to do it. Maybe not all of them would remember, but if they see you, they stop you, and figure out who you are. They check your ID, and then they remember.

Another asylum seeker I spoke with, who had fled Honduras, told me that the mara (the gang) has a motto—*The mara doesn't forget.*

At the ranch, Arnovis kept a low profile. He's gregarious by nature, so he consciously had to avoid making friends. He kept his head down and worked, and he knew how to do that. Hard, hot, grunt work: dragging feed troughs, filling burlap sacks with corn, shoveling out manure; sweat-in-his-eyes and dust-caking-his-feet work for a rich and absent ranch owner. I barely had anything, he told me, just enough to eat and give a little something to my daughter. I didn't have money for pants, for clothes, for anything, but I felt good, because I hadn't worked in so long.

His bosses came to rely on him and told him that a night shift was going to be opening up—an extra two dollars a day for an hour less of work, and he'd be avoiding the sun, too. The job would consist of watering the cornfields. Walking row by row and opening spigots, redirecting, patching, coiling and uncoiling the hoses. Wet, muddy, slippery, witching-hour work. In comparison with working under the bite of the sun, however, the night shift would have been a cinch, but he never got his chance at the promotion.

On lunch break one afternoon, Arnovis was lying in the shade of a mango tree—by himself, as was now usual. A few of his co-workers were gnawing on mangoes under another tree about a hundred yards away. The fruit from those trees were particularly delicious: juicy, green, and sweet. People from the islands would come to eat and collect those mangoes, but the locals knew to be careful: the *bichos*, as gang members are sometimes called, liked the mangoes as well. It's one of the reasons Arnovis kept his distance. He was eating a mango when he noticed about five or six people approaching his coworkers. As they got closer, he saw that they were armed with rifles. Arnovis immediately crawled around to the other side of the tree—no good reason to be seen by bichos with guns—and then slipped into a nearby ditch, eventually making it to the cornfield and out of sight.

About a half hour later he met back up with his coworkers and asked them what had happened.

They interrogated us, one of them told him.

The gang members wanted to know who they were, where they were from. They checked the workers' IDs and then asked them who else was working on the ranch. They even wanted to know their schedules. When they asked if anybody working there wasn't from Isla de Mendez, they told them that yes, there was one. And then they asked for the name.

Arnovis.

They recognized the name. Of course they did. That Arnovis. The only one. From Corral de Mulas.

Tell him we want to talk with him, the bichos told his coworkers. Tell him Cristofer is waiting.

Cristofer was the new palabrero, the local leader, and word was that he was tough.

I asked Arnovis how he had known about Cristofer. You know, he said. Everybody knows. It's about survival, staying alive. He ran through for me which gang controls which village on the islands.

> San Marcos Lempa: MS
> San Morana: MS
> El Marillo: 18
> La Canoa: MS
> San Juan del Gozo: MS
> Isla de Mendez: MS
> Ceiba Doblada: MS
> Corral de Mulas Uno: 18
> Corral de Mulas Dos: MS
> And Puerto de Triunfo is divided down the middle:
>   MS and 18.

Arnovis checked in with his boss, explaining everything, wanting to see if he could get any help or protection.

His boss heard him out, told him that he was sorry, that he understood, that it was screwed up, but that there was nothing they could do. Sorry, he told Arnovis, and then he added that he couldn't work there anymore. It was too dangerous. The boss couldn't put the other workers at risk. He was fired.

He knew then that he needed to leave. And he knew, he told me —he knew right away—that he had to take Meybelín with him.

Arnovis called his brother in Kansas, who told him he would see what he could do about hiring a proper coyote this time.

About getting Arnovis and Meybelín to safety. No kidnappings this time. No trains.

A friend of his brother, it turned out, knew a coyote who could take them in a truck, but he was going to charge two thousand dollars up front, and then another six on delivery. That was how they put it: on delivery. Eight thousand in total. His brother would front the initial fee, but Arnovis would have to come up with the remaining six once he got to Kansas. And they wouldn't go alone: Arnovis's brother-in-law, José, had been looking to leave for months and was going to take his daughter, Darlene, who was six, a year older than Meybelín.

Arnovis now only had to convince Mirna to sign papers permitting Meybelín to leave the country so they could get her a passport.

It all happened so fast. Within a week of the renewed threat and firing, Arnovis, Mirna, and Meybelín were on a bus to the San Marcos terminal in San Salvador. They met the coyote outside the bus station. He was a middle-aged man—large belly, seemed friendly—who pressured them to leave that very day. But they still had to get Meybelín's papers in order. The following morning Mirna signed a notarized letter allowing Arnovis to take Meybelín out of the country, and then they headed to the passport office. José and Darlene were already on their way from Jiquilisco. Two hours later, they said goodbye to Mirna, and the four of them boarded a PuertoBus heading for the Guatemalan border. It was a flurry of goodbyes, signatures, decisions—he barely had time to think—and that's how fear works, more muscle than mind. Get to safety, and *then* find time to reflect. It's okay, he comforted Meybelín. I love you. It's going to be okay. We'll stick together.

They had their first trouble a few hours later. The Guatemalan border guards rejected Darlene's papers. Arnovis and José tried to persuade them to let them pass, but nothing was working, and José and Darlene couldn't continue across the border. In a quick confabulation with Arnovis, José told him that he would get across the river under the bridge, and they'd meet up that night in Guatemala City. Arnovis agreed, but he told me that as the bus crossed the Río Paz into Guatemala, he wondered if he would ever see his brother-in-law again. From the El Jobo bridge he could see the river far below him—women washing clothes on the banks, a horse grazing on the long lime-green grass, a tangle of beached trash. José, meanwhile, said it was all pretty simple. He and Darlene got off the bus when the guards' told them they couldn't continue, walked down to the river, paid to be ferried across, and, pretty quickly, found a so-called chicken bus heading toward Guatemala City.

That night, after José and Darlene caught back up with Arnovis and Meybelín, they bought tickets to Huehuetenango.

Sometimes coyotes act as the bank for migrants: if you wire them their front fee, they hand you cash for the segments of the trip they won't be traveling. Arnovis's coyote, after receiving the two thousand dollars from his brother, handed Arnovis eight hundred in cash, which he hid in his shirt. He would later show me where, in a dark-blue denim Columbia button-down, he had ripped a small hole in the inside double-lining of the left shoulder to slot his money.

In Guatemala City, at eleven that night, the four of them boarded a bus bound to Huehue, where they found a hotel called Sinaí, close to the bus depot. The girls were excited to stay in a hotel for the first time in their lives. Their fathers told them to sleep but let them goof around for a few minutes, bouncing on the single bed. They didn't know where they would be staying the next night, or any of the next nights, and the men sat back and watched as the girls tired themselves out in nervous glee. In the morning, on very little sleep, they caught another bus to La Mesilla and met with the coyote again. Home was already seeming far away to Arnovis. Everything, in fact, seemed distant—Corral de Mulas, the future, the United States, even the conversations he was having with José. They were on the cusp, the knife-edge, every direction a free fall. Only Meybelín was close enough. It's okay, he told her when she looked at him. Everything is going to be okay. I'm here. We're together.

The coyote told them he had to go deliver their money to La Base (the cartel), and he would come back soon with instructions. They waited all day. They bought the girls Coca-Colas to distract them, let them play on their phones, but hardly spoke between themselves. Around eight that night another man came to find them. He drove them to a parking lot where they were loaded into the back of a small delivery truck with about thirty other men, women, and children. It had started to rain.

The truck took off behind a convoy of other trucks loaded with men, women, and children. They drove extremely fast. The roof was leaking, and the packed migrants tried to rearrange and scrunch themselves all onto one side to avoid the dripping water. Arnovis found a wedge between slats of the trailer and was able to catch glimpses of the night passing in flashes of black and wet and green. The convoy only slowed down at the border crossing, where they were waved through with no inspection. And then they started speeding again through the rain, and Arnovis and José held their daughters tightly between their legs, trying to keep them dry, trying to keep them warm and safe, wishing that they would fall asleep. There would be no more hotels.

"What is this country I have come to now?" Ulysses asks. "Are all the people wild and violent, or good, hospitable, and god-fearing?"

It's okay, Arnovis whispered. It's okay. We're together.

11

The strongest weapon ICE has is time, Santos, a Mexican man who was denied asylum and is now in hiding, told me. After a series of emails, Santos finally agreed to speak with me, but only if I used a pseudonym and didn't mention the name of the city where he was holed up. I agreed, and we had a series of email exchanges and phone calls. I also checked his story with his attorney and immigration documents.

Santos kept turning his tale to his lamentable—the word he repeatedly used—twelve hours of terror he experienced beginning late one evening on August 11, 2013. That horror was followed by twenty-six months of torment and humiliation in ICE detention centers, and now the almost constant fear and paranoia he contends with while trying to live a quiet life by himself in a new northern Mexican city, alone, scared to make connections or friends, and scared to share anything of his past.

When he was seven, Santos moved with his parents to Texas, where he lived, went to school, worked, and eventually got married. In 2008, after twenty-five years in the United States, Santos got divorced and returned to a small village and suburb of Juárez between Praxedis and Guadaloupe, an area of Mexico that was rapidly descending into dizzying violence—a scourge of kidnappings, murders, and disappearances conducted by both paramilitary drug-trafficking organizations and the Mexican military and federal police. Personally, though, Santos told me, everything had been going well. He moved onto his family's small snatch of land and lived next to his twin brother, trying to keep his head down and work, though he soon realized the violence was seeping into everything. Every day, he said, we saw commandos driving in their trucks. I didn't realize it at first, but they were sicarios, or vigilante assassins. My eyes were opening that it wasn't a good idea to have come back to Mexico, but you have to move forward, you have to see things positively. I was already there, living with family. They helped me emotionally, physically, financially, in every way possible, he said. And everything was going well, we were living peacefully. I was adapting. But then it got worse, he said, worse and worse, and I saw my first dead body, and then another. You just go out walking and you come across a body without a head, someone hanging from a bridge. And the saddest thing about it is that the kids got used to it, they started joking about it. It wasn't unusual for them to see death. It didn't scare them anymore. They would make jokes about it. And you see the culture that's forming in their heads.

Once, Santos said, I'll never forget, I was in town one day, and the sicarios had left one of those coolers with ice, a big one, and inside there was the head of one of the local bosses. I remember a kid went over to open it and instead of being shocked, he started joking around: Qué bigotes! he said, what a mustache! It was disturbing to see kids joking about something like that.

Every day, or like six times a week, there was a killing close by. Only when you got home and closed the door and you were with loved ones could you feel calm.

But then one day the violence broke into that sanctuary as well. On the night of August 11, 2013, Santos was waiting for his twin brother to get home from the Del Rio convenience store where he worked as a cashier. It was around 11:30 when Santos heard his brother's truck pull up and, as he said, he finally had the peace of mind to be able to fall sleep. He said that he had been reading the Bible, or maybe was on his phone, and had just turned off the lights when he heard another vehicle pull onto the property, and then some people shouting. He went to his kitchen to look outside the window, where he saw what he described as an undercover military truck. You can tell which are military, he said—the newest models. From the kitchen he could hear the voices more clearly and recognized the voice of his cousin, who often got in trouble with the law. Another truck pulled up, skidding to a stop in front of his brother's house. Santos didn't know what to do and had gone back to his bedroom to put on some clothes when he heard three gunshots: *tah! tah! tah!*

Terrified, confused, he went to his front door where he could look out the small window from the darkness of his home. He saw the officers' blue camouflage uniforms, identifying them as ministerial police—military-like federal police, notoriously corrupt, charged with fighting organized crime. And then he noticed, in the bed of the first truck, his brother's unmoving face. Santos went out his back door where he saw, also hiding in the darkness, his nephew, who lived in yet another small house on the lot. Unsure of what they had seen, or maybe not wanting to believe it yet, the two of them decided to walk to the front of the house.

I was wearing sandals, he said, and my nephew was barefoot. He didn't have a shirt on. And, as soon as they saw us, they grabbed us and started beating us, hitting us with their rifles. They threw us against a wall and took my nephew's wedding ring. They stole it, first thing; one of the cops put it in his pocket.

The officers told Santos and his nephew not to get involved with what didn't concern them. And I was like, It's my brother— are we not supposed to wonder what's going on when we hear gunshots? And while they were roughing us up, Santos said, they were taking TVs, computers, anything that was worth anything out of my brother's house and loading it into one of the trucks.

When the officers finished their looting, they shoved Santos and his nephew over to the first truck and pushed them into the bed. And I fell, Santos said, against my brother's leg. I could feel that he was still warm. And I remember, all I remember is that I hugged him, and I was looking for my brother's pulse, my twin, and I couldn't find it. I realized he was dead.

They took off driving, and one of the officers riding in the back with them explained that they were looking for a goat's horn, an AK-47 they'd lost a couple months ago when one of their bosses, El Ingeniero, had been killed. Santos's cousin—currently wedged between officers in the back seat of the pickup—the one always getting into trouble, supposedly knew where it was, but when they raided his house and didn't find it, he told them that Santos's brother had it, which was, Santos assured me, false. When they came into his brother's house they weren't planning on killing him, but one of the officers saw that he was holding something in his hand, and opened fire. It wasn't a weapon he had, it was just a little truck, his son's toy, and the officer, or the sicario, was sort of apologizing about it, and Santos and his nephew and his brother were all lying in the back of the truck, though only two of them were listening.

You know, Santos said, I can't say with any certainty whether these guys were genuinely police or if they were just dressed like police. Some of them were wearing uniforms, but some of them were wearing normal clothes. So I call them sicarios, but at the end of the day, it doesn't matter, they all do the same thing.

We got three live ones and one dead, he heard one of the sicarios say into the radio. They had been riding for what seemed a long time. A voice on the other end responded, Take them to R. After a while, they turned down a bumpy dirt road. They were taking us to a place to disappear us, to bury us, Santos thought, bumping against his dead twin brother as the truck heaved and rattled across potholes.

We got to this spot and they pulled us out, and they started getting all these tools. A saw, a hammer, some chains, who knows what else. And they said something about getting the truth out of my cousin. And then they pulled my brother out of the truck, and his body thudded into the dirt. It was really sandy there,

I remember that. It felt like sand under my feet. And I heard this thud, his last thud, and then I heard them start to dig. And while they were digging the grave for my brother, they were beating my cousin, beating him with a pipe, and asking him where the goat horn was. And at some point my cousin was telling them to just kill him. *Mátame, mátame,* he was crying. They were beating him in the legs, all over his body. And then one of the other guys told us that they were going to let us go. I guess they saw we were honest people. That we were victims, you know. They beat my cousin so long they were getting tired.

You didn't see anything, one of them came up and told us, and you don't know anything. And if anyone asks where your brother is, you're going to say that the Martians took him. And if tomorrow we hear that you opened your mouth, we're going to come and kill you the same way we killed your brother. Just so you know. We're not joking around.

What saved us was God, Santos said. He saved us from the claws of death. Because, I mean, that was a spiritual experience we had. I know it wasn't them that saved us, it was God. He changed their hearts. And, of course, we were saying: No, no, you're not going to hear anything from us. Don't worry about us.

The men put blindfolds on Santos and his nephew and drove them back to their house. They pulled them out of the truck and pushed them to their knees and told them that they were leaving, and that they better not look around until they were gone. If you look at us, we'll kill you.

They didn't look.

And we stayed there on the floor, like they said, Santos told me, on our knees, and we didn't turn around. And when I could hear that the truck had left, I turned around and pulled off my blindfold.

And we went to the—Santos paused to search for a word, or to enter back into that memory; it was dead silence on the phone —crime scene, he said. We went into my brother's house and looked at everything. We just stood there, in a state of shock.

We didn't know what to do, and we kept asking ourselves, What do we do? What do we do? What do we do?

And then my nephew, it was his idea, he said that we should go ask for asylum. And it made sense. We couldn't stay there.

I asked Santos what he had known about asylum before that day. He told me he knew that it existed, but he didn't really get what it was. I knew it was a program for people, he said. But I thought it was more for Central Americans. Not for Mexicans.

He and his nephew changed clothes and washed. They took photographs of the bloodstains and their bruises. They got in his nephew's car and drove to the Cordova Bridge, also known as the Bridge of the Americas, which connects Juárez with El Paso, and over which twenty thousand people and thirty-five thousand cars and trucks cross every day—giving meaning to the name of the city. When they entered through the sliding glass doors they told the CBP officers they wanted to ask for asylum. They could see how scared we were, he said. How sad we were. They could see it in our expressions. They could see the tragedy we had just lived through. They took us in, thank God.

The officers put them into an hielera, where they stayed for sixteen hours, and then a truck came and took them to the El Paso Processing Center.

With the exception of what he heard from his attorney, Carlos Spector, Santos said he received almost no information from the government about how to apply for asylum or what he needed to prove or explain. After about two or three weeks he was given a credible fear interview, by phone, but he didn't understand what it was for. Most of what he learned he picked up from rumors and gossip from the other detainees.

At his hearing on July 30, 2014, ten months after he first presented himself on the bridge and asked for asylum, a judge denied his claim. He appealed. On February 10, 2015, sixteen months after he was first taken into detention, the Board of Immigration Appeals heard his appeal and remanded the decision back to the immigration judge, ruling that the judge did not adequately consider certain facts and did not address whether his persecutors were "government" or "government sponsored." On June 2, after two additional hearings, the judge again denied his request for asylum. Santos appealed again. He then submitted his third request for parole, which was also denied. In December, nearly two years after he presented himself at the border, Spector, his attorney, filed a habeas corpus petition, claiming his prolonged detention violated "the bare minimum of due process in that he has never been granted an individualized bond hearing." The US District Court in El Paso ruled that the government needed to give him a bond hearing within twenty-one days.

Finally, after twenty-six months, Santos was let out on bond while the appeal of his negative asylum ruling went up to the Fifth Circuit. An ICE official put an electronic monitoring bracelet on his ankle and told him he had to report to the ICE office every Monday. A couple months later, as he was trying to adjust back to life in the United States and a life of "freedom"—and with his case still ongoing—an ICE officer called him and told him to come in. It wasn't a Monday, his regular check-in day, and he was nervous. When he got to the office, they put him in handcuffs. That same afternoon, without explanation, he was already back across the bridge, deported.

He's moved three times since he was refused protection and expulsed from the United States. I don't want to be seen or recognized, he told me. I just want to live a normal life, though I know it can't be normal because I'm scared every moment. He's tried to start over but feels he has to hide his past and that, as he told me, he has no ground left to push off from.

ICE's most powerful weapon is time. Their strategy is to make us desperate, break us down, separate us from our family until we enter into crisis and sign our deportation, Santos told me. If you try to outlast them, they ignore you, forget about you.

At one point in our conversation he wondered who had upended his life more—the sicarios who had killed his twin brother and kidnapped him, or the US government who had locked him away for over two years after he asked them for protection.

It's tempting to mythologize migrants, refugees, and asylum seekers—their stories are extraordinary and hard to fully grasp without direct experience, which may be part of why judges, policy makers, and unsympathetic or even well-meaning citizens so often fail them. At the same time, refugees' lives are too varied and singular to be successfully captured in allegory, or even in literature. In his novel *Exit West*, instead of striving toward dramatic verisimilitude to portray the intensity of refugees' journeys, Mohsin Hamid resorts to the rather hokey device of a magical door through which the migrant passes and is beamed to the destination country, skipping the passage altogether. Despite the sheer numbers of refugee stories throughout the world, it's notable that migrant literature overwhelmingly focuses on the struggles of arrival and integration (or non-integration, as Hamid does, to great effect, in *Exit West*) rather than the transit itself. There are plenty of great immigration novels, but few migration novels. German author Jenny Erpenbeck's fantastic refugee novel *Go, Went, Gone* likewise begins post-transit. "Must living in peace—so fervently wished for throughout human history and yet enjoyed in only a few parts of the world—inevitably result in refusing to share it with those seeking refuge, defending it instead so aggressively that it almost looks like war?" Erpenbeck asks. That would be: war against refugees.

Mexican novelist Emiliano Monge stands as one of the few contemporary novelists to—successfully—portray refugees' actual journeys in vivid detail. It is a nightmarish and weird love-story-cum-refugee-novel, and he had to draw on direct interviews with migrants and numerous quotes from Dante to pull it off. At the same time, Monge seems to echo another classic writer who recounted a different era of flight—Frederick

Douglass, who, in his "resistance to Blood-Houndism," described the "panting fugitive" and the "dark train going out of the land, as if fleeing from death."

Channeling classic descriptions of exile and escape, Monge writes of a group of Central American migrants crammed into a trailer and their "*cries of despair ... the tormented spirits as they lament in chorus*," as well as their "howls of such pain they were not human sounds ... and we felt terror take hold once more." In another description, he writes that the migrants were "pale as death and paralyzed with fear."

As the series of migrant caravans in 2018 made clear, Central America is an increasingly uninhabitable place for many, and a lack of American hospitality doesn't make it more inhabitable. *Why* someone's home has been rendered uninhabitable doesn't much matter to the person who can't forge a life there—and yet it's all that matters to an immigration judge, who only offers protection if someone has been persecuted *on account of* five narrow grounds. So while genuine refugees are increasingly, boldly, and creatively refused relief, economic migrants, especially if they are from majority Brown or Black countries, are denied on no grounds at all.

The extremes of poverty—to anyone suffering it—are as "bona fide" as any other reason to flee a home. One example of the hazy distinction between an economic incitement to migrate and a traditional refugee claim was offered to me by Rosa Nelly Santos, director of COFAMIPRO, a Honduras-based organization founded by mothers searching for their children who disappeared after migrating north. After the stolen 2017 election in Honduras, the entrenched ruling party of Juan Orlando Hernández—who torched constitutional law to reelect himself president with funds partially garnered through cocaine trafficking, and at the same time doubled down on his massive privatization schemes to keep his fellow kleptocrats in power—fired opposing party politicians and government workers. Some of those formerly middle-class workers, unable to find new jobs, were targeted for violence and imprisoned. Many of those workers fled north. Upon showing up at the US border and asking for asylum, some of them answered honestly that they were coming for work—but only because they had been politically persecuted and fired from their jobs back in Honduras. Could they qualify for asylum? Not on the basis of lack of employment. Nelly Santos told me of at least two men she knew who had already been denied and deported. Their life in Honduras had become unlivable because of economics *and* politics, yet they found no protection abroad and faced renewed persecution and unemployment at home.

Though refugee stories of escape from racial, ethnic, or religious targeting may provoke sympathy in policy makers and in immigration judges, novelist Chimamanda Ngozi Adichie, in *Americanah*, also probes into a person's "need to escape from the oppressive lethargy of choicelessness," especially in postcolonial countries such as Nigeria. That same oppressive choicelesness holds true for Central Americans, some of whom may have been "raised well fed and watered but mired in dissatisfaction," as Adichie writes, "conditioned from birth to look towards somewhere else, eternally convinced that real lives happened in that somewhere else." Refugee and asylum cases are not the exception to an otherwise free and prosperous world. Rather, they are only some of the most visible embodiments of severe global inequalities and iniquities—whether martial, economic, or climatic.

Banks Miller, Linda Camp Keith, and Jennifer S. Holmes, in their study of asylum claims between 1990 and 2010, note that 89 percent of asylum seekers came from countries the World Bank classified as low-income or low-middle-income countries —meaning that per capita income was less than $4,035 in 2012 dollars. They also note that most of those seeking asylum in the United States, 52 percent, came from countries where "severe repression or egregious violations of human rights are a regular part of life and where murder and torture are common." That is, poverty is endemic to corruption. And, though it's not always the case, both poverty and corruption often add up to violence. Violence, then, especially when it's pervasive enough that you can't escape it by relocating, often incites a refugee claim. As Obinze, the character from *Americanah*, puts it, migrants like him were not "starving, or raped, or from burned villages, but merely hungry for choice and certainty."

Climate change, another form of violence, also interlaces with economic and political claims in Central America. Some of the drought-suffering regions of Honduras—enduring a ten-year dry spell stretching through a corridor of the Northern Triangle —are seeing people move to the major urban centers of San Pedro Sula and Tegucigalpa, where they find themselves newly impoverished and newly extorted by gangs—the de facto political parties of many of the receiving neighborhoods. Frank-Vitale has reported that towns in some parts of Honduras have actually banned new people from moving there in fear that they will bring in the gangs. The result is that, with nowhere else to go, many of them head north. They thus constitute economic-political-climatic refugees.

Many of the Garifuna—Black, mixed-ancestry people living along the Caribbean coast of Central America—migrants who travel north from the once-pristine but increasingly "developed" Honduran coast, are suffering from a poisonous concoction of rising tides, economic instability, political oppression, and racism. Jennifer Ávila, a pioneering Honduran journalist and cofounder of the excellent new media outlet Contra Corriente, wrote of one Garifuna man who got caught up in the 2018 family separation debacle not because he was fleeing gang violence or political persecution but because the rising sea had begun destroying his village, Masca, and he tried to find a new home in the United States. I went to Masca myself to see the sea eating away at the coast and the yellowing, salt-watered coconut trees. Neither fishing—the seas are increasingly fishless, locals tell—nor agriculture can sustain many of the villagers, and they point to a devastating 1998 hurricane, Hurricane Mitch, as the precipitating event. Given the predictions of more frequent and increasingly severe hurricanes, the future of the village seems in existential peril.

Todd Miller leans on Christian Parenti's concept of "catastrophic convergence" to explain how these tides of ecological, economic, and political crises swell together and force people to move across borders. The United Nations estimates that by 2050, 250 million people will be displaced by climate change. "Despite predictions of such startling magnitude"—other estimates are as high as 750 million people potentially uprooted by climate change—"there is no legal framework for climate refugees," Miller writes. "Not in international law, not in the laws of specific countries. Instead, there is more spending on border reinforcement than ever before in the history of humankind."

Guatemala, in particular, is consistently listed as one of the world's ten most vulnerable countries, with severe droughts and erratic weather leading to failed harvests, destructive storms, and dwindling agricultural jobs. I visited one small village, Xeatzán Alto, in the Chimaltenango Department, where dry spells and periodic heavy rainfall have actually washed away entire swaths of the village, and enormous sinkholes prompt people to wonder how long the very ground beneath their feet will remain. One of the migrants I spoke with in Tijuana who fled Honduras in one of 2018's caravans left his home after, for two consecutive years, the beans he and his family planted didn't grow enough to flower. This was after the yearly haul had already dropped from an average of ten 100-kilo sacks to only three sacks per year. It just stopped raining, he told me. There was nothing to do. Nothing to eat.

A 2017 study from the World Food Programme found that, in 2014, an El Niño–provoked drought in the already arid Central American dry corridor "caused a significant increase in irregular migration to the United States." Almost half the families surveyed in the study were found to be food insecure and had already begun implementing "emergency coping strategies," such as selling their land. Unemployment in the dry corridor was over 50 percent in all three countries, and as high as 68 percent in Honduras.

Betsy Hartmann, however, astutely warns against lumping all the blame on the changing climate. In addressing the influence of climate change on the Syrian civil war—an oft-cited and, in Hartmann's view, facile interpretation—she writes, "These political and institutional failures should not be laid at the door of the amorphous mega-agent of climate change." Doing so risks ignoring "the very real human agency behind the war. We scare ourselves to death, or rather into accepting death, destruction, and massive dislocation as the inevitable apocalypse that awaits us in the era of climate change." If massive global changes due to climate change are inevitable, with attending forced displacements of masses of people, we risk political inaction and ennui, consigning the poorest among us, climate refugees —maybe better termed *refugees of late capitalism*—as unavoidable tragedies.

A diverse array of agents—economic impossibility, the climate crisis, plus armed sicarios, government goons, and rivalrous gang members—are uprooting and unroofing millions of people across the globe, rendering them homeless and pushing them to flee across borders. Asylum protocols are not the solution to these complex global problems, but they are a solution to the individuals suffering them.

Sometime after dawn, the truck they were riding came to a stop. A man they'd never seen before opened the back gate and commanded them to jump down. Hurry, hurry. *Get out!* he yelled, but none of them knew where they were being herded, what they were getting out for. Arnovis and José, with their daughters, were near the back of the truck and were among

the first to step down. There were no buildings or anything at
all around, Arnovis told me. Just *monte*—low jungle—and soft
light. The sun was barely up, but it was already hot and humid.
The coyote hustled everybody off the road and into the jungle.
Lie down, he ordered. Some people dropped to the ground right
away; others hesitated.

Don't be scared, the coyote said, but everybody was scared.

They were waiting for another truck to come and take them
to Villahermosa. It would only be a few minutes.

Get on the ground, the coyote barked again. Arnovis and
José laid their extra shirts down for the girls to lie on. There
were bugs and thorns, the ground was wet, and the girls were
nervous. What's happening, papi? Meybelín asked. It's okay,
Arnovis told her. This is what we have to do. We just have to
wait. It will be okay. He and José knew the girls were hungry,
too, or would be when they got over their fear, but they didn't
have any food. The fathers gave the girls some water and told
them to be quiet, that everything was okay. Arnovis told me
how much he kept smiling at Meybelín, trying to show her that
he wasn't nervous, that he wasn't scared, that they were okay.
It's okay, he smiled. Occasionally he would point out a tree, or
look at the horizon, and say, Look, Meybelín, que bonita, no?
Sí, papi. And Meybelín would then tell her cousin, Darlene, to
look at the beautiful tree.

They waited a long time in the monte, the coyotes watching
over them, occasionally shushing them. The mosquitoes were
awful, and when they swatted them the coyotes snapped at
them to be quiet.

Finally—was it an hour, two hours?—another truck pulled
up, just like the one they had gotten out of, and the coyotes
yelled at them to load up, to *hurry, hurry, hurry*. They told them
that they would leave anybody behind who didn't run. They
all ran, cramming into the back of the truck.

This trailer was more enclosed, and the air hardly filtered in.
Someone said they felt like they had to throw up. Someone else

told them to be quiet. It smelled inside like cooped animal, like bodies scared of the slaughter. Meybelín held on to her father and, Arnovis thinks, fell asleep between his legs. After a while he could smell the vomit. It got hot enough that he could feel it affect his breathing, but he wouldn't let go of his daughter.

In another hour they were in Villahermosa. The truck stopped behind a large warehouse and, in a rush, like always, the guides pulled them out of the truck, pushing them into what looked like a used-clothes warehouse. They were split into different rooms, and Arnovis and José and the girls were prodded up a flight of steps and locked inside a small, windowless room, completely bare except for a few scraps of cardboard and some trash.

They wouldn't leave that room, except to go to the filthy bathroom next door, for the next three days, during which, twice a day, young men with pistols tucked into their belts came and gave them food. One young Honduran woman in the group was cradling her sick infant.

The baby was soooo tiny, Meybelín said to me when she heard her dad mention the baby. *Pequeñiiiito*, Meybelín said again. She and Arnovis and I were sitting around the hot pink table after dinner. His mother had just served us coffee, and Meybelín asked for a cup. She felt like talking and told me about another baby in the room, another little one, she said delightedly, seeming to want to distinguish herself, as kids do, from children even younger than themselves. The baby fell asleep on my leg, she said, laughing. Do you remember, papá?

After a while, Arnovis told me, the baby started wailing again and a coyote came in and yelled at the mother to keep it quiet. A Guatemalan man stood up and defended the woman, and the coyote spit back at the man to shut up. Later, the coyote returned with the jefe and another man, who was holding a gun and who had tattoos on his face. Do we have a problem? the jefe asked the Guatemalan man. If you have a problem with someone here you have a problem with me. Is that what you're telling me—that you have a problem with me? The jefe took off his belt as if he were going to whip somebody with it. The Guatemalan said he didn't have a problem.

Three days after they'd been first locked inside, another young man with a gun ushered everybody out of the room. When they hit the staircase they gained a view of the main open floor of the warehouse, which was crammed with more bodies than Arnovis had ever seen all in one place. *Un mul-ti-tud!* of people, he stressed, guessing there were five hundred people choked into that room. José put the number at six hundred.

And everybody was so quiet, Arnovis said. It was terrifying. Everybody scared, and so, so quiet. And then the coyotes started ordering people out through the back door. As the four of them made their way down the stairs they saw a line of tractor trailers parked behind the warehouse, migrants filing into them. They were ushered to one of the trailers where a coyote was collecting phones and giving them their code names. They had become un paquete, a package. Their code name was Ricky. *Four Rickies for El Chino.* Arnovis and José handed over their phones, lifted their daughters into the back of the refrigerated truck, and then climbed in after them.

In the 1990s, the conurbations of San Diego-Tijuana, El Paso-Juárez, and, to a lesser degree, Nogales-Nogales became the targets of an unprecedented border militarization campaign (walls, fencing, Border Patrol agents, and expensive and hardly functional surveillance technology, as well as internal checkpoints and concurrent militia activity) that pushed hundreds of thousands of border crossers through increasingly dangerous desert corridors and into the hands of armed and poorly trained Border Patrol agents who, with negligible oversight, could decide their legal fate. These agents could treat them as they pleased —sometimes respectfully and with dignity, sometimes beating the shit out of them, molesting them, or even killing them. The strategy was called Prevention Through Deterrence and was ostensibly meant to make an "illegal" border crossing so difficult that migrants wouldn't even try. But, as many have since elucidated, everybody knew that it wouldn't work. Anyone with any basic knowledge about why migrants were coming would know that enhancing the difficulty of the route would do nothing to change the root causes.

Indeed, the Prevention Through Deterrence policy was implemented the same year as NAFTA, the open borders (for goods and capital) trade agreement, which wrought catastrophic economic effects on sectors of the Mexican economy and left nearly 5 million jobless—especially in southern Mexico and in coastal fishing communities. With the promise of better paid work and the long-established migrant routes between the United States and Mexico beckoning, it was inevitable that many would head north, and they did.

Greg Grandin called the people pushed out of their homes "NAFTA refugees" and notes that "US economic policy has provoked one of the greatest migrations in history." The simultaneous border militarization and free trade agreement was a sharp prod into the deadly deserts or, for those who made it, into the undocumented shadows of the United States.

It was over a century earlier, in the 1889 Supreme Court case *Chae Chan Ping v. United States*, when the border was first used as a tool to turn back Chinese migrants, and the border has been a racialized tool of marginalization ever since. Justice Stephen Johnson Field wrote in the unanimous 1889 decision, "To preserve its independence, and give security against foreign aggression and encroachment, is the highest duty of every nation, and to attain these ends nearly all other considerations are to be subordinated. It matters not in what form such aggression and encroachment come, whether from the foreign nation acting in its national character, or from vast hordes of its people crowding in upon us." The language—"all other considerations are to be subordinated"—set the grounds to ignore the Constitution and treat refugees like enemy combatants, echoing two other Chinese Exclusion cases granting "plenary power" to the legislative and executive branches to enact whatever immigration laws they please. Plenary power was invoked in 2017 and 2018 as the Trump administration issued executive orders and DOJ policy memos meant to ban Muslims from entry into the country, separate children from their parents, and generally throw the bolt on any noncitizen they wanted to lock away, deny entrance to, or deport.

Racism pervaded these early policies and decisions, with scholars pointing to *Plessy v. Ferguson*—the Supreme Court legalization of "separate but equal"—as the critical backdrop for the Chinese Exclusion and plenary power arguments. In 2003, the Supreme Court further articulated the doctrine in *Demore v. Kim*, carving out a space of legal exclusion, stating that "Congress may make rules as to aliens that would be unacceptable if applied to citizens."

The actual act of crossing the border was only deemed a crime beginning in 1929, after a focused effort was made by Secretary of Labor James Davis and South Carolina senator Coleman Livingston Blease, who Kelly Lytle Hernández calls in *Migra!* "a proud and unreconstructed white supremacist." Unlawful entry thus became, for the first time, a misdemeanor punishable by six months' imprisonment and up to a $250 fine; a second unlawful entry was deemed a felony, punishable by two years' imprisonment or a $2,000 fine, or both. Today's border enforcement still carries that stink of punitive racism. One of the first immigration enforcement moves after 9/11, for example, was INS acting deputy commissioner Peter Michael Becraft implementing a new parole policy targeting Haitian asylum seekers: no Haitian could be paroled out of detention without direct approval from INS headquarters in Washington, even if they had passed their credible fear interview. But *why*? Why did INS target Haitians in the aftermath of 9/11? Though Haitians played no role in the 9/11 attacks, US immigration services have long held a special animosity toward some of this hemisphere's darkest-skinned immigrants.

The US District Court of Southern Florida heard a challenge to the post-9/11 denial of parole and ruled against the Haitians citing a 1977 decision, *Fiallo v. Bell*, which, again echoing the concept of plenary power, stated that "over no conceivable subject is the legislative power of Congress more complete" than it is over the admission of "aliens." Attorney General John Ashcroft established a similarly pedigreed policy in 2003 with Operation Liberty Shield, which targeted asylum seekers from thirty-three Arab-Muslim countries (supposedly where al-Qaeda and al-Qaeda sympathizers were known to have operated) and was a clear precursor to Trump's Muslim ban. The countries included Afghanistan, Algeria, Bahrain, Bangladesh, Djibouti, Egypt, Eritrea, Indonesia, Iran, Iraq, Jordan, Kazakhstan, Kuwait, Lebanon, Libya, Malaysia, Morocco, Oman, Pakistan, Philippines, Qatar, Saudi Arabia, Somalia, Sudan, Syria, Thailand, Tajikistan, Tunisia, Turkey, Turkmenistan, United Arab Emirates, Uzbekistan, and Yemen, as well as Gaza and the West Bank. Though Ashcroft's ban was struck down, the Trump administration, after a couple tries— adding a few non-Muslim-majority countries to their ban list —successfully rammed a similarly spirited policy through the courts.

The plenary power of the executive to exclude and expulse as it pleases trickles down to the frontline agents. The same Border Patrol whistleblower who spoke to me about agents failing to screen for asylum seekers as they "rolled" them described Border Patrol's culture of "kick ass and ask questions later," and detailed multiple incidents of senior agents physically abusing migrants in the desert. One example he shared with me involved a field training officer kicking a water bottle out of the hands of a four-year-old boy who had been walking for days in the desert. Another officer repeatedly kicked a group of migrants to try to force out of them a confession about smuggling. And the Border Patrol horse patrol, he explained, is notorious for "tuning up" migrants (beating them) on their way back to station. Agents also occasionally lit on fire or urinated on migrants' personal belongings.

The 2001 Patriot Act; the 2003 creation of ICE; the doubling of the Border Patrol's ranks from 2003 to 2009; and the multiple-decade agenda of using the fear of terror as a motivation to try to "seal the border," normalize the state of exception, lengthen and layer the wall, and continue to militarize immigration enforcement—all of these measures turned an already dangerous crossing into a veritable gauntlet and added a row of teeth to Prevention Through Deterrence. And the bureaucracy—the most efficiently violent apparatus of the state—followed suit. Migrants were prosecuted for entry without inspection in kangaroo courts called Operation Streamline, which overlooked asylum seekers' claims of fear, fed migrant bodies into the prison industrial complex, and engorged the already bulging pockets of private prison companies. As immigration judge Dana Leigh Marks—who argued *INS v. Cardoza-Fonseca* in the Supreme Court, sparring with Justice Scalia—famously quipped about asylum cases, "We do death penalty cases in a traffic court setting." (The kangaroo courts of Operation Streamline, it's critical to note, were inspired by the "walrus courts" that Haitian asylum seekers were subjected to onboard Coast Guard cutters in the 1990s, when INS agents conducted credible fear interviews shortly after interdiction at high seas and then shipped the Haitians to Gitmo.)

You can trace the century-long buildup and subsequent post-9/11 crackdown not only in the overall estimated crossing rates (which are connected to the US economy as much as the situation in sending countries) but also in the fees the cartel-controlled coyotes charge migrants. According to the Mexican Migration Project, from the mid-1970s until the early 1990s, the costs for paying for a guide hovered around $1,000. But this price obscures the fact that as recently as ten or fifteen years ago, you didn't even necessarily need a coyote. If you met someone who knew the trails, or if you had previously walked them yourself, or were desperate enough, you could sally north on your own. I've heard a number of migrants talk about crossings in the early 2010s costing as low as a few hundred dollars, whereas the price for a clandestine crossing today can be as high as $10,000. Arnovis and Meybelín were charged $8,000, and, since they arrived to the United States, even though they didn't get to remain, they still have to pay, with Arnovis's brother in Kansas currently paying off the debt in monthly installments of $450. Most Central American migrants I speak with these days report costs of at least $6,000. What caused what is at least a six-fold increase?

Once drug-trafficking organizations saw that, as a result of US border militarization, it was increasingly difficult for migrants to cross, and that human smugglers (who used to operate independently) were charging higher fees, they recognized the potential for market expansion. Just as the Mexican cartels have diversified their business model, expanding from drug trafficking into the kidnapping, crude oil, and even timber markets, they also encroached into people smuggling and trafficking, co-opting coyotes and forcing them to pay fees to cross "packages" (such as the "four Rickies for El Chino" as Arnovis and family were designated) through their territory. This is why the safe house where Arnovis was confined in Piedras Negras was not run by coyotes alone but the cartels. Or why when Arnovis and José met with their coyote in La Mesilla, Guatemala, he had to go and pay off La Base before they could get into the truck. The cartels typically charge coyotes between $100 and $500 per migrant, according to what I've heard. Without the border enforcement buildup and militarization, it's certain the cartels would have continued to prey on individual migrants, but uncertain they would have entered whole hog into the market. If you were to overlay a chart of border deaths onto a chart of smuggler fees, you would see that deadliness and price redden together. The cartels, that is, have US border policy to thank for raking in the spiking profits.

Though having to negotiate with one violent organization (the cartels) to avoid being caught by another violent organization (the US Border Patrol) affects all migrants who attempt to cross the border, it has unique ramifications on asylum seekers. Asylum seekers have the legal right to present at a designated port of entry and make a claim for protection—a right not afforded to an "economic migrant." Of course, a right, even one enshrined in law, doesn't guarantee its application, and many asylum seekers are turned away from ports of entry by Customs and Border Patrol officers. Once you submit yourself into the services of a coyote, however, you cannot choose how and where you will cross. Most coyotes guide all the migrants they smuggle over the wall, across the river, or through the desert, and don't make special provisions for asylum seekers—though that's beginning to change. And, as we've seen, US policy incentivizes asylum seekers to make the more dangerous trek into the arms of cartel-controlled coyotes who guide them into the wilderness. Otherwise, they are deemed "arriving aliens" and are ineligible for parole.

There is one way, however, that "arriving aliens" can get out of detention: after passing their credible fear interviews, they can appeal to ICE for parole if they fit into one of five categories: they are pregnant, were witnesses to a crime and are willing to testify, are minors, have serious medical conditions, or are "aliens whose continued detention is not in the public interest." The Obama administration, for the most part, didn't see it as in the public interest to keep "arriving alien" asylum seekers in custody, and generally directed them to be released on parole. Within a month of the Trump administration taking over, then Secretary of Homeland Security John Kelly issued a memo ending the so-called catch-and-release policy to stop offering parole to "arriving aliens." The justification was that the practice "undermine[d] the border security mission."

Where and how asylum seekers present themselves matters; even identical circumstances driving an asylum claim will be treated differently depending on how and where the claim is made and what court the claimant lands in. In Arizona and Georgia, for example, asylum claims are granted only 10 percent of the time, whereas in New York, the grant rate fluctuates between 45 and over 90 percent, depending on the judge. Nationwide, 2017 saw a precipitous drop in the overall grant rate, to only 33 percent of all asylum claims. That was down from a rate that had gone from about 40 percent granted in 2001 to 60 percent in 2012. The 2007 study *Refugee Roulette* described how Colombian asylum applicants in Miami had a "5 percent chance of prevailing with one of that court's judges and an 88 percent chance of prevailing before another judge *in the same building.*" That is, depending on which judge you get, your chance of receiving a positive asylum decision can increase by a factor of 18. In another arbitrary twist of fate, if your judge is a woman instead of a man, you have a 5- to 8-percentage-point higher likelihood of gaining asylum.

Miller, Keith, and Holmes put it succinctly in *Immigration Judges and U.S. Asylum Policy*: "US economic and material interests influence grant rates more than human rights conditions." Conducting the most comprehensive study of asylum decisions to date, the authors reveal that both the amount of military aid the United States provides to a country and the amount of trade with that country negatively affect asylum outcomes. As we saw and continue to see in Central America, the more the United States trades with and offers military aid, the less likely judges are going to believe an asylum seeker, even if that very aid and trade have helped to provoke that asylum claim in the first place.

But many asylum seekers never even get their chance in court, as Customs and Border Protection officials simply turn them away, tell them to come back later, trick them into signing voluntary deportation forms, or rip away their children and threaten them with years in detention. One woman reported to the *New York Times* that an agent told her, "There is no asylum here." Another asylum seeker told me that an agent said to him, simply: "Trump ended that."

"I had always hoped that this land might become a safe and agreeable Asylum to the virtuous & persecuted part of mankind, to whatever nation they might belong," George Washington wrote in a 1788 letter, often cited by immigrant rights advocates. But Washington—who happens to be my seventh-great-uncle —wrote another letter, five years earlier, to the officer in charge of New York City maritime traffic, lamenting the fact that fugitive slaves, including "some of my own," might be fleeing with the British. He wrote: "if by Chance, you should come of the knowledge of any of them, I will be much obliged by your securing them, so that I may obtain them again."

The United States has built in, into its deepest foundation, the contradiction of claiming to be the land of the free—of "safe and agreeable Asylum"—and of engaging in the racist persecution of those clambering for freedom. It is a land of selective welcome and outright refusal.

There was barely enough room to sit, not enough room to stretch out. The smell again—cooped body, fear of slaughter. It was very cold. After they had handed over their cell phones, the coyotes had given each of them one green apple and a small package of cookies. No water. Arnovis and José dressed their daughters in all the clothes they had, held them between their legs, told them to rest. It's okay, Arnovis whispered to Meybelín. I'm here for you. It's just going to be a little while.

It would be fifty-two hours. Fifty-two freezing, cramped, long-rattling hours they were locked inside the truck trailer. It smelled and the smell got worse—the air thick with breath and cold sweat, the reek of piss and uncleaned bodies. People panted and whimpered in the cramped, unnatural dusk. During the day, light filtered through the trailer's roof, but at night it was pitch black, and the darkness let out a soft moaning Arnovis could hear over the thrum and rattle of the road. No one told them how long it was going to last, or even where they were going.

There were three five-gallon paint buckets, with plastic bags as lids, for the human waste. The girls each peed a couple times, with Arnovis or José holding them over the sloshing buckets, their small hands clenched around their fathers' necks. There was nothing to wipe with, no water to wash their hands.

A day in, sometime after the first night, Meybelín went limp, and Arnovis, scared out of a stupor, was worried she wasn't getting enough air. He tried to shake her, but his arms were numb. He willed through his heavy nerves, blood sluicing into his hands, and gripped his daughter very tightly. Papi, she whined. It's okay, he told her. Papi, she repeated. As feeling tingled back into his limbs, he couldn't tell if she was trembling or if it was the rumble of the truck. It's okay, he said, still gripping her too hard.

Fifty-two hours.

José estimated it was fifty-four.

At what point did you eat the apple? I asked.

I don't remember.

But you definitely ate the apple?

Yes.

I tried to think of another way of asking: What was it like? Weren't you nervous?

Yes, Arnovis told me. I was scared for my daughter. His words came out slowly: I asked myself, a thousand times I asked myself. What had I done?

We were having this conversation in his kitchen, late one night under the single insect-buzzed light bulb. We were both in plastic chairs. The deeper we got into the story, the slower he seemed to be speaking—each word laboring out of his chest, through his throat, heavily shaped by his tongue and lips. The arm of his plastic chair was broken and had been repaired with twine. His elbow kept slipping off. It was the first time I had seen him cry.

We don't have to talk about it, I said.

But Arnovis kept talking. He told me about how much he regretted taking her, that she didn't deserve to be in that truck, she didn't deserve to have to remember that experience, didn't deserve for that to be part of her childhood. And I was crying, he told me, because she couldn't see me in the dark of the trailer and it was so cold, and it lasted so long, and I didn't know when we were going to be safe again. I don't know what I've done to her. I was trying, he said, and paused again. I was trying to keep her safe.

In the summer of 2017, a truck carrying fifty-four migrants on its way north from the US-Mexico border was discovered in a Walmart parking lot outside San Antonio. Thirty-one of the migrants crammed in the trailer were diagnosed at the hospital with severe heat exhaustion, while eight of them were already dead. Two more would perish in the following days. *Intercept* journalist Ryan Devereaux described the migrants' intense struggle after being locked into the truck: "Told to step inside, the trailer's door was closed behind them. It was pitch black and already hot, the man recalled, and there was no food or water. At approximately 9 p.m., word came that they would be taking off soon. The refrigeration was working, they were assured. It was about an hour before people began struggling to breathe. They pounded on the trailer and took turns taking in air through a single hole in its wall."

Twenty-two of the surviving migrants were considered key witnesses to provide testimony to a grand jury and various law enforcement agencies. Some of them were jailed, and at least two of them were kept for over an hour in the same holding cell as the driver. A father who had ridden in the truck with his son—who had fallen into a coma—reported being "aggressively questioned" by ICE agents. The survivors were officially eligible for U visas, granted to those who have suffered a crime and cooperate with US law enforcement, but DHS turned them over to ICE agents who sent them to detention centers without informing their lawyers. Some of the survivors were deported. A quick Google search turns up dozens of cases of migrants being packed into truck trailers, while surely there are many more that pass undetected and are never written about. Sometimes there are over a hundred people packed inside. Sometimes the air conditioning works. Sometimes it doesn't, and passengers die, of suffocation or of heat stroke.

In his 2015 novel *The Jaguar's Children*, John Vaillant describes migrants riding in the back of a water truck abandoned in the Arizona desert. At one point, Hector, the narrator asks himself, "What does it mean when the only proof of living is the pain you feel?"

Arnovis's memory of arriving to Reynosa after over fifty hours cramped in the back of a truck trailer was hazy. He was suffering from extreme fatigue, dehydration, excessive cold, hunger, and days of suppressed agony and worry for his daughter. Someone gave them water when they arrived, yes. He remembers that. He urinated, yes. There were men with guns, yes. He breathed. They breathed. They warmed themselves. He wouldn't let go of Meybelín.

He remembers the coyotes breaking up the group of migrants, making calls, organizing "the packages" for the next coyotes. I got fifteen for *Emperatriz*, one coyote spoke into the phone, and a driver came and picked up fifteen of the migrants. I got six for *El Patron*. If you don't pick up your *Maymelo-nine* in fifteen minutes we're sending them to La Base, and you fucking know what happens at La Base.

Arnovis and José and the girls were some of the last to go, but finally a coyote came and picked up his package of *Four Rickies*, and then drove them to another safe house. Darlene's stomach had begun hurting. Meybelín was quiet. None of them had eaten anything in over two days but an apple and a package of cookies.

No, they had not been expecting to be in the trailer for so long.

No, they would not have gotten inside if they had known.

And no, this was not the hardest part of their trip.

The new safe house, guarded over by a couple of the seemingly ever-present young men wielding guns and cell phones, was on a residential street. They ate that day, but not much, not enough, and Darlene still wasn't feeling well. The next morning they were still hungry, but there was nothing left to eat in the house. They asked one of the young men for more food for the girls.

I don't know, the man told them. That's not my job, but you're leaving soon. You can get some food when you get there. But they didn't leave that day. Arnovis found some old potatoes in a kitchen cabinet and cooked them on a hot plate. The girls complained, and José and Arnovis were running out of ideas on how to console or distract them. Darlene ran into the bathroom and vomited. There was nothing to flush with but a bucket of dirty water. There was no toilet paper. The taps didn't work, and they only had one bottle of water left between the four of them.

Arnovis told me that for that entire week he thinks he slept less than ten hours, nodding off momentarily in the back of the trucks, or the warehouse, jerking back awake, shivering with cold, trying not to wake Meybelín. Something seemed to break in both Arnovis and José at that last safe house. Maybe it was the thirst, or the lack of sleep—those most elemental needs. They both returned to this day, this morning, repeatedly. No water, no food, and the vibrations of the truck seemingly having shaken something loose in all four of them. They had been struggling for ten days to shelter the girls from the horror closing in on them. Oh, look, how pretty, Arnovis would tell Meybelín when they were sprawled out on the jungle floor. Look at that big tree. Those are our friends, these men. They have guns to protect us. Look at that little girl in the warehouse, he told her. Isn't she cute? Her pretty shoes. We have to be quiet now, but we're going to be okay. Just a little bit longer. Eat my cookie. We'll wash your hands when we get there. It's going to be okay. Yes, it's going to be okay. I'm here with you. It's going to be okay.

The fathers bought them juice and soda when they could, let them play with their phones, when they had them. The girls stayed close together. They hugged each other, whispered to each other—not like they did at home, not shrieking gleefully and tumbling over each other, combing each other's hair, but still comforting, holding onto each other, falling asleep on each other.

But then they were out of water, Darlene was stomach sick, and they had just suffered a fifty-two-hour stint inside a refrigerated truck. It was the first time, Arnovis told me, that Meybelín broke down, broke into sobs. He told me how impressed he had been with her. That he hadn't realized how strong she was. That she hardly complained. And I could see tears coming to his eyes again as he told me this, but I think, he said, that she was really sad, sad and confused. She must have been so scared, and I didn't even have water to give to her.

Later that afternoon one of the coyotes came and told them they were leaving.

We need water, Arnovis told him.

When you get there, the coyote responded.

We need water now. He and José insisted. And the guy was getting mad, and he was going to kick us out, or leave us behind, Arnovis explained. If you have money, buy some water, he told him. But they had no money. Think of the kids, José pleaded, and one of the other coyotes came up, reached into his pocket, and gave him a handful of pesos. Buy some water, he said. We'll stop on the way to the river.

"If you cross this border unlawfully, then we will prosecute you," Attorney General Jeff Sessions decreed in April of 2018. "It's that simple."

But nothing was or is simple about it.

Sessions's justification for terrorizing and breaking apart families was the so-called "zero tolerance" policy, which belongs in scare quotes because, given the complexity and vastness of the border, there is always only *partial* and *selective*, rather than "zero," tolerance. The idea behind the policy was the absolute reification of the border itself, with the border being a contingent *idea* rather than a geographic fact, a point that Greg Grandin expertly makes in his book *The End of the Myth: From the Frontier to the Border Wall in the Mind of America*. Grandin quotes one government official in the mid-nineteenth century calling the border a "zigzag, every-varying line." The flexing of nationalism and nationalist discourse, that is, manifests as much in the halls of the Capitol as at the geographic borderline. A border represents, Grandin writes, "the absurdity of human efforts to force the concrete to conform to the abstract, to take the world as it is and try to make it be as it ought."

It's also worth noting that the Refugee Convention, to which the United States is signatory, is explicit, in Article 31, in that states "shall not impose penalties, on account of their illegal entry or presence, on refugees who, coming directly from a territory where their life or freedom was threatened." Likewise, according to Article 26, signatory states "shall accord to refugees lawfully in its territory the right to choose their place of residence and to move freely within its territory." The zero-tolerance policy Sessions was wielding against families was in direct contravention of the letter and spirit of the Refugee Convention.

The same month that Sessions rolled out the zero tolerance policy, the Border Patrol apprehended a total of 38,237 people; to prosecute all of them would have drained the resources of the Justice Department and further crammed both the slogging courts and brimming detention centers. According to a report from Make the Road New York and the Center for Popular Democracy, if the zero tolerance policy were ever able to be fully implemented, the number of people in private, for-profit detention facilities would increase by up to 580 percent. Even with current proposed expansions in capacity, including the construction of "tent cities," DHS has nowhere near the room to hold every person they apprehend. So the DOJ has to *choose* who to prosecute, and, especially in 2018, they chose families with children.

Statistics reveal that less than a third of the more than thirty-eight thousand migrants apprehended by Border Patrol agents were criminally prosecuted in the first full month of zero tolerance. In total, over twenty-four thousand adults without children were apprehended, whereas only slightly more than forty-five hundred adults *with* children were caught, with, initially, three thousand total children separated from their parents. That means that the DOJ could have prosecuted just as many people for crossing the border without detaining or separating a single child from their parents. They could have even doubled the number of prosecutions and still not separated a single child from their parent. Instead, prosecutors targeted families, detaining over three thousand of them, at least, and then separating children from their parents.

Sessions announced the policy the same month that Arnovis was eating a mango on a lunch break, saw a huddle of thugs stride up with guns, and decided—knew—that he had to flee, and that he was going to take Meybelín with him.

The administration had been contemplating family separation since 2017 and ran something like a pilot project in the El Paso sector the same year. I interviewed a woman there who had been separated from her infant son while she was still breast-feeding him. She told me that after eight months of detention, when she was finally released and saw her son again, he didn't recognize her.

Alan Shapiro, pediatrician and cofounder of Terra Firma, a medical-legal program that offers medical, mental health, and legal help to undocumented children, wrote in an affidavit to a lawsuit that family separation may not only lead to "irreparable harm and trauma" to the children but also has a "doubly harmful" effect, first traumatizing the child and then depriving them of their primary source of stress mitigation: their parent.

Despite it all, despite the vicious crackdown, in September of 2018, the number of family units crossing the border increased. Contrary to the logic of deterrence, neither militarizing the border nor brutalizing the people who are forced to cross the border will stop them. If people need to flee, they flee.

Some suspected that the policy was as much a financial boon to some of the administration's corporate pals as it was a floundering and cruel attempt at deterrence. Between the announcement of the policy and DHS's June 22 request for information about the possibility of detaining an additional fifteen thousand people in family jails, the stocks of GEO Group and CoreCivic, the two largest for-profit immigration detention corporations, increased 5.9 percent and 8.3 percent, respectively. Currently, ICE forks over approximately $2 billion a year to for-profit companies to detain migrants. John Kelly, who was secretary of DHS in 2017, and then White House chief of staff as the family separation policy was being implemented, left office in late 2018. Less than six months afterward, he joined the board of a company, Caliburn International, to which the Trump administration—while Kelly had been part of it—had awarded a $222 million dollar contract to operate a child detention center.

Arnovis and Meybelín, along with José and Darlene, made their way down to the south bank of the Rio Grande in Reynosa on a hot, cloudless afternoon. One of the coyotes joked that they were going to have to swim across, but, as they approached, they saw a man pumping up a green, yellow, and black Intex Seahawk 4 inflatable raft. After a few minutes of pumping, the raft was sledded to the river's edge, and the coyote told them to get in. The boat, though, wasn't completely inflated, and the muddy river, even if it appeared calm, had hidden currents—and they knew it. Arnovis unbuttoned his shirt and untied his shoes, just in case he needed to swim. When the four of them were in—Arnovis in the stern, with Meybelín in his lap, and José in the middle, stabilizing the sides of the raft with his arms and with Darlene in his lap—a coyote jumped in the prow with a handle-broken paddle and they shoved off. In the stern's exterior hull, Arnovis soon realized, there was a small hole through which air was hissing. He reached over and stuck in a finger.

I was explaining everything to her, Arnovis told me. Look, mi amor, he said to his daughter, this is the United States. She thought the bridge looked like a snake, and asked, Papi, why don't we cross on the bridge? Because, mi amor, we don't have permission to cross on the bridge. So we're going to cross underneath, and then we'll look for a police officer to help us.

Worried about the safety of the girls, and remembering that Arnovis had gotten kidnapped the last time he tried to cross into the United States, his brother in Kansas had asked the coyotes for proof of crossing before he would send the "delivery" payment. One of the coyotes snapped three photos with his phone as the foursome were disembarking on the north side of the river. Months later, Arnovis's brother sent me the photos. In two of them, you can see Arnovis reaching over the side of the visibly limp raft to plug the hole. José, pushing his hands deep into the sidewalls, seems to be trying to use his body as a brace. The last photo is of the four of them standing in the dirt of the United States, none of them smiling. José looks like he's been crying; Darlene is puffy-faced and pale; and Arnovis is staring at the lens with a haggard, exhausted, almost angry look. Meybelín, her arms raised slightly to the sides, seems the calmest among them, but also on the cusp of ferocity: she could be posing as a superhero. In the background, the river water hazily reflects the sunlight, catching the green and yellow of the thick brush on the opposite bank. Above and behind them, a long bridge—the McAllen-Hidalgo International Bridge—connects the two countries.

After pausing for the photo, they scrambled up a steep path, cutting through thorns. The coyote told them to walk straight for about twenty minutes and they would see la migra. They walked for an hour before they spotted a Border Patrol truck.

When they saw us, Arnovis told me, they called out, Avanzan, avanzan, move forward. We got to within about twenty yards, but I know you can't just approach police in your country. They were looking at us, and they yelled again, Avanzan, avanzan. And so, we walked up, but, you know, respectfully.

There were two Border Patrol trucks and a van. Arnovis held Meybelín by the hand. The officers waved them forward and lined the four of them up next to the van and asked who they were, what relationship they had to each other, and where they were from. Five other migrants were already inside the van. When the officers loaded them in, they told Arnovis and José that they had to go in the front, and that the girls had to go in the back. There was wire mesh splitting the seats in two sections. It's okay, they told their daughters, we'll be right here. The women sitting in the back made room so Meybelín and Darlene could be closer to their fathers.

Arnovis worried Meybelín was going to have a breakdown—they had hardly lost physical contact for the last two weeks, and so he tried to distract her the way he had been. Look, he told her. Look how beautiful it is. Beyond the steel mesh protecting the window, two Border Patrol officers stood in the dirt of Texas hill country, hands on their gun belts, spitting like cowboys. Meybelín looked back at him. When are we going to get there? she asked. Soon, mi amor. I'm right here. Soon.

After a bumping, hour-long ride, they pulled through a series of gates and into a large parking lot and were let out. Arnovis went up and grabbed his daughter. She seemed cold, a little pale. An officer gave them juice boxes and a sandwich, and Meybelín took a large bite and slurped the sugary juice through the straw. She had been eating so poorly. He needed to get her to safety, he thought, to his brother's house in Kansas, where he could get a good meal in her. And then she could rest, and he could finally sleep, and then it would finally be true, what he had been telling her all trip, that it was okay, that they were safe.

In 2018 photos and audio published from the Border Patrol's short-term holding facilities shocked much of the nation and the world: wailing children sprawled over thin cushions on concrete floors, dog-pound cages overfilled with men, women, and babies, and Border Patrol agents laughing and joking on the other side of the cyclone fences. Arnovis and José, too, were shocked by the conditions they faced. A 2018 report by Freedom for Immigrants collected over eight hundred instances of hate and bias perpetrated in immigrant detention centers, highlighting examples of detained immigrants being called "monkey," "porch monkey," "King Kong," and "fucking blacks." After a man asked for underwear and socks in the West Texas Detention Facility, the warden told him: "Shut your Black ass up. You don't deserve nothing. You belong at the back of that cage." And though the worst treatment still is reserved for Black, gay, or trans migrants, all migrants suffer in immigration detention centers. A 2018 ACLU report cited instances of Border Patrol agents threatening to kill and sexually assault children in their custody.

The first glimpse inside the holding facility reminded Arnovis of the used-clothes warehouse in Villahermosa, where armed coyotes prodded migrants like they were pigs and barked at the infants. Except that in the Border Patrol facility, instead of rooms, there were cages. He told me: the fear was dense.

It's okay, Arnovis told Meybelín again. I'm right here.

The were inside, but they still had to wait about an hour for others to get transferred before space would open up for them in one of the cages.

It's okay, mi amor.

We were in shock, Arnovis told me. We were inside cages. For what?

Besides whispering to Meybelín and Darlene, José and Arnovis didn't speak to any of the other migrants. A little while later they were transferred to a closed-room hielera. Nobody explained anything to them. There was a window on the door where they could see Border Patrol agents at their desks. They were eating, laughing, and joking around, Arnovis said. Soon, they came around to hand out the "cookies," the silver polyethylene sheets that serve as disposable blankets and keep migrants from suffering hypothermia—though many still get sick. There weren't enough cookies to go around, and Arnovis and José didn't get a blanket. Later, when some of the other migrants left, Arnovis took their crinkled silver sheets out of the trash so they could use them. After a while, Meybelín and Darlene, exhausted, fell asleep on the floor.

When stories started breaking in May and June of 2018 that children were being taken from their parents, the administration denied that it had implemented a family separation policy. Then, as the stories and criticism proliferated, they justified the policy by claiming the Flores settlement (an agreement that the government wouldn't detain minors in unlicensed facilities for more than twenty days) was forcing them to separate families. DHS secretary Kirstjen Nielsen referred to the Flores agreement as "legal loopholes" that "hinder the Department's ability to appropriately detain" family members, and, the following year, the Trump administration issued an order to cancel the agreement, seeking the indefinite detention of immigrant families. In 2018, Attorney General Jeff Sessions even used the Bible as justification: "I would cite you to the Apostle Paul and his clear and wise command in Romans 13 to obey the laws of the government because God has ordained them for the purpose of order." As historian Casey Strine has pointed out, however, a reading of the actual intent of the first-century letter reveals that Paul was encouraging Romans to welcome back the Jews after the emperor Claudius had exiled and forcibly removed them six years previously. The letter also contains perhaps the most famous Pauline directive, which Sessions didn't mention: "Love your neighbor as yourself. Love does no wrong to a neighbor; therefore, love is the fulfilling of the law."

In order to deport as many people as quickly as possible, the administration coerced parents, including asylum seekers, by taking away their children as a way to get them to sign voluntary deportation papers. A complaint filed by two major lawyers' associations alleged that the government was using physical and verbal threats, solitary confinement, restriction of feminine hygiene products, and the denial of food and water to convince parents to sign documents—almost always untranslated—that they did not understand.

One Guatemalan mother separated from her five-year-old son for over a month described her experience: "They said they would take us to El Pozo or 'the Well' as punishment if we kept crying about our children. They said I would be punished because I refused to eat in the mornings. They would tell me that they were going to also put me in El Pozo. I did not know what that was. The women told me it was an ice cold room that was dark with no windows." The parents, the complaint made clear, were being punished for missing their children.

Another mother commented, "I bet ICE treats their dogs better than they treated me."

Yusuf Saei, a public interest fellow at Muslim Advocates, one of the organizations suing the government on multiple fronts for its separation practices, explained to me the "disabling trauma" of family separation, and the parents' subsequent "alterations in cognition" that turned asylum-screening interviews into what he called "junk proceedings." One woman, whose son was taken from her for two days, told me about Border Patrol officers pressuring her to sign deportation papers: It was the worst experience of my life. I couldn't sleep. I didn't bathe. I couldn't eat the food. The AC was so, so, so, so cold. There were thirty-five people in there. It's so, so bad. They move you from one hielera to another to another, and you don't even know where you are.

After about twelve hours inside the hielera, a Border Patrol agent called Arnovis out of the room and told him to sit down at a desk, behind which another officer was typing on a laptop. How are you? the officer asked without looking up.

Good.

Good to hear. Have you ever been in the US before?

Yeah.

The officer, still typing, told Arnovis that he had a long file. He read him his rights and then told him to sign a paper. Arnovis was unsure what to do—the paper was in English, and there was no translation.

The officer explained that his signature only confirmed that he had been read his rights, and, hesitating another moment, Arnovis signed. The officer sent him back to the hielera. A half an hour later they called him out again, this time with Meybelín. Another officer asked Arnovis some of the same questions the last officer had asked him, and then turned to Meybelín. The officer called Arnovis's sister-in-law, a legal permanent resident living in Kansas, and asked if she knew Meybelín and if she would be responsible for her if she were released into her custody. After hearing her answer—that yes she would take Meybelín—he told her he'd call back in a few days. The officer then proceeded to take their photographs and fingerprints. Arnovis thought they were going to let them out, and that soon they would be in Kansas.

And they never asked you if you wanted to apply for asylum?

No.

Or if you would be scared to return to your country?

No.

Nothing like that?

No.

Or why you came to the US?

Nothing.

Back in the hielera, every four hours they pulled them out of the room to be counted. Arnovis held onto Meybelín, trying to get her to sleep, but, with the lights always blazing and people always coming and going, he told me, it was like they were driving us crazy. I grabbed a couple extra blankets that people were throwing away, and I think it was like twenty-four hours later, with Meybelín asleep on the floor—I laid another blanket on top of her—when they were pulling us out for another count, Meybelín looked at me and said, Papi, I can't.

I can't handle it, she told me. She sounded like a grown-up, Arnovis said. What's the matter? I asked her. Papi, I can't. I don't want to be here. And I told her, Mi amor, just hold on, we're going to your aunt's soon. But she just kept looking at me and saying I can't, I can't, I can't, I can't, I can't.

The officer ordered them to come out. He wasn't mean, but he was firm. They could have counted us in the room, but they made us come out, every time. They were doing it all on purpose. Arnovis was ashamed, he told me, but didn't know what to say to her, so he just told her to hold on, that he loved her, and then Meybelín covered her face and cried.

A couple hours later, an officer called Arnovis and José out of the room, but this time it wasn't for the count. An officer told them, Look, we're going to get you out of here because your daughters aren't eating very well. And it's cold for them.

They were sent back into the room and then called back out again a little while later. There was a problem. In the next bus there was only space for the two girls, so they would have to be split up. But, an officer reassured them, they would send Arnovis and José on the next bus. It was normal, they said. Plus, the girls couldn't go to court anyway, where Arnovis and José were being sent for prosecution. After court, they promised, they would send them to be reunited with their daughters.

Don't worry, the officer told Arnovis. We're going to take better care of your daughter than we're taking care of you.

The officer handed him a small slip of paper explaining that he was being prosecuted for crossing the border illegally, and that "his son or children" would, meanwhile, be transferred to the Department of Health and Human Services.

How crazy, Arnovis told me when we were sitting in his kitchen. We were both jawing cheap mint gum that had lost its flavor after a few chews. Arnovis had an open plastic baggie of cigarettes that he had bought from his brother-in-law's store, where they sold Super Cola and sweet bread and small envelopes of coffee and loose cigarettes out of their front window. Arnovis didn't use to smoke very much, but, these past few months, he had been smoking a lot. How crazy it all was, Arnovis said.

I said to her—Arnovis told me, once he was back in the hielera—Look, mi amor, you're going to go with them for a little bit, maybe one night, and they're going to give you a bath—she hadn't properly bathed or showered since Guatemala—and something to eat. And I'm going to come in another bus. But you'll be with Darlene. And we'll be there very soon.

Papi, Meybelín told her father, I'm hungry. Okay, he said, they're going to feed you soon. Do you hear me? You're going in the first bus, but we'll come right after you.

I'm hungry, Meybelín said again, and she looked like she was about to cry again.

That was the last conversation Arnovis would have with his daughter for a month. For most of that time, he didn't even know where she was. When I asked Meybelín if she knew where she had been sent after she was separated from her father, she shook her head. Did they tell you where you were going? No, she said, they put us on a plane.

That was your first plane ride?

She nodded.

Did you like it?

No.

12

The same month that Meybelín was shivering on the floor of the hielera, in June of 2018, Trump took to Twitter and opined: "We cannot allow all of these people to invade our Country. When somebody comes in, we must immediately, with no Judges or Court Cases, bring them back from where they came."

A few months later, as caravans of mostly Central Americans proceeded through Mexico, Trump called the migrants "an assault on our sovereignty," claiming that "our border is sacred." Meanwhile, as the United States worked to deny asylum claims, or not hear them in the first place, thousands languished in hastily organized, unsanitary refugee camps in Tijuana, where they lacked basic services like water, reliable shelter, and access to bathrooms. I spent a week walking through the camps, reporting and doing some volunteer work. Trash floated in puddles, bottles full of dark urine were scattered everywhere, and sopping blankets and rain-pulped sheets of cardboard piled up in corners. Among the aisles of tents out of which resting legs spindled, there issued a chorus of constant hacking and coughing. Without access to bathrooms or clean water, many of the migrants and refugees were sick. Amazingly, despite the squalor, most also kept their spirits up.

As they were blocked from asking for asylum at the ports of entry, they increasingly took to the deserts, scaling walls on the outskirts of Tijuana or trekking east into the wilderness. It was an extension of Prevention Through Deterrence, the 1990s policy still in effect that funnels migrants away from urban crossings, and it was aimed directly at asylum seekers. Make the process dangerous enough and—the erroneous logic goes —they'll stop coming. But they kept coming.

Couldn't Arnovis, or any of the other caravaneros taking part in the Central American exodus, have gone somewhere else? Couldn't he have asked for asylum in Mexico, or Spain, or Costa Rica?

David Miller coins an unwieldy term in his influential book *Strangers in Our Midst: The Political Philosophy of Immigration*: "particularity claimant," referring to those asylum seekers who have a specific claim on a country because of past cultural, colonial, or political ties, or because of military or economic interventions. Some migrants and refugees may simply be trying to go *anywhere* safe where they can stake a viable life, but many have a tie or claim to a specific country, and head there. As Mae Ngai puts it, "Migration to the United States has been the product of specific economic, colonial, political, military, and/or ideological ties between the United States and other countries." The process calls to mind Sri Lankan novelist A. Sivanandan's succinct phrase, "We are here because you were there."

Central Americans certainly have a particular relationship to the United States, which used the region as an "ideal testing ground" to stage "an experiment"—of engaging in regime change and squashing popular uprising by providing advisors and materiél without committing substantial numbers of ground troops—as a 1988 army report described the US role in El Salvador. The experiment was not without its repercussions, and Salvadorans, Hondurans, Guatemalans, and Mexicans flee specifically to the United States because the US, in no small part, is why they need to flee. In the late '40s, the US even went so far as to use Guatemalans as actual laboratory subjects, purposefully infecting them with syphilis and other STDs. Iraqis fleeing Iraq today, to give one example out of a multitude, have a similarly particular claim to the United States and should be considered "particularistic refugees."

After decades of such migration flows, many Central Americans also have family or community in the United States. Chimamanda Ngozi Adichie portrays the same relationship between the British and asylum seekers from former British colonies in her novel *Americanah*: "The wind blowing across the British Isles was odorous with fear of asylum seekers, infecting everybody with the panic of impending doom, and so articles were written and read, simply and stridently, as though the writers lived in a world in which the present was unconnected to the past, and they had never considered this to be the normal course of history: the influx into Britain of black and brown people from countries created by Britain."

Similarly, the United States has been intimately linked to El Salvador for well over a century—first as a major importer of the country's indigo, then its coffee, and then, at the height of the Cold War and as El Salvador suffered through a scourge of poverty, repression, and feudalistic inequality, as a backer of the brutally repressive elite and their military henchmen, who tortured and murdered peasants, clergy, labor leaders, teachers, and opposition groups to maintain their grip on power. The centuries-long simmering tension was brought to a rolling boil when the 1979 coup (the fifth in the course of fifty years) put a military junta in charge and the people took to the streets and the mountains to revolt. The military, with political, financial, and tactical support from the United States, sought to quash the budding insurrections.

US politicians had seen El Salvador as an ideological fulcrum for years, wanting to make sure the country didn't "fall" to communism. And though some members of the Salvadoran rebellion were inspired by Marxism, and paltry support was indeed coming from Cuba, most of the Salvadorans organizing against the government rose up because they were tired of living under the heel of extreme poverty and stomach-turning levels of inequality. In the late '70s unemployment was peaking in El Salvador at over 50 percent, and almost 80 percent of arable land in the country was owned by 0.01 percent of the population. In 1983, only 6 percent of the population earned more than $240 a month. As Raymond Bonner points out in his seminal book on the Salvadoran civil war, *Weakness and Deceit*, in that same year, a market basket of basic goods cost $344 per month, or 60 percent more than 94 percent of the population earned in a year.

"We believe that the government of El Salvador is on the front line in a battle that is really aimed at the very heart of the Western Hemisphere, and eventually us," Ronald Reagan intoned in 1980. Bonner notes, however, that a contingent of Green Berets had been in the country as early as the 1960s, and US training of the Salvadoran military dated back to at least 1957, though there was no clear military or national security motivation. Why were they there? Perhaps William Howard Taft captured the US stance toward Central and South America best in 1912: "The whole hemisphere will be ours in fact as, by virtue of our superiority of race, it is already ours morally."

But for what concrete reason would the United States be sending elite military units to a tiny coffee-producing country with a population far less than that of Chicago? And why, once the war began, did the United States start cutting checks? (Over half a million dollars a day was paid out, on average, during Reagan's term, while at its height, military aid reached one million a day.) Why did it send attack helicopters and train killers who raped and murdered nuns; assassinated the country's beloved and recently beatified archbishop, Óscar Romero; and engaged in genocidal scorched-earth campaigns in villages throughout the country? As Greg Grandin lays out in *Empire's Workshop: Latin America, the United States, and the Rise of the New Imperialism*, "The history of the United States is cluttered with 'preemptive' interventions that even the most stalwart champions of U.S. hegemony have trouble defending."

The outright US war with the tiny island of Grenada—the invasion was roundly condemned by the United Nations as a "flagrant violation of international law"—might be the most glaring, absurd, and revealing example of imperial hammering, but the proxy wars for the genocides waged in Honduras, El Salvador, and Guatemala were more consequential. Of the over $4 billion in "aid" the United States sent to El Salvador during the 1980s, 70 percent of it went to its military. (Today, those inflowing dollars wouldn't even have to be converted; since 2001, the official Salvadoran currency has been the US dollar.)

James J. Phillips applies the term "sacrifice zone"—first coined to describe the United States' willingness to sacrifice the Marshall Islands and parts of Nevada for atomic bomb testing— to Honduras, and it fits for the whole Northern Triangle: rich land for mineral and resource extraction, the battle site of America's "Drug War," and the dumping ground for disposable excess laborers.

"All told," Grandin summarizes, "U.S. allies in Central America during Reagan's two terms killed over 300,000 people, tortured hundreds of thousands, and drove millions into exile." During this same period the number of destitute people in the region grew from 11 percent of the population to 33 percent—another 165 million people. Critics see the incredible and incredibly destructive expenditure in Central America as an attempt at a Vietnam "do-over," or as inoculating the United States from the "Vietnam syndrome"—a timidity to use US force abroad. In her book *Salvador*, Joan Didion quotes a US embassy officer making a bald admission: "If it weren't for public opinion ... El Salvador would be the ideal laboratory for a full-scale military operation." Basically, after taking one on the chin, the United States wanted to win a war, and El Salvador seemed like the place to do it. The "experiment," however, came at the cost of massive human suffering, death, and displacement.

While seventy-five thousand people, at least, were killed during El Salvador's civil war (in Guatemala the number is closer to a quarter million), approximately 30 percent of the entire population fled between 1980 and 1992, the majority leaving for the United States. Despite the official unwelcome, today, around 15 percent of all Salvadorans live in the United States. To arrive safely, some people had to rely on what Renny Golden and Michael McConnell called "the new underground railroad" —a series of sanctuary churches set up to protect Central American refugees when the government wouldn't. Robert White, a former US ambassador to El Salvador, captured the reality: "When you finance and train a gang of uniformed butchers and they begin wholesale killing, wiping out whole villages, the people don't emigrate, they flee."

Today, it is primarily the gangs—the Mara Salvatrucha and Barrio 18, both founded in the United States—that drive people to flee. These gangs, just like the murderous government henchmen of the '80s and '90s, are partially (though less directly) funded and trained by the United States. Beyond the commonly cited intervention, incarceration, and deportation policies of the US government that led to the rise of the "Central American" gangs— it's also worth taking a look at the underlying conditions in urban America that helped spawn them. African Americans in Los Angeles, who had themselves arrived to the city in large numbers after fleeing the Jim Crow South in the 1940s during the Second Great Migration, had long been relegated to second-class Angelenos, with housing codes redlining them into corners where the police hounded and harassed them. In the following decades, as Koreans and other Asian Americans moved to LA, they were met with racial animus not only from the police but also from African Americans. James Ellroy captures the terror of anti-Asian sentiment in LA in his novel *Perfidia*, set in the years during the Japanese internment rage, which was led— in both real life and in the novel—by the LAPD. By the 1960s, in South Central and downtown LA, minority groups were fighting for the few scraps of economic dignity the city was offering, and were increasingly pitted against each other. Enter Central American refugees: the next oppressed group hoping for salvation, or at least a bit of safety, in SoCal. As they were discriminated against by the police and squeezed by other minority groups, some Central American refugees, unsurprisingly, began organizing themselves into self-protection units or street gangs.

A transformative moment for the nascent gangs took place during the Rodney King riots in 1992. The peaking ethnic tension between Korean Americans and African Americans, especially as played out in corner-store conflicts and in competition for jobs and housing, exploded along with a rising fury against the vicious and long-corrupt police. A deepening Black unemployment crisis spurred by, as Mike Davis sums it up in *Magical Urbanism*, "persistent residential segregation, workplace discrimination, collapsing inner-city schools and rampant criminalization of Black youth," along with ongoing deindustrialization, spurred Black communities to see both Mexicans and Central Americans as competitors. At the same time, the "early 1990s recession, whose national epicenter was Los Angeles County, devastated the barrios," Davis reports, with Latinos suffering the biggest loss of median household income "registered by any ethnic group since the Depression." Combined with the effects of cutbacks in federal aid, cities like Compton suffered terribly, and the general "socioeconomic decline exacerbated festering Black-Latino tensions."

The young MS-13 gang, as the Martínez brothers explain, "exploited the ethnic jockeying in an attempt to get closer to Chicano gangs." Uprooted, marginalized, and under attack, young men lacked both safety and community. Sent to prison in disproportionate numbers, they did what they could to survive, including allying with already established gangs, which is how the Mara Salvatrucha was born. When US immigration authorities started rounding up and deporting gang members to LA's transnational suburbs in Central America, the doubly transplanted gang members found fertile soil and a weak state in which to rapidly expand. Today, according to a 2018 International Crisis Group report, the gangs control one-third of all municipalities in El Salvador. Between 2014 and 2017, there were twenty thousand murders in the country, more than in Libya, Somalia, or Ukraine.

War, in the classic martial sense, is not raging in Central America today. But the "Drug War"—that ineffectual police and military bonanza in which officers and agents have been killing and incarcerating the hemisphere's poorest and brownest for almost a century—is a key ingredient in destabilizing Central America. Though the "Drug War" goes back to the 1930s when Harry Anslinger, the morphine-addicted head of the Bureau of Narcotics (later redubbed the DEA) staged his racist crusade against Billie Holiday, it has been ramped up to its current form by the same administrations that used Latin America as their "empire's workshop" and began seeding chaos into American cities. From 1981 to 1985, DEA funding rose by over $1 billion from $860 million to over $1.8 billion (a 72 percent increase). In that same period, federal funding for drug treatment efforts dropped 16 percent, from $404 million to only $338 million. The whopping funding package was mixed with a police-media blitz painting primarily inner-city Black men and women not as victims but as perpetrators, and then shutting them into cages. As Michelle Alexander explains in *The New Jim Crow*: "Mass incarceration as we know it would not exist today but for the racialization of crime in the media and political discourse." A quick glance at headlines or, depending on where you live, a quick turn about your block will show you that the estimated trillion-dollar, decades-long war certainly hasn't been waged, or at least certainly not won, against drugs. That is because drugs are more prolific and as deadly as ever: in 2017, more than seventy-two thousand Americans died of drug overdoses, an all-time high and a tenfold increase from a decade earlier.

As America's "War on Drugs" racked up victims in the United States in the 1990s and 2000s, it was exported to tally further failures abroad, first in Colombia, where the US State and Defense Departments sent just shy of $5 billion between 2000 and 2008. "Overall levels of violence in Colombia increased markedly with the launch of Plan Colombia," Dawn Paley writes in *Drug War Capitalism*. "In 2002, its second year, there were 673,919 victims of the war—largely Colombia's poor and working majority—the highest recorded number for any year in the past decades." The enormous crackdown on drug trafficking and guerrilla units in Colombia in the early 2000s redirected trafficking from motorboats speeding through the Caribbean to truck trailers long-hauling it north through Central America and Mexico. In the mid-'80s, more than 75 percent of cocaine on its way to the United States was intercepted in the Caribbean, with barely any seizures in Central America. By 2010, the routes had completely switched, with over 80 percent of US-bound cocaine seized in Central America.

The increased business helped small-potato Mexican trafficking organizations branch out from marijuana and begin cultivating other drugs, turning Mexico into a country of drug producers, drug consumers, and drug exporters. The United States pivoted in response, establishing the Plan Colombia–inspired Mérida Initiative to fund primarily the Mexican, but also Central American, government crackdowns. It spent $1.6 billion to arm and legitimize known human rights violators, torturers, and assassins—the Mexican military and police. Paley notes: "Tellingly, homicides in Mexico peaked in 2010, two years after the Mérida Initiative began." By 2019, the homicide rate increased even more, with nearly 8,500 murders in the first quarter. And it wasn't just internecine cartel fighting. In 2015, a migrant showed me a video he took while riding on top of the Beast, capturing Mexican federal police using migrants as target practice, shooting at Central Americans clinging to the top of the train. One of the men in the video, Beylin Sarmiento Guzman, was killed. Though it's the only instance I know of that has been captured on video, I've been told other stories of Mexican police taking potshots at migrants riding the trains; in the summer of 2019, Mexican police shot and killed at least two Central American migrants. Funding for the Mérida Initiative, meanwhile, continues, with $139 million doled out to Mexico in Trump's 2019 budget.

Without shrinking the demand, interdiction efforts actually bolster trafficking organizations: as producers and traffickers of the drugs are winnowed, competition decreases and those who stay afloat are able to charge more and expand their business portfolio—especially to people smuggling, people trafficking, and kidnapping. As the United States developed crop-spraying campaigns in Colombia and Mexico, for example, in efforts—allegedly—to eradicate drug production, the prices of the drugs went up, and the cultivators and smugglers who survived were primed to make a lot of money, and they did—reaping extravagant wealth in the form of diamond-encrusted pistols and presidents stuffed into their waistband.

Another critical component to the shift in the drug trade and the "cartelization" of Mexico was NAFTA, the free trade policy that resulted not only in war in the southern state of Chiapas but also in massive levels of unemployment and the building of highways and other transportation infrastructure—basically a whip-crack for poor Mexicans either to hightail it to the United States or enter one of the few employment options available, the drug trade. NAFTA further developed "the idea of a narcotics industry intertwined with neoliberal transformation," Paley writes. The overlap between migration and drug trafficking is striking: two phenomena together demonstrating that where there is a human need (migration) and a human desire (intoxication), humans will find a way to meet it, no matter what walls, operations, foreign funding, or acronymic agency you try to police them with.

To further complicate the picture, as Gary Webb revealed in his blockbuster 1996 series of articles in the *San Jose Mercury News*, CIA agents were catalyzing the drug trade to try to help Nicaragua's extreme right-wing guerrillas, the Contras, oust a democratically elected president. As Webb and other writers revealed, the CIA was supporting drug traffickers as a way to fund a rebellion. But the US facilitation of the Central American–US drug trade, some have contended, also enriched the Crips and other gangs in Los Angeles by supplying local crack dealers with product whose distribution tore at the fabric of mostly poor urban communities, which is exactly where fleeing Central Americans were landing.

James Phillips explains how the United States employed "criminal gangs and gang activity to fuel chaos and insecurity in order to topple governments." In other words, early gang development was seen as being in the US "interest." In the 1980s, US agencies, Phillips writes, "found clandestine ways to arm the Contras through arms-for-drug trades with known drug lords in Honduras who had connections with Contra camps and safe havens in that country." The Central American gangs originated not merely as a response to conditions in Central America and Southern California but through deliberate US midwifery. Not only are they an unfortunate sequela of the "War on Drugs," but they are a distinct political creation.

Gangs may be created—think of Dr. Frankenstein's monster, or the Taliban—but they are not so easily disbanded or controlled. For one thing, gangs operate autochthonously, varying according to the specific demographic makeup, economy, and relationship with the police, as well as national and international anti-gang and drug policies. Throughout El Salvador and Honduras I heard varying accounts of how the gangs collaborate with or operate exclusively apart from drug-trafficking organizations and the police. In Corral de Mulas and the surrounding villages and islands, for example, there were at least two major military police operations targeting members of the army and local and national police for drug trafficking and connections with transnational criminal organizations. These soldiers and police officers, according to a number of different people I spoke with—including journalists, residents, and the mayor—worked with the same gangs they were supposedly working against. On one night I spent with Arnovis and his family, forty soldiers, police, and business owners in nearby Puerto Triunfo were arrested for connections to drug trafficking. As the news started to trickle in that night and the next morning, the family wasn't surprised. Some of the officers who were arrested had been regulars at one of the two local restaurants in Corral, just a short sandal-dragging stroll from their home.

Earlier that year, in April, just a month before Arnovis and Meybelín fled, three police officers and an administrator of the National Civil Police were among seventeen arrests in nearby Usulután for participating in a network that transported cocaine from Colombia to the United States. A few months before that, the police intercepted 1,750 pounds of cocaine in a ship, and in 2016, two Ecuadorans and one Colombian were arrested in Puerto Triunfo with almost 1,500 pounds of cocaine. That same year, in Operation Shark, national police arrested 314 gang members from the Revolutionary 18s, a rival faction of the 18s. As Arnovis explained it to me, and as the mayor of Puerto Triunfo confirmed (the mayor of Puerto also presides over Corral), the gangs on the islands have a symbiotic but auxiliary relationship to the narcos, who work directly with the military and police. According to the mayor, an ex-army captain still referred to as Capitán, these were only "rogue" actors and not representative of the army as a whole. Typically, the gangs work as security, or are contracted for menial tasks, such as cutting the grass on the clandestine runway for the drug planes, or loading or unloading packages.

In rural parts of Honduras, as I learned, it was different: the narcos, in complete control of some departments, permit almost zero gang activity. They don't want gang scuffles to heat up the plaza, as it's often described—a wave of crime and violence on a gang's turf inviting a crackdown—and getting in the way of their business. That seemed to be the case in Olancho, where I spent a few days interviewing returned asylum seekers in the offices of the Lutheran World Federation. They kill them like flies, said one young recently deported man, to explain how narcos treat gangsters, echoing Arnovis's mother's line about being killed like dogs. It was the same, again, in a mountainous tract of the Yoro Department—the narcos establishing complete operational control—where Edwin, a nervous and desperate asylum seeker I met in the summer of 2018, was from. We spent the day together in a small town, where he told me his long and tragic story about multiple attempts on his life. His cousin was murdered by the same narcos, as he called them, as had shot his brother and threatened him after the three of them turned down an "invitation" to collaborate. He also told me about fleeing with his young son, Jaime, and their ongoing separation. Edwin had been tricked into signing his deportation papers after they'd arrived to Texas. Shortly before we met, Jaime had recently turned five while still in Office of Refugee Resettlement (ORR) custody in Chicago.

This isn't life, Edwin said at one point. I wanted to bring my son to safety, that's it. I wasn't trying to live large. I'll go to the US as a slave. I don't care. I just needed to leave.

When I had asked, earlier, if Edwin had tried going to the police for protection, he'd told me, The police don't exist. Later in the conversation, he mentioned that the police had shown up at his parents' house one day, looking for him. The police work with the narcos, he said.

The vice president of the Honduran Congress, Marvin Ponce, admitted in 2012 that, as Edward Fox reported, "up to 40 percent of the country's police force was tied to organized crime." Researcher Dana Frank quotes a former police commissioner acknowledging that "it's scarier to meet up with five police officers on the streets than five gang members." In 2018, Juan Antonio "Tony" Hernández, the brother of the illegitimate president of Honduras, was arrested in Miami on drug and weapons charges. Prosecutors alleged that he was a "large-scale drug trafficker" who had worked between Colombia, Honduras, and the United States to import "multi-ton" loads of cocaine. He was later found guilty of the charges. The president himself, as well as his wife, were directly implicated in profiting from the drug trade.

"The mere fact that perfect policing does not exist in the applicant's home country," Attorney General Sessions wrote one month before Edwin and Jaime fled Honduras, or "that the country in question has an extremely high crime rate, or that certain populations are more likely to be targeted by private criminals, does not itself establish the home government is 'unable or unwilling' to curb the persecution."

Given the United States' extreme reluctance to provide protection—even while emboldening and excusing the persecutors—couldn't Edwin have gone somewhere else? Couldn't he have asked for asylum in Mexico, or Spain, or Costa Rica? What is the *particular* relationship between Honduras—the Northern Triangle country expelling the most asylum seekers—and the United States that Edwin would specifically want to stake his asylum claim here? The answer is complex, as it is with El Salvador, but perhaps a good place to start is by remembering the fact that the United States established its banana republic in Honduras over a century ago—the term itself was coined by short story writer O. Henry after a visit to the country—and since has worked to establish free economic zones where sweatshops, gang crime, murder, and rape—along with foreign trade—flourish.

The US history of meddling in Honduras is as seedy as it is in El Salvador or Guatemala, though because the country has not experienced an all-out war or revolution, the abusive relationship is often overlooked. An obituary of an American mining magnate dating to the late nineteenth century referred to him as the "King of Honduras," an epithet that neatly captures the Taftian viewpoint of Honduras as open for the taking. Through a series of US-led reforms and militarization over the next 130 years, Honduras's economy was channeled into two tracks: monocrop export agriculture and sweatshops. The manorial banana economy followed much the same path as in Guatemala, and, today, palm oil industry captains are following the example of the banana barons to suppress, exploit, and kill intractable workers. Those barons have received significant support from the United States.

In the 1960s, for example, the AFL-CIO labor union teamed up with the CIA to create the American Institute for Free Labor Development (AIFLD), with the supposed intent of providing training to Latin American labor leaders, though they actually worked in line with American anti-communist efforts to stave off a left-leaning government in Honduras. The AIFLD's major goals, according to James Phillips, were to "prevent 'communist' infiltration, and … to control or neutralize labor activism, and to foment labor unrest against 'communist' governments" with the aim of "keeping labor movements docile and subservient to business elites." The AIFLD effectively hamstrung a labor movement that could have curbed the obscene levels of exploitation that exist today or acted as a counterweight to the violent US-backed authoritarian administrations that have ruled Honduras for decades.

By the 1980s, the United States was using Honduras as a staging ground to run its military "experiments" throughout Central America. As Adrienne Pine puts it in *Working Hard, Drinking Hard*, her book on violence in Honduras, "In 1981, US military aid to Honduras, a small country with a population of 4.2 million that was not at war, was $8.9 million. By 1984 US military aid leveled off at $77.4 million, earning the country the dubious nickname 'USS Honduras.'"

The United States continues to support the politicians, generals, and business captains who despoil and militarize Honduras, following in the footsteps of Ronald Reagan, who enthusiastically backed brutal iron-fist quasi-dictators and bestowed, for example, a Legion of Merit medal to cutthroat military officer Gustavo Álvarez Martínez. Trained in the United States, Martínez was commander of Battalion 316, a death squad that worked in cahoots with the CIA and was notorious for torturing, and sometimes assassinating, political opponents. The year before Martínez received his medal from the United States, according to Pine, career diplomat John Negroponte (a confidant of Martínez and the future ambassador to Iraq) ordered an officer in the US embassy to delete information about Honduran military abuses from the annual Human Rights Report so that Congress wouldn't pull the funding plug. Reagan and Negroponte even praised Martínez for "encouraging" democracy in Honduras. (Reagan took the same stance toward Guatemalan general and president Efraín Ríos Montt, convicted of genocide and crimes against humanity, though Reagan thought he got a "bum rap.")

At the same time as the war shifted from anti-communism to "anti-drugs," the United States began seeing Honduras as a potential source for neoliberal expansion, leading the IMF and World Bank in funding infrastructure projects to construct maquiladoras. These Honduran private-public corporations, jointly backed by the IMF and the United States, proceeded to build roads and factories to produce and export goods— mainly textiles—but neglected to fund sewage, water, garbage, or electricity projects for the neighborhoods where the maquila workers lived, effectively creating gang-incubating slums. After the IMF made a nearly $200 million loan to Honduras in 2014, it recommended "reducing the wage bill of the Honduran government," as Dana Frank reports. The stipulations on the loan also included major reductions on spending on public health and housing. The next year, according to the United Federation of Honduran Workers, around ten thousand public employees had lost their jobs. And while much is discussed about how NAFTA created the need for southern Mexico to begin importing corn from the United States, the same massive influx of cheap produce took place in Honduras, with beans, after the IMF's restructuring plan tanked Honduras's agriculture industry and the country had to start importing the traditional staple from Ethiopia. Pine summarizes that, after maquilas came to Honduras, real wages haven't gone up, and "the country has not seen the improvements in education, employment, public health, and security that are supposed to be part and parcel of development." Instead, development heralded unprecedented levels of crime.

To combat that crime, US-backed President Hernández infamously promised to put a soldier on every street corner, even while those soldiers and police officers terrorized and murdered citizens. Illustrating a direct connection between police abuse and the United States, Spanish journalist Alberto Arce reported how, in 2011, the soldiers who shot and killed fifteen-year-old Ebed Yanes—who had scootered around a checkpoint on his way to meet a girlfriend—were US-trained, US-funded, and operating with US equipment. One of the top military officials who later tried to cover up the Yanes murder was a student, just like Gustavo Martínez, at the Western Hemisphere Institute for Security Cooperation, the Georgia-based combat training academy formerly called the School of the Americas.

One afternoon as lowering rain clouds menaced in the sky, I met one young Honduran maquila worker, Antonio Ramos, for coffee and banana bread right after he got off his shift. Antonio lives in the same gang-controlled Rivera Hernández neighborhood where I met El Mini-Me and El Mortal outside Tienda Emily. He makes his living at a nearby maquiladora sewing official NBA jerseys and earning less than ten dollars a day. A little more than a year before I met him, he left college and fled Honduras after he was targeted by the gangs and the military police, who showed up at his house one day and tried to coax him into one of their trucks for questioning. With the help of his grandfather, he refused. The incident stemmed from an earlier schoolyard dispute that one young soldier wouldn't let drop. After narrowly escaping falling into military custody—potentially a black hole of torture or dismemberment—Antonio made it to the United States but was denied asylum and quickly deported. He told me that, now, he almost never leaves his house, except to go to work. For a couple months after our meeting, he updated me regularly, sending me photos of new gang graffiti outside his home and describing the sounds of the previous night's shootouts.

Two years after the 2009 military coup that the United States deemed legitimate, the same year that its funding for Honduran military and police increased by 50 percent, then president Porfirio Lobo sent seven thousand troops to occupy the Lower Aguán Valley, where campesinos had been fighting back against ruthless palm oil corporations. As typical for a coup, the consequences weren't just a shifting of who gets to wear the sash, but a violent targeting of political opponents and the already marginalized populace. As the Honduran military and private security forces they worked with were arresting, terrifying, and sometimes slaughtering peasants in Lower Aguán, the US Rangers conducted a month-long training course for the Honduran military. The *New York Times* even published a headline making a direct connection between the catastrophe of the US Middle East policy to the catastrophe of its Central American policy: "Lessons of Iraq Help U.S. Fight a Drug War in Honduras."

The US-seeded corruption and instability of the Honduran state, along with the US-funded drug demand and drug war, all led, in part, to Edwin and young Jaime's departure. The US response when they knocked on the door and asked for protection was to lock them up. They then deported Edwin and transferred Jaime fifteen hundred miles north. In November of 2018, after more than five months of being separated from his family, locked in an ORR facility in Chicago—in many of these facilities social workers are prohibited from touching or hugging the children; even the children themselves are not allowed to hug each other—Edwin's son was released and given over to the custody of his aunt in New York. Edwin sent me photos of the day of his release: Jaime is wearing a backwards cap, holding a crowded string of welcome balloons, and hugging a stuffed puppy.

Gracias a dios, Edwin wrote me, from Honduras. When I asked about his own situation, however, he told me he's still in hiding. He's glad that Jaime has been released, but he doesn't know when, or if, he'll ever see him again.

13

I had a suspicion, Arnovis told me. There were a thousand suspicions in my mind. But I still thought I was going to see her again. I thought maybe the next day. But then after a day, I thought, Okay, maybe she's sleeping in day care. Maybe she really needed to sleep. And okay, one day, one night, but then before I went to court, they took me to another detention center and I asked, Where's my daughter? And they told me, I didn't you know had a daughter. Meybelín, I told them. Who's Meybelín? She's my daughter.

Something so horrible to hear—that they don't know. And they said that she wasn't showing up in the system. So I told them to put in her last name, in case they got confused. Still she didn't show up. It was horrible. What happened to my daughter? Who had her? Who knew where she was?

ICE had transferred Arnovis and José to the Rio Grande Detention Center. Before they took him to court, they did another preliminary interview and he told them, again, that he wanted to ask for asylum.

You know what, they told me, here in this country, there is a law, and we have zero tolerance for those who break it. I told them that I couldn't go back to my country. That has nothing to do with us, they said. Whether you have a kid or not, they said to me. You just bring your kids like they're a ticket for you to stay.

It's painful to hear someone tell you something like that, Arnovis said. That you're using your child like that. I was detained for twenty-three days without knowing anything about my daughter, without hearing my daughter's voice, without anybody telling me my daughter was all right, or showing me a photo. Twenty-three days of terror.

In Flannery O'Connor's 1955 novella *The Displaced Person*, the grumbling xenophobe Mrs. Shortley succinctly defines a refugee: "It means they ain't where they were born at and there's nowhere for them to go—like if you was run out of here and wouldn't nobody have you." Mrs. Shortley also articulates the perennial fear of the receiving population, when she has "the sudden intuition that the Gobblehooks, like rats with typhoid fleas, could have carried all those murderous ways over the water with them directly to this place. If they had come from where that kind of thing was done to them, who was to say they were not the kind that would also do it to others?"

Arendt has an even more compact definition for the refugee: an "outlaw"—someone who is betrayed and exiled by the state.

In 2014, the UN General Assembly called for a summit to address the growing number of displaced peoples around the globe. World leaders met in New York for a day of roundtable talks and came up with a nonbinding resolution that could be confused for a term paper from a precocious undergraduate. Among its astute observations: "Since the earliest times, humanity has been on the move," and "We are witnessing in today's world an unprecedented level of human mobility." The declaration nodded at "the root causes" of the exodus, with the signatories promising that "we will ensure a people-centered, sensitive, humane, dignified, gender-responsive and prompt reception for all persons arriving in our countries ... We will also ensure full respect and protection for their human rights and fundamental freedoms."

But that "full respect and protection" is not what's taking place. In response to the millions of people arriving to their borders and shores, nations continue to trample human rights, ignore root causes, and engage in a state-centric, insensitive, undignified, gender-biased, dragged-out reception or flat-out refusal. In 2018, the UN published another "milestone" migration agreement that, even while it expressly states that it is not legally binding, garnered 163 signatories to "operationalize the principles of burden- and responsibility-sharing to better protect and assist refugees and support host countries and communities." The compact itself—sounding like a boardroom presentation with its "multi-stakeholder and partnership approach" and "innovative financing schemes"—states that it is "entirely non-political in nature." As previously mentioned, the United States did not participate in the compact because, as UN Ambassador Nikki Haley put it, "the global approach … is simply not compatible with US sovereignty."

The 2014 declaration is right that "migration should be a choice, not a necessity," but the statement also seems to betray a hopefulness that reality rapidly lays to rest. It is not a choice, and hasn't been a choice for the last thirty years for millions of asylum seekers, including those from Central America and Mexico. Relying on the UN to administer a solution, relying on the "leaders of the world" to continue to hold roundtables and drop fifty-page highfalutin declarations—especially as the largest instigator of refugee claims, the United States, refuses to participate—as more people continue to be uprooted, will result in more of the same: we will see, in south Texas and Mexico, more and more of the kinds of refugee camps that are in Kenya and Uganda, and more and more people around the world will be uprooted and left bereft of both rights and roofs.

In March of 2016, the UNHCR published *Eligibility Guidelines for Assessing the International Protection Needs of Asylum-Seekers from El Salvador*, in which the agency recognizes that family members of gang members are "reportedly treated with suspicion and have been attacked and killed." The guidelines argue that contradicting a gang is a political action, in that the gangs have de facto political control of some Salvadoran cities and towns. The report concludes, "Depending on the particular circumstances of the case, UNHCR considers that family members, dependents and other members of the households of gang members may be in need of international refugee protection on the basis of their (imputed) political opinion."

"Instead of supporting people running from harm," the US government has "built a machine designed to psychologically break them in the hopes that they will give up and go home," Sonia Nazario wrote in 2018. Or, as one Border Patrol agent, according to an ACLU report, put it to an asylum seeker: "I'm going to take you back to the river so that you can die."

In July of 2018, the US Citizenship and Immigration Services agency (USCIS) issued a policy memorandum, "Guidance for Processing Reasonable Fear, Credible Fear, Asylum, and Refugee Claims in Accordance with *Matter of A-B-*," after Attorney General Jeff Sessions referred the case to himself, further delineating who is afforded protections on the basis of "membership in a particular social group." Sessions used the case to overrule a separate Board of Immigration Appeals (BIA) case, arguing that "married women in Guatemala who are unable to leave their relationship" are not "members who share a common immutable characteristic, [are] defined with particularity, and [are] socially distinct within the society in question."

Sessions added, quoting his own ruling in *A-B-*, "In cases where the persecutor is a non-government actor, the applicant must show the harm or suffering was inflicted by persons or an organization that his or her home government is unwilling or unable to control, such that the government either 'condoned the behavior or demonstrated a complete helplessness to protect the victim.'" He pointed to cases almost identical to Arnovis's: "Groups comprising persons who are 'resistant to gang violence' and susceptible to violence from gang members on that basis," ruling that they "are too diffuse to be recognized as a particular social group." Sessions concluded: "Victims of gang violence often come from all segments of society, and they possess no distinguishing characteristic or concrete trait that would readily identify them as members of such a group."

In a previous case, *Matter of Acosta*, which was decided in 1985, the BIA defined the slippery concept of persecution of a particular social group as "persecution that is directed toward an individual who is a member of a group of persons all of whom share a common, immutable characteristic." *Immutable characteristic* was itself, then, defined as a characteristic "that the members of the group either cannot change, or should not be required to change because it is fundamental to their individual identities or consciences." The UNHCR explains the immutability approach as "a characteristic or association that is so fundamental to human dignity that group members should not be compelled to forsake it."

The BIA, years later, further articulated "particularity" such that "social visibility"—but not of the "ocular kind"—"is an important element in identifying the existence of a particular social group" and that it must have "well-defined boundaries" and be "recognizable" as a discrete group by others in the society.

Does someone fleeing a gang threat have such a "particularity" that makes them members of a discrete group? I tried to put that question to Arnovis's family. His mother looked at me and smiled. I thought I hadn't explained the question well enough, but when I started to try to reformulate it she stopped me. Everybody knows, she said. Todos saben. And she said it in a way that I knew that was going to be her final answer. But other people, I said, your neighbors in Corral, know when somebody, *particularmente*, is threatened by the gangs? She waved away my question. Todos saben, she said again. In a town as small as Corral, how would they not know?

Though it may be a settled matter for Sonia, for the US government, the question remains: Is opposition to a gang an immutable characteristic? Can you change your position to the gang —or even join—and not change *who you are*? The UNHCR guidelines state, "In a cultural context where it is risky for people to oppose gangs, often in closely knitted neighbourhoods that are effectively controlled by gangs, gang resisters may be set apart in society." Corral de Mulas is a closely knit neighborhood controlled by a gang. Neighborhood news—storms, engagement announcements, school concerts—is disseminated by the loudspeaker affixed to a tower next to the school, and if you're out of earshot or are out fishing, you hear the news as soon as you see your neighbor. Everybody knows, as Sonia told me. Todos saben.

But what was *immutable* about Arnovis such that *on account of* it he was persecuted? Was his mere resistance, his mere existence outside the gang structure, enough to qualify him as socially distinct? *What he did*—the elbow to the mouth—incited the persecution, but then *who he was*—refusing to join MS, his ongoing presence in Corral, the *immutable* history of his past offense and his living resistance to becoming a soldier or pawn in the gang's structure—led to his ongoing persecution, rendering life for him in Corral both insufferable and untenable.

He also might have qualified for asylum not because of his particular social group but on grounds of his political opinion, which the UNHCR defines as "any opinion on any matter in which the machinery of State, government, society, or policy may be engaged." The guidelines continue: "In certain contexts, expressing objections to the activities of gangs" may be construed as forming a political opinion. "It is important to consider, especially in the context of Central America," the guidelines specify, "that powerful gangs, such as the Maras, may directly control society and de facto exercise power in the areas where they operate ... Some jurisdictions have recognized that opposition to a criminal activity or, conversely, advocacy in favor of the rule of law may be considered a political opinion."

The gangs in Corral—one persecuting Arnovis, the other beckoning him—regulate commerce through extortion and taxation. They also monopolize the legitimate use of violence within the territory. They are, in sum, the state, and they are Arnovis's persecutors. If he had remained in Corral when he was first targeted, Barrio 18 would likely have found him—as they had found his brother-in-law Miguel—and similarly pulled him into the street and put a pistol against his head. Except, in his case, they probably would have pulled the trigger. Or maybe, first MS would have found him and pressured him, again, to join, and instead of threatening to stick a gun in his mouth or put a machete to his neck, as Arnovis's old acquaintance Peluca had warned, they would have actually put the gun in his mouth or swung the machete.

So his options: join MS and stick his neck out for Barrio 18, or run.

Arnovis was taken to court, where, along with approximately thirty other migrants, he pleaded guilty to the charge of illegal reentry to the United States. Before and after court, ICE agents repeatedly pressured him to sign a voluntary deportation form. He refused, and refused again, and was transferred to a for-profit detention center run by GEO Group, one of the two largest private immigrant detention corporations. He asked the guards over and over again about Meybelín. They told him that they didn't know anything, that their job was just to guard over him and give him food, and that's it. ICE officials, including his deportation officer, Officer Torres, as he remembered him, only came to the detention center twice a week. The first time Arnovis met Torres, he told him he'd look for Meybelín. The next week, when Arnovis saw him again, Torres didn't have any new information.

They had no idea what I was going through, Arnovis told me. I was filled with anger, and at night I cried. I couldn't sleep. Everybody else in there was asleep, and I was just sitting there. Those were such long days I was living.

After three weeks of emptiness, insomnia, and accelerating

thoughts swinging between fury, self-reproach, helplessness, and a frantic sadness, a new deportation officer showed up to tell Arnovis that he needed to leave the country. If he stayed to try to fight his case, she told him, he would be locked up for three years, and his daughter would be locked up for three years, too, and the best thing for both of them would be for him to sign his deportation papers.

The officer handed him a sheet of paper. There was a paragraph on the top in English, and then some blank lines below. I'm going to tell you what to write, she told him.

They were in a room with fifty bunk beds. Ninety-nine other men were sitting on their bunks or on the floor or at a row of benches along the wall or in the bathrooms in the far corner. A constant chatter of squeaking, cracking, coughing, thudding, snoring, sighing, groaning, flushing, and farting filled the room. There was no peace, calm, reprieve, dignity, or decency. Not at night, not during the day, not when the guards yelled for quiet or when ICE officers sat with you on benches and talked about your fear, about your persecution, about your daughter who was either in Florida or New York, about your six-year-old daughter going to prison, about how long you were going to spend locked up if you didn't write and sign what they told you to write and sign. Arnovis and the officer were sitting on one of the benches along the wall. There was no table to write on. Three years in immigrant jail, Arnovis thought. Three years without Meybelín.

The officer told him, Write what I tell you to write. She said, Three years you will be locked up. Three years your daughter will be in custody.

Three years, Arnovis thought.

The officer handed him a pen. Write what I tell you.

He flattened the paper against the wall.

The officer started speaking, Yo, Arnovis Guidos Portillo ...

He doesn't remember exactly what he wrote, except that he wrote what she told him to write.

They had won, that was how he saw it. They had made him miserable enough that being anywhere would be better than being where he was. He wasn't going to find Meybelín while being guarded over by GEO Group guards who didn't speak Spanish, who didn't know where his daughter was, and who couldn't even confirm that he had a daughter. He needed to get out.

14

It's hard to weigh the competing emotions—the current misery of confinement, the fear of future death—as detained asylum seekers pressured to give up their cases are forced to do. Humans recoil from death as well as from captivity. We want to live and we want to live free. We want both.

Since detention standards were changed in 1996, the US government, in direct refutation to the Refugee Convention, has locked up hundreds of thousands of asylum seekers who have broken neither domestic nor international law. The idea is to use them as an example of the misery the government is willing to draw on the bodies and minds of those seeking its protection, in order to convince future asylum seekers from even trying. When former White House chief of staff John Kelly first introduced the idea of family separation in 2017, he said, "Yes, I'm considering" family separation "in order to deter more movement along this terribly dangerous network. I am considering exactly that." But deterrence—prolonged detention, family separation, or forcing migrants to walk through the remote deserts—doesn't work. Bertha, for example, a sixty-three-year-old Honduran grandmother fleeing to save her and her granddaughter's life, came to the United States knowing that they would likely be detained. And they were. Even after Bertha's granddaughter was released, ICE kept Bertha locked up for almost two years.

~

I met Bertha in a small echoic room in the El Paso Processing Center, in her eighteenth month of detention. Boggled as to why ICE would detain, for such a long time, a shy grandmother with developing health complications who poses neither flight risk nor security concern, I asked her lawyer, Ed Beckett, if he knew why the government hadn't released her.

They're just assholes, Beckett told me. Cruel and unusual punishment, that's about it. I think she's a prime example of deterrence.

At her first asylum hearing in the low-ceilinged court inside the El Paso Processing Center, Bertha was denied asylum but was offered protection and relief from deportation through the Convention Against Torture. But then, a few days after the hearing, and before she was released, the judge suddenly changed his mind and reversed his decision. As Beckett helped Bertha appeal, she was kept in detention.

I've been in here eighteen months, she told me in the spartan interview room. I'm from the department of Cortés. I came to the bridge on November 18. We were in the hielera for one day, and then they sent us here. I came ... I fled. We came together. My granddaughter was only fourteen, her name is Yariela. The gangsters wanted her to be their wife. But I couldn't let that happen. And then they wanted to kill me. They said they were going to kill me. We left the next day. I knew ... well, I'm scared to return to my country, that's what I told them.

I asked her what the security situation was like in her hometown.

I lost my grandson on October 11, 2013. They disappeared him. We don't know where he is. I raised them both. Their mom was already here, in Houston. And when we had to leave, we just left, without hardly anything. We ran out of money in Guatemala. We had to go asking for money, asking for alms, for food. I was asking God for help. We traveled by bus. I wouldn't know how to take a train. We were hungry sometimes, but people treated us okay. They gave us food.

They respected me because of my age. An *abuelita*. A little grandmother.

That's why we left. Because a gangster was trying to make my granddaughter his wife. I turn to ice when I think about going back there.

I came to ask for protection. I didn't kill anyone, she says. She began counting on her fingers, starting with her thumb, then index finger. I didn't rob anyone. I don't do drugs, don't have anything to do with drugs. She held up all five fingers to me, and then dropped her hand. I'm clean. A good woman. My daughter is the only one who helps me with some money, for the vending machine, for phone calls, but I can't stand anything from the vending machines anymore. I can't stand the soda ... I'm just asking God to get me out of here. And my granddaughter. She asks me, she's so sad, she asks me, Mami, she calls me, why don't they let you out? And she starts to cry. You raised me. Please come here with me.

You can't make a complaint or go to the police back in Honduras, Bertha told me, because they'll know. They have a system, they can track you. I was looking for my grandson after he disappeared, but trying not to make too much noise. And we never found him. I imagine that they killed him, dropped him off somewhere, in some ditch, that's how they do it. You can't try to talk to the police or they'll disappear you. If you see something, she said, and then zipped her lips with a finger.

I don't know why there's so much violence. I can't explain it. It started around, around 2000. It wasn't like this when I was a girl. Everything was much calmer. But it's so bad now. Everybody, so many people are leaving. They told me they had to separate us, but they didn't tell me where they were taking her. I was so ... I never expected to be here so long.

To kill time I read the Bible. I also like to play Monopoly. I used to play with this other woman, from Honduras. We played a game last night. But she left today.

I asked her who won.

She smiled, embarrassed. I did, she said. I'll miss her a lot. She went back to Honduras, just today. I lie in bed and read the Bible. The Psalms. My dad died when he was ninety-one years old, and he told me, hija, for this, your tongue, she said, and stuck out her tongue, they'll kill you … for talking, for saying what you see. The gangs, they were taking money, war taxes. They charge you for everything. There wasn't any more money for food.

Here, in detention, we wake up at five, we have breakfast. Lunch at eleven. And dinner at four-thirty. But sometimes I'm hungry at night. At home we ate at nine. I get hungry at midnight. Sometimes I buy something from the vending machine, but I don't like those crackers or cookies anymore. I don't even like soda. I go to bed hungry. Lights out at nine o'clock. There's count three times a day. At ten in the morning, at three-thirty, and at nine. At count we have to be quiet. We have to lie in our beds and we can't talk. If we make noise we get in trouble. At night though, it's hard to sleep. If someone's snoring, she says, laughing and putting her hands on her cheeks, we have to deal with it. There's always someone in the barracks with us. One of the guards. They're not mean, but they talk strong if we're loud, if someone's talking during count. She paused to think. Sometimes, to pass the time, I draw. I draw flowers, princesses, little animals, things like that. Curlicues. Just to pass the time.

It's not good to be in here. This situation … it's like a purgatory. It's like we're never going to leave. I just think I'm never going to leave. If I get out I'm going to do what I always do, follow the right path. Be good. Do right. We're all the same. You have to treat people nice. I hope, I hope that God forgives the United States. They have no heart. We're people. We're old women. We can't be here. I don't know why they don't let us go. I just don't know why.

Bertha started telling me about her favorite Psalms, but then one of the guards interrupted us. Our time was up. I told her I would read a couple of her recommendations, and, as I scribbled into my notebook and the guard stood watching us, she told me to read Psalms 23, 91, 102, 27, and 71.

It had been a long time since I read any of them, and, at my hostel later that night, as I began to read them on my computer, I wondered at first if all the Psalms referred to danger and searching for refuge in times of trouble and old age, or if she had just selected those that so precisely fit her situation.

I will say of the Lord, He is my refuge and my fortress. Surely He shall deliver you from the snare of the fowler. He shall cover you with His feathers, and under his wings you shall take refuge. You shall not be afraid of the terror by night, nor of the arrow that flies by day, nor of the pestilence that walks in darkness, nor of the destruction that lays waste at noonday. For my days are consumed like smoke, and my bones are burned like a hearth. My heart is stricken and withered like grass, so that I forget to eat my bread. My bones cling to my skin. I am like a pelican of the wilderness, I am like an owl of the desert. I lie awake, and am like a sparrow alone on the housetop. Do not cast me off in the time of old age. Do not forsake me when my strength fails. You prepare a table before me. You anoint my head with oil. My cup runs over.

In the summer of 2018, after twenty months of detention, Bertha lost her appeal and was deported alone back to Honduras. When I think of her now, I think of another poem, the line from Keats—*Where but to think is to be full of sorrow*—and of Saint Romero, who was reading the twenty-third Psalm, one of Bertha's recommendations, during mass on the day he was assassinated in the San Salvador cathedral. "May God have mercy on the assassins" were the archbishop's last words.

Sixteen hours after the army sniper pulled the trigger and killed Romero, on March 24, 1980, the US House Foreign Operations Subcommittee began hearings on the $5.7 million in military aid that the archbishop had begged President Carter not to send, which he said would "surely increase injustice here and sharpen the repression that has been unleashed."

Though the vote was postponed, the military aid was eventually approved.

Joan Didion described the administration's account of the Salvadoran government's progress toward human rights, on which the US aid depended, as hallucinatory. The adjective also would apply to ICE's self-proclaimed compliance with its own standard of guaranteeing "safe, secure, and humane environments" for what it calls "custodial supervision."

15

He's been on a plane twice in his life—both times, Arnovis was in chains.

I was in shock, he said.

He was leaving Meybelín behind, by herself, somewhere in "Florida or New York," as the ICE officer had told him.

Along with about a hundred other migrants, after landing at the airport in San Salvador, Arnovis was unshackled, loaded onto a bus, and driven to La Chacra, the migrant reception center. He was scared to be home, he said. He didn't want to move, didn't want to be there, or be anywhere but with his daughter. Inside La Chacra for the second time in a year, a social worker helped him call a US government number and, to his amazement and relief, they eventually got someone on the line who offered to help track down his daughter. They spent hours trying. Finally, after getting nowhere and accepting that there was nothing more he could do, he walked across the dirt and gravel parking lot, exited the large green door, and saw his father, once again, waiting for him under the brilliantly spilling magenta bougainvillea.

It was so sad, he told me. So, so sad to see my father in front of me. I couldn't bring myself to say that I didn't have my daughter anymore. I just told him that I failed. I failed, I said. And then I saw my mother, and we all started crying.

And then Arnovis noticed the cameras. All these gringo reporters—what are they doing here? he wondered. It seemed like a joke. They're making a disaster of my country, he thought. He wanted to scream at them.

Joana, his partner, and his brother-in-law, Miguel, were there, too, and they all hugged him. It's okay, they said. It will be okay. Miguel told him that a journalist had been talking to his wife, who had also come along, and he thought maybe she could help. It was Sarah Kinosian, a journalist writing for the *Guardian*. Though he didn't want to talk to anybody, Arnovis relented, and Miguel called Sarah over. She introduced herself to Arnovis, asked a couple questions, and got his number. Maybe she would visit him in the next couple days, she offered, so they could talk some more. Fine, Arnovis said.

The family piled into the borrowed car and started the long drive back to the islands. After crossing the Bridge of Gold over San Marcos Lempa, with another hour yet to drive, the family decided to stop to eat pupusas. Arnovis, still wanting to be nowhere except on his way to get his daughter, as he put it to me, didn't even step out of the car. He was sitting alone in the heat of dusk when he saw his dad hurrying back toward him.

Arnovis, his dad said, it's Mey, and he handed him a phone.

The first thing she told me, Arnovis said, was: Papi, why did you leave me here?

My god. I didn't know what to say.

No, mi amor, I didn't leave you.

Then why didn't you bring me with you?

At a loss for words—like they were sucked out of his soul—he lied. The airplane broke, he told her, hardly knowing where the idea was coming from. The airplane that was going to bring you back with me broke, but as soon as they fix it, they'll pick you up and you'll be back with us.

When, papi?

Soon, mi amor. Soon.

They spoke for maybe three minutes, and then Arnovis's dad took the phone to talk to her. After he hung up, both father and son were crying. Crying and crying, Arnovis said.

They didn't know if they'd ever see her again. They'd been hearing stories. Horrible stories. The US government, they'd heard, had been kidnapping thousands of children.

When the United States deported Arnovis, ICE hadn't returned his Salvadoran ID card, and though he didn't want to leave his home, and was scared he would be seen, he knew he needed to travel to Usulután, the department's capital, to procure a new ID, though he put it off for a few days. Kinosian had, by now, put him in touch with Jonathan Ryan, the executive director of RAICES, an immigrant rights legal services organization based in Texas, who told him that Meybelín was not in "Florida or New York," as an ICE officer had told him, but in Phoenix, and that they would send someone to talk to her and try to get her either released to Arnovis's brother in Kansas or have her sent back to El Salvador.

In those first few days, the Salvadoran Foreign Ministry called Arnovis and told him it was going to get his daughter out, giving him a tentative timeline of three months. He was in shock. Meybelín, six years old, by herself in America for three more months. He started planning to head north again. He was going to go find his daughter. His idea, he told me, was to cross again into the United States and turn himself in so he could talk to a judge. But something stopped him: a sudden wave of media attention.

Just a few days after his deportation, the first article on Arnovis, by Joshua Partlow, came out in the *Washington Post*. The following day, Kinosian published an article in *The Guardian*, and Arnovis became one of the primary faces of the family separation crisis. In the photos published by both outlets, Arnovis appears in a blue 2015 Old Navy American flag T-shirt. He appears crying or tearful, and either sitting on Meybelín's small bed, wiping his face, or, in one photo, looking younger than he is—pale, thinned by shock, mouth slightly open, and eyes staring blankly up—leaning against the door frame of his one-room hut. Daylight filters in between the slats of the palm-rib wall behind him, and Arnovis looks nothing like the strong, hardworking man who had built that very home. Only his hand in the photo, holding up his black cell phone as if waiting any moment to receive a call from his daughter, betrays any sign that he was not defeated.

Besides going out for essential tasks—to get the new ID, or sign papers to facilitate RAICES securing Meybelín's release—Arnovis wouldn't leave the family home. His fear, along with his hopes, was compounded by a flood of journalists drawing attention to him. In addition to the *Post* and the *Guardian*, Reuters, NPR, *Newsweek*, TeleSur, PBS, Telemundo, Univision, *El Faro*, and the *Chicago Tribune* would cover Arnovis and Meybelín's saga and separation. Every day he was getting calls from reporters and producers. I, too, called him from a café in San Salvador and, after talking a while, asked if I could come and visit. I wanted to give him space to tell the story in his own words, and a few weeks later I published an oral testimony account of his saga in the *Nation*.

In the midst of that journalistic crush, even as he was hoping that the attention would help him get Meybelín back, he also worried that the blitz would alert his persecutors.

And then, soon after the first stories went up, he got a call from Ryan at RAICES, who told him that Meybelín was going to be on a flight home the next day. He was shocked, felt a sudden hollowness in his chest—the need to *do something*. Not knowing what, however, he simply walked across the yard to the kitchen. His dad was the first person to receive the news, and then he called the rest of the family together.

They moved into action, stringing balloons from palm to palm, figuring out how to get a car—so many family members came that they ended up borrowing two vans—and preparing Meybelín's favorite food: rice and beans, which is also what they eat nearly every day. Arnovis ordered a piñata in the form of a little girl. At the airport the next day the family was met by a battery of international press, and Arnovis gave multiple statements on camera. He seemed nervous but spoke in a measured, confident manner. And then the Salvadoran government informed him that Meybelín was going to be handed over to her mother, and Arnovis wouldn't be allowed to receive her. It was a moment of confusion that was quickly corrected.

Their reunion was inside the airport, out of view of the press. Arnovis said that he and Meybelín literally ran toward each other. Having her in his arms rattled that desperate need into his chest again. He was burning with emotion. Love, shame, fear, confusion, relief, and love again, which is how he described what he felt in that moment. The family was given a police escort back to Corral de Mulas.

The first time I met Arnovis and his family, a few weeks after he had been deported from the United States—and recently reunited with Meybelín—I had hired a driver to take me to Corral de Mulas. There are no buses that service Corral, and I didn't yet know how to arrive by boat. My driver was Antonio Montes, a photographer and a professional driver for Reuters correspondents in El Salvador. He drove an early model Scion with a hand-grenade-shaped gear shifter, and told me a terrifying story of his adolescence in San Salvador during the war. Once, with his whole family huddled under a kitchen table fortified with bed mattresses, a bomb fell into his backyard. It did not explode, but, thirty feet closer, and it would have crashed through the roof of his home. After the raids ended that afternoon, the family abandoned the house. Unlike millions of other Salvadorans in those years, however, their first internal displacement didn't lead to further flight to the United States.

Antonio's father is a scientist at a nearby dairy farm, and through him Antonio knew one of the islands' ranchers who owns a large ranch close to Corral de Mulas. Antonio described to me the wide gulf between the millionaire ranchers who keep vacation houses on the islands and live in either San Salvador or the United States, and the peasants who earn seven dollars a day, or less, to work the land and tend the cattle. In *Weakness and Deceit*, journalist Raymond Bonner describes the grossly stratified society in rural El Salvador during the 1980s as "like Appalachia or the American West—in the 1800s." In two of the departments where support for the revolution was strongest, Morazán and Chalatenango, there were only five doctors in the 1980s, or one for every ninety thousand peasants. Today, Corral de Mulas and the neighboring villages on the islands don't have much better access to health care. If you get sick on the weekend or at night, you have to find someone with a boat to take you to Puerto Triunfo—the small city with the nearest hospital—which is, at least, a thirty-minute lancha ride away. In the late '70s, the population as a whole only ate 82 percent of the daily caloric requirements. In 2018, 14 percent of children under five years old suffered from chronic malnutrition.

As Antonio barreled down the empty roads—at one point he swerved violently to dodge a *zumbadora*, a neotropical whipsnake, slithering rapidly across the pavement—he described how most of the islanders admire what they see as the largesse of ranch owners, who swing into town a few times a year bearing gifts of basic food baskets or toys for the kids. One of the ranchers recently rebuilt one of the schoolhouses and bankrolls an impeccably groomed soccer field on the school grounds. Education levels, meanwhile, remain extremely low on the islands—most of the locals leave school after ninth grade, some even earlier—and there are few job opportunities outside of grunt labor or small-boat fishing. The same morning that Antonio was driving me to Corral de Mulas, one of the ranchers had thrown a small "party," offering a bit of food and coffee to the locals, making a short speech, and sending each family home with a packet of generic rice crispy treats already melting in their plastic.

After talking to Arnovis for a few hours in thin plastic chairs in the shade, Arnovis's fourteen-year-old niece, Cecilia, brought us each one of the rice treats. Arnovis didn't eat his, but I was hungry, and pulled open the plastic to reveal a melted chocolate mess. Even the glue holding the thin plastic together seemed to have melted. This was the biannual kindness the rancher bestowed on the villagers.

When I first arrived, the house was quiet, the family seemingly waiting out the late morning heat. Arnovis's father and sister were at work, and the carcasses of a few "welcome home" balloons still hung from a wire. Meybelín was facedown in the kitchen hammock, sound asleep. She seemed babyish, her arms straight down at her sides, feet crossed at the toes. Arnovis and I talked for about four hours. He told me about his trip, what Corral was like, Meybelín's nerves, her fear of being apart from him, and his worry that the gang would find him again. When Meybelín woke—with indentations hatched into her forehead from the hammock strings—she came over to sit on Arnovis's lap but wouldn't meet my eye.

The family seemed happy that Meybelín was back, but two members were still locked up. José had been transferred to south Texas's Port Isabel Detention Center, known as the Corralón, and Darlene was in a shelter somewhere in Florida, or so they thought. The Corralón has a long history: first as a US Navy station, then a Border Patrol academy and location of the Office of Public Safety, a wildly euphemistic name for an international police and military training academy that ran programming similar to the School of Americas—notorious for training Latin American military and police officers later accused, and sometimes convicted, of crimes against humanity and genocide. The Port Isabel school, also sometimes simply referred to as the "bomb school," offered its international pupils lectures such as "Assassination Weapons: A discussion of various weapons which may be used by the assassin." Robert S. Kahn, writing about the detention center in 1984, explained how "virtually every man processed through Los Fresnos immigration prison [Port Isabel] was told that if he applied for political asylum, he would have to stay in jail for a year or more." Kahn continued: "As the refugees stood naked with chemicals on their genitals, prison guards misinformed them about US law to discourage them from seeking political asylum."

At one point during our talk, Arnovis shuttled up a tree to retrieve Meybelín a coconut. His mom served me fried fish in a bowl, with lime and homemade tortillas. In those hectic weeks of return, two friends of the family from Corral, both hounded by the gangs, decided to flee north to ask for asylum.

On my second visit to the family home, a few weeks later, shortly after arriving and being served a limeade and a bowl of beans with more fresh tortillas, Meybelín was excited to play with the new yellow soccer ball I had brought her, at her request. I was surprised when Arnovis suggested, or maybe just conceded to the suggestion, that all of us—Arnovis, Meybelín, Ale, Pedrito, Cecilia, Joana, Sonia, and me—go to the beach to kick it around. It was the first time I'd seen him off the family property, except for a brief ride in Antonio's window-tinted Scion, and I wondered if he would be nervous. He brushed it off and told me he'd be okay.

About a ten-minute stroll from the house, passing under the shade of a stand of huge mango trees by the school, we arrived to the beach where, beyond Mothersalt Island, we took in the view of the Chaparrastique volcano hovering prominently across the bay. The day was windless, with hardly even a wrinkle in the warm, brackish water—the mangroves, volcanoes, and sky mirrored almost perfectly on the surface. We played a version of keep-away, with Meybelín and Pedrito repeatedly distracting themselves and covering themselves in wet sand or running to splash like excited dogs in the water. I've played soccer all my life and can recognize when someone has a good touch. Arnovis has an easy command of the ball and a fluid, hard shot. After the sweat and sand started stinging our eyes and we had worked back up an appetite, we all waded into the water to bob in the bay and let our bodies cool. For some reason, maybe simply in the face of the immensity of the quiet bay and the volcano, we were all whispering.

As we walked back home, evening was beginning to settle in the village. A cluster of women were slicing thin strips of banana to fry in oil and sell for fifty cents a bag on the side of the road. Skinny cattle were returning from their day of grazing, followed by skinny men on horses or bicycles. Meybelín was walking between Arnovis and me, holding each of our hands. At one point she tried to get Arnovis and me to hold hands as well, but, slightly embarrassed, we resisted her giggling attempts. And then, from behind us down the road, a flock of young men on bicycles approached. I turned to see what they were about as they slowly rode up and overtook us. They all seemed to be in their late teens, and all of them turned to look at us as they rode past. There is such little traffic in Corral de Mulas that a passing car, or even a person on foot, piques interest. Most of the boys, it seemed, looked at me curiously, probably wondering who I was. I noticed, too, that Arnovis didn't once turn his head to look, even though a number of the boys, maybe all of them—they were high schoolers on their way to the soccer field—knew the family and most called out some form of salutation. It was odd, I thought, and I later asked Arnovis about it.

Every time I see someone, he told me, I get nervous.

But you knew them all?

Yeah.

And are any of them involved in the gang?

You never know. I don't want them to see me. And I don't want to be seen.

He who fears he shall suffer, Montaigne wrote, already suffers what he fears.

How he was going to live in such a small village without being seen, Arnovis didn't know. But for now, he was going to lie as low as possible. If they come for me, he told me, they come for me.

Another critical worry was the money the family still owed the coyote—six thousand dollars, which, at that point, his brother in Kansas was struggling every month to pay off in installments. Originally, Arnovis was going to be working in the United States, earning US wages, and paying it himself. Paying it off now seemed impossible.

The next four days in Corral we spent talking, eating, and making short forays to the beach, the turtle hatchery, or the family's cashew and corn plot. Arnovis would occasionally squat against a palm tree and have confabs with his brother in Kansas about heading back to the United States—this time to try to sneak across.

A couple weeks later, before my third trip to Corral, Arnovis sent me a message asking to talk. He'd been stopped by a few young men who told him they knew that a bunch of gringos had been coming to his house and giving him money. They said he had received six thousand dollars, and he needed to start paying them higher taxes. We both thought it was suspicious that they cited the exact number the coyote had charged him. Arnovis told them he didn't have any money, which seemed true. Later, when discussing his finances, he told me that he'd done some rough budgeting, and besides money for Meybelín's school supplies, a little bit of gas money for the motorcycle, and food, there was nothing left. Not a dime.

The men who stopped him told them they would investigate. Arnovis said that they could go ahead, and that they wouldn't find anything, that nobody had given him any money.

I was in Corral again on another night, about a month later, when *El Faro* published a short video documentary on Arnovis and his separation from Meybelín. It was the most thorough Spanish-language publication to date, providing details about Arnovis's initial threat—the elbow on the soccer field—which hadn't yet been described in a Spanish-language media outlet. Arnovis's brother caught it on Facebook, where it was being passed around by other folks from the islands. Furious, he called

Arnovis, insisting that the video was putting him and the family in danger. The call unsettled Arnovis, and he was convinced, again, that he needed to leave immediately. What if they come tonight? he wondered. What do I do?

Earlier that same evening, the whole family was discussing going to a village party being thrown at the nearby restaurant, El Delfín. It seemed like they all wanted to go but were nervous or embarrassed to say so. It was like before a high school dance: Are you going? Are you? I'll go if you'll go.

Arnovis, though, never considered it, even as a few of his friends had been texting him, asking him to come. It's hard when people invite you to do things, he told me, or tell you about work, and you can't go, and you don't even want to say why. And they invite you again later, and you have to refuse again, and then, after a while, they stop inviting you.

In the end, nobody from the family went to the party, but we could hear the music blasting, and some of his cousins danced a bit in the yard. (The next night, the family set up a circle of chairs and danced and laughed with each other, pounding their bare feet into the dirt. Despite my reluctance, and to their enormous glee, I danced as well. Arnovis was the only young person who didn't dance. Nor did Joana—out of respect, she told me).

The article, the phone call from his brother, the noise of the party, all of it had been stirring up his anxieties and fears. He looked pale and sleepless the next morning.

He said to me at one point, unprompted, Some mornings when there's no coffee or bread, and you realize you don't have the chance to go out and work in peace and you can't even sleep at night ... Misery. It's misery. Think about it. You wake up in the morning and you want to drink a cup of coffee. But you can't. And you can't even go buy any because you don't have a dollar in your pocket.

Indebted thousands of dollars to his brother and to a coyote who may or may not have ties to a local gang, unable to work, but needing food and to provide what he could for Meybelín,

Arnovis had no good options. As he considered what to do, he filled his time building his sister's house, just a few minutes' walk away, helping out with corn or cashew harvests, and trying to hatch a plan.

It's the same thing as before, he said. If I stay I might get killed and Meybelín will have nobody. If I leave, maybe I can at least pay for her school, or send for her to come after me.

One day he told me, definitively, that he was going to Mexico, that he was going to wait in Mexico for a few weeks, and then pass into the United States. At his request, I helped him look into trying to ask for asylum in Costa Rica, but, in the end, he didn't think it would work.

I have no proof, he told me. We'd been discussing the requirements for asylum. Nobody will believe me.

The fear pressing in on both sides froze him. In the following weeks, if he was slow in responding to a WhatsApp message I sent him, I feared the worst. Once, his father called me, and for a moment I was sure he was going to tell me that they had come for Arnovis.

Can I Live?

16

Volo ut sis.
I want you to be.
—Augustine

There is no better argument for the need for asylum than, when you are not granted it, you are killed. Legitimating the fear and the need for protection after you're dead, however, doesn't help. In 1984, Ricardo Ernardes escaped multiple attempts on his life in El Salvador. After his cousin was murdered, he fled to the United States and asked for asylum. When he was denied, he told the *Los Angeles Times* that the judge "can see the concrete proof by my death when I get home." Which would be, of course, too late.

I first came across a story of someone who was denied asylum, deported, and then murdered while reporting a story for *The Nation* in 2017 about "asylum-free zones," certain US court districts —Atlanta, Oklahoma, Arizona, and Charlotte—where immigration judges deny practically all asylum claims. According to a petition filed before the Inter-American Commission on Human Rights, huge portions of the country had turned into zones where "asylum seekers are systematically denied protection" regardless of the dangers they are fleeing. I spoke with a private attorney in one of these asylum-free zones, Elizabeth Matherne, who told me about one of her clients from Guatemala. Despite receiving death threats, the man was preparing to testify against a drug trafficker before a US Attorney. The day before his testimony to the FBI, his brother in Guatemala was stabbed; the attack, though not fatal, served as a warning. The man went ahead, cooperating with the FBI. Afterward, when he was applying for asylum, his claim was accompanied by a letter of support from the FBI agent he had worked with. Despite what Matherne described as a clearly credible claim, the judge denied him asylum and ordered him deported. And then he was gunned down. Nine days later, his brother was murdered as well.

According to one calculation in 2015, there had been 932,444 people officially denied asylum since 1992. By 2019, that number had reached well over 1 million people. For how many of them was deportation not just a denial of welcome and protection, but a death sentence?

Another client of Ed Beckett—Bertha's attorney in El Paso— was a cotton farmer in the Valley of Juárez who owned and worked a plot of land that abutted the border with the United States—prime real estate for drug traffickers expanding their operations west from Juárez. One day, in 2016, a group of men came and offered him a choice: either you give us your land and work for us, or we kill you.

I first met Beckett in his office in the back corner of an industrial strip mall between Border Patrol and ICE facilities on the outskirts of El Paso—one of those near-the-airport locations with bare parking lots, fields of concrete, and businesses without signs. His office was decorated in classic car and cholo art; a US Marines Honorable Discharge certificate hung from a wall. On the floor was a toddler-size Elmo chair and a box of diapers. Beckett, with slicked-back hair, was wearing black pants, a black shirt, and black Converse shoes. He was a lively, entertaining speaker, and I basically told him what I was interested in and sat back and listened. Over the course of a couple hours, he mentioned four former clients who had been killed after either being denied asylum or after suffering prolonged periods of detention and having given up on their asylum claims.

He told me the farmer in the Valley of Juárez, after being approached by the drug traffickers who wanted his land, thought about it for a second, and then said no. I'm an old man, what do you want me to do? I'm fifty-seven. I'm not involved in any of that. I just want to farm. The drug traffickers told him: You're warned. If we see you on this land again, you're fucking dead.

So what does he do? Beckett asked me. He realizes how serious they were, and he comes to the United States and asks for protection. He's an old man but he's not dumb, he's not going to ask for protection from the Juárez police.

The threat had come to the farmer in the middle of the Juárez-Sinaloa war, in which competing paramilitary drug-trafficking organizations were fighting for control of the Juárez corridor, with the Mexican government helping out the Sinaloa side. The farmers who lived along the line, who had been growing cotton for generations, were pushed into the crossfire. They were killed, decapitated, disappeared, dispossessed of their land. Their houses were burned, taken over, or abandoned.

The plot the farmer didn't want to hand over had been passed down to him from his grandfather. This is what we do, he told Beckett. We grow cotton, this is how we make a living, I can't just leave.

But then he left.

You would think it would be a slam-dunk case, Beckett said, but the judge asks me, Do you have witnesses to corroborate the threats? But, Beckett wondered aloud, who the hell is going to come forward if you're a witness? Would you be willing to write an affidavit against the Sinaloa Cartel? Hell, no.

After the farmer presented himself at the border, he was detained and eventually sent to Sierra Blanca, the same hole where Santos suffered and where Martín saw rats and snakes, couldn't handle the horror, and finally asked to be sent home. The farmer, who was used to the open air—the dirt, the sky, and his cotton—soon became sick. He couldn't handle being caged. After a few months, he wanted to go home. Beckett tried to convince him to stay, that he had a good case, but the farmer told him he couldn't take it anymore. I'm really sick, he said. This is a horrible place.

I tried to convince him, Beckett told me, but he said, No, no, no. He was begging me. Please, please, please. So, you know what, he's my client. So I write the letter asking for deportation. He gets deported.

They found sixty bullet casings surrounding his body, Beckett told me. Sixty high-caliber casings. AK-47 and M-16, that's what they shot him with.

The *Diario de Juárez* reported on the murder in an article with an anonymous byline—for the safety of the reporter—on Thursday, September 29, 2016: "Man Executed with 60 shots in Praxedis."

In January of 2018, *New Yorker* writer Sarah Stillman published an article about asylum seekers murdered after being deported. Stillman and a team of researchers at the Global Migration Project at Columbia University counted over sixty recent cases.

In her article, Stillman profiled Laura S., who had fled to Texas after suffering terrifying domestic abuse in Mexico. One day she was pulled over for supposedly driving between the lanes. When the cop asked for her license, and she couldn't provide it, he called the Border Patrol. Laura panicked, beginning to cry. "I can't be sent back to Mexico," she said. "I have a protection order against my ex—please, just let me call my mom and she'll bring you the paperwork."

"Sorry," the cop told her. "I already called."

Later, when Laura was being deported, she supposedly told the Border Patrol agent, "You're sending me straight to the slaughterhouse."

Soon after her deportation, her ex found her, T-boned the car she was driving in, dragged her out, and bit off a chunk of her ear. The following day she went missing. Her body was eventually found in an incinerated vehicle.

Later in 2018, Maria Sacchetti wrote in the *Washington Post* about Santos Chirino, who told a judge during his asylum hearing, after fleeing repeated death threats from MS-13, "I'm sure they're going to kill me." Chirino's uncle wrote a letter to the judge: "Death is waiting for him." His brother wrote: "He can never go back." The judge, noting that Chirino didn't report the death threats that had come in against him to the local police, didn't believe him and ordered him deported. Though his attorney encouraged him to appeal, Chirino couldn't stand being locked up and was sent back to Honduras. A few months later he was shot in the throat and killed. His brother, who was with him, had his head bashed in and was also killed.

Another *Post* investigation chronicled the murder of Ronald Acevedo, who was tortured and killed just days after his deportation. According to the article, "he expressed a willingness to return to El Salvador only after immigration officers told him that he had no chance of gaining asylum and could spend many more months in detention."

Researcher Elizabeth Kennedy collected accounts of at least forty-three Central Americans deported to their death between 2014 and 2015.

In 2015, *The Guardian* cited eighty-three such cases.

In 2016, *The Hill* reported on three Hondurans who were deported and then murdered.

In 2018, *World Politics Review* counted seventy deportees murdered in the previous five years in El Salvador alone.

Some of these murders, among the various reports, are likely counted twice, but it is even more likely that many murders after an asylum denial are never counted. Few people keep such a tab.

Sos tumba, they told him.

Tomorrow your mouth will be full of flies.

In the summer of 2018 I met one young man, José Ricardo Cortés, who, after fleeing El Salvador with his mother, began going through a troubled phase in southern Ohio and Kentucky. He was made fun of because he was one of the few Latino kids in his middle school, and struggled to "correct" his accent and fit in. He started drinking, ran away from home a couple times, and got in trouble with the cops. He spent some time in juvenile detention and was eventually deported. Upon return to the Mejicanos barrio of San Salvador, he was targeted again: he didn't fit in, he had a funny, gringo-tinged accent, and the local gang picked on him and tried to get him to join. After they told him they were going to kill him, his aunt contacted Beto, the community organizer who had shown me around the neighborhood a few times, and asked for help finding him a safe place to crash. Beto helped him sneak out to a cheap, tiny hotel, basically a flophouse, in another part of town. José started dreaming of heading back to the United States. He would do it right this time. He would finish high school, get a job, put his life in order. He wanted to get the small tattoo of a diamond removed from under his left eye. He stopped drinking.

I met José at his hotel one morning and we spent a few hours talking. He had been looking for work—keeping his face tattoo covered under a small circle of a Band-Aid—but was struggling to find a steady job. As we wrapped up our conversation, he asked if I could spot him a couple bucks—he hadn't eaten that day, and it was already mid-afternoon. We walked to a nearby mall and I told him I'd buy him a meal at the food court. He chose Taco Bell—a few Doritos Tacos, and churros for dessert—because it reminded him of home. I didn't talk to José again after that day, but a couple months later, Beto contacted me via WhatsApp and told me that he'd been murdered. He sent me a photo of him in his casket. A mortician had patched a bullet hole in his face with off-colored makeup.

Being deported to your death isn't a new phenomenon. In the early 1980s the United States knowingly and sometimes deliberately tried to deport Salvadorans back to their deaths. As Robert S. Kahn reports, multiple Salvadoran deportees were denied protection and sent back to their deaths, including José Humberto Santacruz Elias, who was deported on January 15, 1981, and "disappeared on arrival"; José Enriquez Orellano, who was shot three times in the chest and then decapitated two weeks after he had been deported; Octavio Osegueda, who was shot to death in 1983 the day after he was deported; and a sixteen-year-old who, after being deported, was abducted by the US-trained Atlacatl Battalion—the same one that carried out the El Mozote massacre—and was never seen again.

In 1984 the ACLU submitted to the US House Subcommittee on Rules a list of 112 deportees who were either murdered or suffered human rights abuses after their deportations. In the appendix of the report is a February 20, 1981, Warrant of Deportation signed by the INS district director of Laredo for Santana Chirino Amaya. On September 1 of the same year, the Salvadoran newspaper *El Diario de Hoy* published a note that Chirino Amaya, twenty-four years old, was found decapitated near Amapulapa, San Vicente.

In 1991, after being held in detention in Guantánamo Bay, Marie Zetie was supposed to be transferred to Miami but was "accidentally deported" back to Haiti, where she was murdered.

In another case, in 2004, sixteen-year-old Edgar Chocoy fled Guatemala after gang members robbed, beat, and threatened to kill him. At his asylum hearing, he told the judge that if he was deported, "Wherever I'm going to live, they'll find me." Seventeen days after the United States sent him back to Guatemala he was shot in the back of the neck.

In the summer of 2018, I spent a long, hot, sad afternoon in the small city of Catacamas, in the Olancho department of Honduras, talking to Sobe, a woman whose son, Ronal, had been murdered thirty days earlier. After witnessing the murder of a friend, Ronal received multiple death threats, and, after a terrifying few weeks in hiding, fled north. Having crossed the border into the United States, he was detained for eleven months, denied asylum, and deported. And then he was killed. At one point in our conversation, Sobe mentioned to me that she now feared for the young man who had witnessed her son's death. He wasn't safe in Honduras; nor, she speculated, would he likely find safety in the United States. What she feared, what seemed possible, was an ever-widening cycle of witness, threat, flight, denial, and death.

Many of the organizations I spoke with told me about cases of people murdered after seeking asylum. INSAMI, an organization in El Salvador that helps deportees readjust to the country, had accounts of twelve such cases, but the director was hesitant, and eventually refused, to share details or put me in touch with family members. The organization Cristosal also had multiple recent cases of murdered deportees but were worried about the safety of family members and wouldn't share details. I spoke with two men who had lived most of their lives in California and, after their deportation, had founded an evangelical church and an American football league in San Salvador. One of their cousins was shot, eleven times, soon after he was deported. After a miraculous recovery, he went off the grid and into hiding, refusing to answer phone calls, even from his family, out of fear.

I met a man in the COFAMIPRO office, an organization run by mothers whose children have disappeared, in El Progreso, Honduras, who showed me the bullet wound in his belly. He was a taxi driver who couldn't pay the gang's extortion fees. Fearing for his life, he fled to the United States and asked for asylum. Soon after he was denied and deported back to Honduras, he was shot three times, right in the gut. After he finished telling me his story, he began begging for help, weeping and lifting up his shirt repeatedly to show me the thick scars.

According to a 2014 Human Rights Watch report, "US border officials ignored [asylum seekers'] expressions of fear and removed them with no opportunity to have their claims examined; others said border officials acknowledged hearing their expressions of fear but pressured them to abandon their claims."

In a city in Honduras, talking with yet another official, I was given an explanation about *emergency evacuation*. (Since this person didn't want me to divulge either his name or the name of his organization dedicated to this work, I'll call him Orlin.) When an affiliate organization identifies a person in serious danger, Orlin explained, they reach out to him and he goes to the family's home to conduct a clandestine interview and risk assessment. In just over two years, the organization has already worked with nearly one hundred fifty clients.

We're not coyotes, Orlin told me. We don't take people across borders. Rather, he and his crew accompany them to bus stations or find other means of transport to ferry them to safety. I asked him if sometimes he doesn't just get somebody in his car and secret them out of a community himself. He replied that sometimes his organization takes recent deportees to a safe house, typically cheap motels, and pays for a few weeks' stay while the person can plan their next move—the next attempt to flee.

When I asked what drove him to do such dangerous work, he told me that his second cousin was killed after asking for asylum and being denied and deported. The family, he said, wouldn't talk to a journalist. They were too scared.

In Mexico the numbers and stories of those murdered after being denied asylum may be even harder to tabulate—there are more deportations to Mexico, more overall murders, and the asylum grant rate for Mexicans is so low there are likely dozens of cases a year, but they get lost in the quotidian forced displacement and pervasive violence that makes isolating such cases almost impossible.

Most immigration attorneys I spoke with about the issue told me they typically lose contact with their former clients after an asylum denial. More than one attorney, fearing the worst, told me they were scared to know what had happened to their clients after deportation. Anne Pilsbury, of Central American Legal Assistance (CALA) in New York, didn't want to know what had become of one of her clients who had such a pressing fear for his life that—after he had been denied asylum and deported—he fled to the United States again, was denied again, and deported again. She couldn't bring herself to call his family to find out if he was still alive.

I was planning to visit one Long Island resident to hear about the story of her son, who was killed after being deported back to Usulután—a short boat and bus ride from Arnovis. But she canceled our meeting at the last minute. The one-year anniversary of her son's murder was approaching, and she told me it was still too hard to talk about. Sometimes, she said, it was hard to talk at all.

17

Don't open the door. You do not have to unlock that door. Do not call the police.

Church elder Anne Glenn was speaking to a couple dozen parishioners in front of a "sanctuary training" PowerPoint presentation being projected onto the wall behind the altar of St. Andrew's Presbyterian church. Just outside Austin, in a cramped backroom of St. Andrew's, was where Hilda Ramirez and her twelve-year-old son had been living in sanctuary for more than two years.

You do not need to talk to ICE, Glenn said.

The general atmosphere among the mostly older, all-white crowd was of polite nervousness. How do we know someone is with ICE? they asked. What if the warrant is signed by a non-sitting judge? Will they break down the door?

In the first days after Ramirez and her son moved into the church, unmarked white trucks came and parked in the church lot. There were also Fish and Wildlife vehicles that rolled by, and the pastor, Jim Rigby, received multiple calls from numbers ID'd by his phone as belonging to Homeland Security.

Hilda and Ivan had sought refuge at the church because the US government not only denied them protection but was trying to deport them. The church, in sharing their roof—protecting them from their persecutors in Guatemala and the US government—was following a decades-long tradition of opening doors to refugees. Golden and McConnell, in their book *Sanctuary:*

The New Underground Railroad, call the practice America's "prophetic tradition."

There was a period, in October of 2016, eight months after Hilda and Ivan first entered the church, when they were granted "deferred action," a temporary stay from deportation, though without any change in their legal status. Despite the momentary and meager reprieve—increasingly, in the Trump era, people with deferred action protection were rounded up and deported—Ramirez was still nervous. She decided to continue living in the church, though she would occasionally leave to run an errand. The next month, her deferred action status was revoked, Trump won the presidency, and, fearing deportation back to the country where their lives were in danger, she and her son, again, secluded themselves in the refuge.

I met Hilda after Glenn wrapped up the sanctuary training, and together we lingered in the church benches as some members shuffled out and others settled in for the 10:45 Sunday service. I'm tired, Hilda said. She told me she has trouble sleeping at night. Most of the people in the congregation don't speak Spanish (though volunteers from Grassroots Leadership, the Austin-based organization that connected Hilda to the church, help with translation and other services), which makes it hard for her to relate to a lot of the members, though together they've forged a strong rapport.

After some initial concern about how they would be able to reoutfit an office into a living space, the congregation came together like worker ants, as Pastor Rigby explained it. If they refused to open their doors to Hilda and Ivan, then Rigby didn't see it fit to call themselves a church. His exact words were: If someone comes to your door and is fleeing violence, and you can't find a fucking couch for them, then let's not call it a church. Rigby's sermon on the day I visited was 2 Corinthians 3:6—"The written law kills, but the Spirit gives life." He delivered that sermon just a few weeks before Jeff Sessions would use a different Pauline letter to insist that Border Patrol agents "obey the laws of the government because God has ordained them for the purpose of order," and begin separating children from their parents.

In her first days in sanctuary Hilda cut off the GPS monitor that had been strapped to her ankle. To give them some peace, the church installed extra poles on a chain-link fence and put green cloth-screens on the fence to offer more privacy. Members also created a Google Group to attend to their food, health care, and education needs. They bought Hilda a cell phone and arranged for a counselor to speak with her. The women threw her a makeup party.

Rigby told me, It's hard for people to realize, however much she likes us, and we like her, this is still prison. Every night they go to sleep not knowing if there'll be an interruption in the night that will take them away. At first, every time there was a siren, every time somebody would knock on the door, they would just panic. In his sermon, Rigby said that Hilda and Ivan are open windows of the soul.

I returned to the church the next day, and Hilda and I were able to talk at length. She was wearing a traditional Guatemalan skirt and blouse; when she sat next to me in the chair, her feet dangled off the ground. For a while, as we spoke, she was braiding the hair of Grassroots Leadership worker Alejandro Caceres.

Hilda was taught to spell and write her name in a fifteen-day course a volunteer gave to her back in Guatemala. Thirty years old, she had never gone to school, though she speaks two languages fluently, Mam and Spanish, and is rapidly learning English.

Hilda's childhood, as she explained it, was full of work and violence: her dad beat her mother; her dad beat her brothers and sisters; and her dad beat her. As a child she tended her father's sheep, and, when she was ten, she moved to Guatemala City on her own, making as little as fifteen dollars a month to take care of her sister's child. Later, after a series of escapes from her family and continued forced domestic work—living in homes where she was mistreated, poorly paid, and hardly fed—eating little more than rice and beans—she escaped again and soon became pregnant. She didn't want to tell me about the work she did for a couple years, or how she met the father of her child, but those years were no reprieve from violence or hardship. Eventually, after Ivan's father repeated his threats against her and her son, she fled—first to Mexico, and then to the United States. I needed to find a safe space, she said. That was all. That was why I came.

But instead of a safe space, she and Ivan found more fear and more violence. Only twelve years old, Ivan has spent nearly a quarter of his life in some type of confinement. Though he now leaves to attend school, when I first met her, Hilda hadn't stepped outside the building, including the fenced-off section where she has started a small garden, for the previous five months. I was able to check in over a year later, in the summer of 2019, and she and Ivan were still in sanctuary. In July of the same year, ICE began sending fines to people who had taken sanctuary in churches. Tabulating $799 for every day she refused to comply with their deportation orders, ICE sent Hilda a fine of $304,000.

ICE comes for me even in my dreams, she said.

Hilda giggles as she recounts to Alejandro and me how she used to braid hair for food in the Karnes family detention center. Oh, yeah. I did braids. I can do pretty good braids. I practiced a lot. People in detention would line up for me to do their hair. Sometimes they'd give me a soda. That's usually how they paid. Or sometimes beans. Because there was a little store inside and they let you buy beans or rice. A little packet of beans would cost like two dollars. Everything was so expensive. A soda cost, I don't remember, like fifty cents.

I ask her what her hometown, Concepción Tutuapa, in the Guatemalan department of San Marcos, was like. Well, she says, it's a city, but really small ... I don't know. How many people? Maybe three hundred. That's the bigger area. In my village there's like a hundred people. I think, maybe forty or fifty families. There's the village, and the courthouse ... and the church. And a market. Yeah, that's all there is.

People farm. That's what they do for a living. They farm potatoes, corn. There used to be a Catholic church, and now there's an evangelical church, and others, too. There are a lot of churches now. Sometimes there are good people, people who work, and sometimes there are people who exploit you, like when you work a ton, and you earn hardly anything at all. I left there not because of lack of work. In my village there was a lot of work, a lot of farming and all that.

Distracted by her braiding, she asks Alejandro, Does it hurt? No? Tell me if it hurts. I'm scared to hurt you.

Well, my dad, Hilda says, picking back up her thread, had me taking care of the sheep. That was my job. So, I took care of them. But then, after a while I went to the city. I went to help my sister because she was already living there, and I went to take care of her baby. I was ten years old. And then I worked for a while with some other people.

They paid me a hundred quetzales a month [less then fifteen dollars]. I never went to school. Not even in the village. There's a school, but the problem is that my dad never let me go. You know, in the villages there are a lot of people who don't believe in school. That it's a waste of time. And so my dad never went to school, and he used to say, I've got land and I'm living well. I eat well. I didn't need school to get that. School is just a waste of time, sitting there in a chair, wasting time. That's what my dad would say.

But I wanted to go to school. Really wanted to. I would go and listen to what the teacher said. I would go behind the school to listen and learn as much as I could. I would take my sheep and leave them by the school and lean close to listen. At first I learned how to write my name. I didn't know what each letter was called. I just saw how it was shaped. In my head I knew how to draw each letter of my name, but I didn't know, like H-I-L ... but I knew at least how to write my name.

And the I went to the capital the first time, and, well, I didn't have time to study because ... I had to be with my little niece, and my sister didn't want ... she didn't buy me books or anything like that. She was, I think, eighteen years old. And I was ten. So, when I was like eleven or twelve I went back to the village because my dad wanted me to come home and get back to herding his sheep. My sister went to school, because my dad let her study.

Jim Rigby comes in with a tray of coffee and peppermint candies. As I pour us both a cup, Hilda finishes Alejandro's hair. Finished, she says, in English, and then adds cream and sugar to her coffee. If I see someone else drinking coffee, I can't resist, Hilda says. I tell her that I'm the same, and then, after a few sips, ask her why she left Guatemala.

Well, because of the life I was living. The situation with my family. I was seeing my dad beat my mom. And it was terrible for me. I didn't want to be there, watching that. There was no respect. Well. The way he was, my dad, he was like people used to be, I mean, I think he was a good dad, but ... he yelled at us. At all of us, my brothers and sisters. So I went to the capital to work again. I went with this woman who was going to the capital to visit her family. And I stayed a few days with her and then I found some other people to work with. Working in a home, it's the only thing I could get. Because in a factory you need Spanish. You need to be able to speak Spanish and to know how to write and all.

It was hard for me to speak in Spanish. Now I speak it very well. Well maybe not *very* well—there are still things I don't understand. But I found this woman who was about to graduate, and she needed to give literacy classes. She needed to help an adult who hadn't ever gone to school. I studied with her for two weeks. The vowels were really hard for me, the ABCs. But

I was learning a little, so I learned about how to put the letters together. But I couldn't keep on studying because I had to work for my bosses. I had to start working at five in the morning and I didn't stop working until eleven at night. So there wasn't time to study. I had to work so much, cleaning the house, washing the clothes, helping the woman cook. And since the people sold cars, I had to cook for their workers as well. Sometimes there was a little discrimination, but I felt okay, because there weren't fights or arguments or anything like that. I was fifteen. They knew I didn't go to school, and they would always just say, Clean this. Do this. Did you already do this? They paid me three hundred quetzales a month [about forty dollars].

I bought myself clothes, because I didn't have enough. They gave me food, but I could only eat chicken once a week. It was just rice and beans. Rice and beans every day. Rice and beans, rice and beans, rice and beans. I was only with them about a year, a year and a little more. I can't remember, and then I went back home. Because my sister found me, and told me I had to go back home. They knew a little bit about where I was, but then my dad told me I had to come home. So I had to go. I heard that my mom was better, and I thought everything was going to be marvelous. I thought if I brought money back to my dad, he was going to be nicer, and wouldn't hit me or mistreat me. So I brought him some money. But he still treated me the same. Well, my mom is an alcoholic, or was an alcoholic, because she has since died. Back home it was all the same. My dad was just … really bad. And so I escaped again. I was sixteen years old. I tried to make a life.

And then, after I had Ivan, *his* dad started threatening me, and then his grandfather started threatening me. They wanted to take my son from me. So, I was thinking of going back to the capital, but I needed to go somewhere farther, because they were following me. They were stealing from me, and breaking in through my window, leaving me threatening letters. So there was nothing else to do. There were no other options. Because I was changing from one place to another to another to another to another. And they followed me. For a whole year. My son was growing up. When I had to leave, when the threats and the extortion got more serious, he was already eight. They wanted to take my son from me. Because, they said, he was theirs. He was their blood.

I couldn't go to the police because the grandfather of my son was the mayor of the village. So it would have been impossible to ask for help. So we just left. Headed to the US, I had to pay for a coyote to cross the border. But then in Mexico we were alone. We crossed on a raft, and then passed through, at Mesilla, to go to Chiapas. And we stayed there a while. I worked in Mexico for a bit, she says, and falls into a long silence. After a while I ask her what she did for work in Mexico.

It was, she says, pausing again … hard. I don't like to talk about it. But I felt a little better, for my son, because we were far from his father. We couldn't be there anymore. It was …

She stops and giggles nervously, and then takes a peppermint candy. In the end, she says, I went to Mexico, and then I came to the United States. She seems content with the description.

I paid, I think, Hilda says, three thousand dollars to cross into the US. At first I had to pay half, but then they, these men who had us in a house, they told my sister she had to pay more. That was in, what was it called? Reynosa. When we got to Reynosa it … it was really scary. There were a lot of bad people around there. They were looking at you mean. It seemed so dangerous. When I first got off the bus in Reynosa, the man who helped me cross, the coyote, he called and told me, Walk to this store, stay there, and don't talk. Don't get nervous. Just wait for a man to come and pick you up. But I was like … she shows me her trembling hands to demonstrate.

I mean, who was I trusting? Is this person a good person? I didn't know who he was. And I was looking for him like, Is it him, or him, or him? And I was there with my son. And then this man came up to me, and said, Are you Ms. Hilda? Yeah, I told him, that's me. Don't look at me, he said. And I was like, Ay, I was so scared. Come with me, he said. And we followed him and got in his car, and I was so scared for my son. I asked myself, What am I doing? Who is this man? Is he a child of god or is he a criminal? There were other women, but they took them somewhere else. And so we got into the car and we drove away. Then they told me, Get out here, get out and run into that house. And don't look at anything. Don't look to the sides, just get out and run into that house. Get out! *Go, go, go! Move!* And so I got out and ran with my son and went right into the house. And the day had been so bright and it was dark inside so I couldn't see anything at first, and I ran into somebody and they said, Hey, watch out! There were *a ton* of people. And it smelled like: Ooh! There were like a hundred people inside, and everyone was just like *Shhh.* And I was the only one who had a child. The only one. There were a lot of men, some women.

My son was scared. He was holding onto me so hard, and I just told him, Don't talk, m'ijo. It's going to be okay. And we were hungry. Because they gave us a little food, but it was rotten. It was rice, sort of like rice soup. And the bathroom, you couldn't wash yourself. There was a little bit of water. And there was a toilet, but it was full of … Yeah. Horrible. Four days we spent in there.

My son slept on my legs. Everybody was on the floor. I just was trying to keep him calm, so he wouldn't talk, so he was okay. The good thing was that I had bought a few things in the store. I'd bought a juice, some cookies. Because we couldn't leave. That's all he could eat. I was trying to distract him, but … He didn't speak. He was just looking. Just watching. This other woman was whispering to us a little bit. I didn't speak to any of the men. A lot of them seemed … I didn't want to talk to them. We couldn't open the window. We couldn't leave. Nothing …

~

Hilda decides she wants a break. After coming back, a few minutes later, from her room, she shows me the GPS ankle bracelet that she had removed soon after coming into sanctuary. She hands it to me and asks, Do you think that this thing is recording our voices? Sometimes, she says, I was scared that it was listening to me. Because they told me that I had to keep this thing, the charger, close to my bed. I put it on my nightstand. But it's never turned off, she says, and shows me the small green light still glowing at the base of the charger. It's always on. Maybe we should look it up on the internet, see if we can find anything out about it.

After a bit of chitchat—the weather, some wholesome church gossip, her dinner forecast—she falls back into her story, picking up in the safe house in Reynosa. Like four days, I think, she says, we were in the house. And then my sister paid so we could leave. We crossed in a little raft, about ten of us. The raft, one of those inflatable things, it was about to sink. It was already filling up with water when we got to the other side. We were so scared because I don't know how to swim. My son doesn't know how to swim. He was so scared. He hung on to me, just so, so scared.

After we got across, we saw the truck right there in the road. We ran straight to la migra. A couple people tried to hide, but the Border Patrol officers told everyone to come out, and they did. And they asked us some questions. Right there on the side of the road, they registered us, and then loaded us into the truck. They asked where we were from, how old we were, and asked for our papers. They never asked if I was scared to go back to my country. They just asked us a few questions and then loaded us up and took us to the hielera. It was like a prison, full of chain fences, and we got in and they registered us again, and they took my sweater, they took everybody's sweater—even from the kids—and they threw them all in the trash. And I thought, well, these people are so nice; they're going to give us new clothes, new sweaters, because we got wet crossing the river, but no. They put us into this room—there were a lot of rooms—and it was so, so, so cold. We were in there for three days.

I ask her if at that location they asked her if she was scared to return to her country. She says that they did, but I didn't know what asylum was, she says. Not until later, when we were in the detention center. They asked me if I wanted asylum and I said, No. I don't want asylum. Because I thought asylum was for old people. Where people get sent when they're old. So I just told them everything, my whole story, and they sent me to the detention center. They interviewed me in Spanish and didn't tell me exactly what asylum was. I didn't know what to say. They asked me stuff and I didn't know what they were saying. They said, Are you coming for domestic problems? And me: What is *domestic*? I didn't know what *domestic* was. I just told them what happened to me.

I asked for a lawyer, but they wouldn't let me have a lawyer. I did my credible interview and they ruled it negative. So I had to stay there and fight my case. They wanted to deport me, but first I had to go see a judge, and I went in front of the judge and well, he believed me.

When the judge gave me my credible, he set my bond at ten thousand dollars. And I didn't have that much money, so I had to keep on, do the whole process there in detention. And at the end of my asylum process, they gave me a Mam interpreter, but it wasn't the right language. I really didn't understand much. The problem was that when you say Mam, you're talking about a lot of languages, and they're not all the same. Some Mam is more like Quiché, and another Mam is so different it's like you're trying to understand English. At the hearing, I just understood a few words here and there. So we just stayed in detention, for eleven months.

I ask her about the hunger strike I had heard she'd participated in. In April of 2015, seventy-eight women, including Hilda, all detained in the Karnes family detention center in Texas, went on a hunger strike to protest their prolonged confinement and the conditions in the detention center.

It was really intense, she says. I think we were so brave. I never imagined I would be inside a prison and do something like that. We just wanted our freedom. Our kids were tired and sick, and the food was bad, and there was the bad treatment. There weren't doctors. Well, there was a doctor, but it was a person who didn't really ... It was like for everything that happened you would go to the doctor and he'd ask, How are you feeling? And I'd say I'm feeling like this or like this. Oh, drink a bit of water, he'd say. My son, I told him once, started getting so many bloody noses, and he was feverish, and was always hot, and he kept vomiting, and had diarrhea. A lot of kids and adults fainted in the detention center. I didn't ever faint, but I sometimes felt, you know ... She rolls her eyes, lolls her head back, pretending to faint. And the doctor would just say, Oh, you just need to drink some water.

There was a woman who had been transferred, Hilda continues, and she had already been in detention for a year, and then eleven more months there, in Karnes. She was so frustrated. Her children had been killed back in Guatemala, and she was really sad and wanted to get out and was asking for help, but immigration wouldn't let her out, and she got pretty sick, and she was talking with some of the other women, and she was just going out of her mind. So, for those of us who were in better health, we decided to do something. We had to do something, because if we just stayed like that, how were we going to get out? They were mistreating us, giving us bad food, restricting our food. If there was bread they wouldn't give us two pieces of bread. That's not right, our kids were weak, and we had a meeting, and one of us was really brave. I don't remember where she was from. But she was the leader, and then we got together and had a meeting and decided to strike. We collected signatures, and we asked for help from some of the people who were outside. And then when immigration realized we were on strike, we said, Okay, now we have to lift up our voices.

So immigration got us all together, put us all in this room, and they told us that if we were going to do that kind of thing, that they were going to hurt our children. They were going to take our children, separate us. And they were going to put red uniforms on us, the kind they use for criminals. So a lot of us got scared. They threatened us that they were going to send us to a real prison, and we got scared. Oh! Immigration always talks mean to you. It's like going to the army. They yell at you. They don't talk to you like I'm talking now, slowly. They don't talk like that. They yell, scream, You don't have rights here. Here you're immigrants, you don't have any rights, you're not American! Oh. That's the kind of way they talk. That's how they talked to us.

I was in the middle of appealing my case, she continues. They'd already denied it, and then they denied it again. So, I was about to be deported. But they were just playing with us. Because when the deportation order finally came, and when the appeal was decided, they came and told me, You want to get out of prison. Give us ten thousand dollars and you're free. But I didn't have that much money.

It was so much time inside prison for my son, dealing with hunger, and horrible food, and the guards yelling at us, all the bad treatment. Why were they treating us like that? I don't know. At one point I told the consulate I was scared to go back to my country. I mean, how was I going to go back? I already tried to hide myself, and they found me. I mean, if you're not a mother, and they kill you, they kill you and that's it, but if you have a child, and you try to take care of him ... Do you understand? You don't want anything bad to happen to your child. You can't live with that. So, I was scared for my son. He was my only family. My only son. I didn't want to be separated from him, or for him to get hurt.

Hilda pauses again, and tells me that they finally let her out, put an ankle bracelet on her and released her and Ivan. A few months later, Hilda says, my lawyer told me that ICE was coming for me, and they were going to deport me. And so there was a press conference, with President Obama, and he said that he was going to deport everybody who had already lost their cases. So I didn't have any choice but to come here. I told Alejandro that I was scared, that I had no peace. I was scared every time I opened the door or looked out the window. I couldn't sleep at night at all. So I knew I needed to come into the church. I didn't think about how long I would be in here. I just wanted safety. I wanted my son to be okay. That's why I came in here.

The first night? Well. You know. I came to see the church, and I saw how nice it was. And everybody, she says, switching to English, was saying, Hi, how are you? And I'm: Oh! How nice, switching back to Spanish. I saw how sweet they were. They were happy to have us here. But I still dream. ICE comes for me in my dreams. They don't give me peace. Oh, I hope to God that we can leave soon and have peace someday, a normal life. That's what I want most. To have a normal life. Really, it's sad. Really sad that we can't be calm, that we have to live like this. It's not normal.

I ask her how she explains their situation to her son.

Look, m'ijo, she says, as if speaking to him. Immigration is looking for us. They want to take us away. And so we have to go to a church to hide. He was already used to how dangerous it all was. I tried to explain it to him so he would understand … I showed him a photo of the president. And I said, This is who is in charge of the United States. And he wants us to leave. He's going to send immigration agents to take us away. He said, Why? Sometimes it's hard to explain to kids. All they say is *Why? Why? But why?* I told him, Look, son, they don't want us here. Because we don't have papers here. I wasn't born here. You weren't born here.

As she's describing her explanations to Ivan, he comes out of a back room after his tutoring session.

Hi, he says to me, shyly. He has a round, gentle face, with slightly puffy, dark eyes. He is very skinny, and when he smiles his whole torso straightens.

Hi, I say to him. How are you?

Good.

I'm John.

Hi, John.

How was tutoring? Are you learning a lot?

A little bit.

Do you prefer to speak in Spanish or in English?

Yeah. Spanish is good.

How old are you?

Twelve.

How long have you been in the US?

Three or four years.

What's it like living in a church?

I feel good in here. The church is helping me.

You went to school today?

He nods.

What did you do in school?

First, I went into the classroom. I put all my books away, like I'm supposed to. And then I learned some math, and then science. And then I studied reading. And then sometimes we do experiments. Yeah.

And you're studying English?

He nods again.

Your mom told me that you're giving classes to her as well.

He laughs. Yeah.

You're her teacher?

Yeah. I'm teaching her what I learn at school.

I ask him what he thinks of this, of he and his mom living in the church.

Well, he says. I don't like that immigration is trying to, um, capture us. I'd like to live in a normal house. Like everybody. With my mom and me. To go to school, like normal. And my mom can stay in the house, or go to work.

Do you talk about your situation with your friends?

Sometimes. When they ask what it's like to be here, I tell them.

Do you remember your journey to the US?

Yes. The only thing I remember about the trip is how hard my mom was trying to get money to come here. And then a coyote came. He helped us cross the river. And we were poor then. And I was wearing pants that were too big for me. They didn't fit. They were too wide, and every time I had to run my pants were falling down. We were in a boat and then we had to run, and my pants were falling down.

Were you scared?

Yeah. Especially when we were crossing the river. Now I know how to swim, but I didn't know how to swim before, and the boat wasn't pumped up all the way, because we were in a hurry, and we were sinking, and I was scared we were going to sink and something was going to happen to us. We could have died. I got scared, and when we got off the boat we ran, because we saw an immigration boat, and we ran more and my pants were falling down and then we saw immigration and we stopped.

Were you scared of them?

Yes, I was really scared of them. I thought they were going to hurt us … They locked us up.

What do you remember about the detention centers?

First we went to one that was called la hielera, and there we didn't have any friends because we weren't there for very long. We were only there, I don't remember how long. And then we were put into the perrera, the dog pound. These big cages where they put you, and then they call out names, at like three in the morning they wake everybody up and call out the names of the people who need to line up, and they put you in the trucks. They called our name and we had to get up and go into the truck and they took us to the detention center.

Was that detention center more comfortable than the hielera?

Not really, because the food was bad. And every time someone came to see what it was like they gave us pizza. And they would give us everything. They gave us toys, and they treated us really well. And they told us not to tell the people that we were suffering. When the visitors left they would take the toys back, they would take all the nice things away.

And is it still hard living here, in the church?

Yes, but I prefer living here than there, in the detention center.

What do you want to do when you grow up?

There are a lot of things I want to do. I'd like to be a soccer player, an actor, a designer, an architect, or a construction worker. If I can't do one, maybe I can do one of the others.

Ivan seems ready to go back to his room, but I ask him one more question. Why do you think some Americans don't want other people to come here?

He thinks for a moment, and then says, Maybe because they never saw someone suffer. Or they just don't know what it's like for us.

18

And for a few seconds all that can be heard are the whisperings of the men and women crossing the borders.

—Emiliano Monge

For nearly three months after he was deported from the United States for the second time, Arnovis hardly left the family property. When he did venture out, he kept his gaze down, avoided contact with neighbors, and didn't reach out to old friends, or to anybody else. By late August, he couldn't handle the isolation and started sneaking out for a few hours of paid work: installing a barbed-wire fence with mongollano posts, clearing a plot of land, or harvesting cashews. By late September, after having burned through a number of long-term projects—he had even finished building his sister's house—he was desperate for steady income. Despite the perceived danger, he went back to the ranch in Isla de Mendez, where he'd worked earlier in the year. His old boss gave him his job back, offering seven dollars a day for the same hot grunt work—harvesting corn for cattle feed, lugging around tubs and sacks, rolling out lines of barbed wire, hind-slapping cows into their corral, and shoveling manure.

Meybelín, meanwhile, still seemed touchy, not her old goofy self. She'd engage by kicking around her yellow soccer ball, disciplining the pig, or playing with the puppies, but she was quieter than before, would stare off into space, throw uncharacteristic tantrums, and turn nervous when Arnovis left her side. The whole family kept a close eye on her, and Arnovis worried that the effects of the separation and the journey were lying dormant, and would erupt at some point later in her life. Meybelín liked to remember the little babies she saw in the safe houses in Mexico, or the long, snake-like bridge they passed underneath at the US border, but what other details, he wondered, what other moments did she remember, or forget?

Arnovis wasn't sure if the gang knew he was back. Probably they did, but what could he do? He started thinking about trying to head north a third time—a fourth if you count his first deportation from Mexico. He told me, repeatedly, that he was ready to leave—the next few days, the next week, the week after that—but plans never materialized. He waited for his pro bono attorneys, in Texas, to see if they could find a way to parole him into the United States, though the bar for being granted protection with a prior deportation would be significantly higher, and, even if he were allowed to remain in the US, he would not be eligible for citizenship and could never leave the country without losing his protected status. He waited for WhatsApp messages from his lawyers that came weeks late. Hang tight, they told him. We're looking for options. Options never came.

One day, in October, picking up some gasoline for the chainsaw and the water pump—there's no gas station in Corral, though a few families sell fuel in gallon-size water bottles—he saw two young men he didn't recognize. Hey, vato, one of them called to him. Loan me two dollars.

It wasn't a loan. It was a tax.

Sure, he said, and handed over a couple bills.

You from here?

Yeah, Arnovis said. The two gang members were both side-eyeing him as he turned and walked away, a bottle of light-yellow combustible fluid in each hand.

I asked if he was nervous during the interaction. He said he was. You get used to it, he told me, but not really. You expect it, he corrected himself, but you don't get used to it.

~

Beto, my Mejicanos cicerone, told me about a tactic that's sometimes used for tax collection in the capital city. A gang member sashays up to you in that smooth-limping, gangster walk, digs into his pocket, and then pulls out a single bullet.

You see this. See this bullet? The tax collector pinches it between thumb and forefinger, holding it up to the sky. The bullet only costs a dollar, he says, but will take you to a whole other world.

If you want to stay in this world, at least for today, you better fork over two dollars.

Arnovis wants to stay in this world. He needs to—for Meybelín. When the tax collectors come to collect, he pays.

~

In the evenings, at the Sudanese camp behind the supermarket of Calais, France, Daniel Trilling reports in *Lights in the Distance*, men would sit around the fire and burn their fingertips. "They were mutilating themselves to avoid detection by the Eurodac police database ... 'You put one end of a metal pole in the fire,' [one of the men] said, 'and wait for it to go red-hot. Then take it out and run your fingertips along the glowing end, one by one, for an hour or two, until they're too blistered to be recognized by a scanning machine.'"

Identity is as singular as a fingerprint, but harder to blister away. If you are persecuted because of an immutable charac-teristic, because of who you are, you may qualify for asylum. Asylum seekers looking for protection from the state are asking: Can I be? The answer comes back: Yes, but only if you cannot be. We can only grant you permission to be here if, because of who you are, you cannot be there.

What pieces of their identities—leaving their home, their culture, their language, their family—are asylum seekers willing to burn away to stay alive? What gauntlets of suffering are we forcing them to run before we are willing to bring them in under our roof?

In order to live, you must be unable to live.

~

In 1959 Otto Kirchheimer described the concept of asylum as "situated at the crossroads of national and international law, compassion and self-interest, raison d'état and human capacity for shame." Nations may have pushed, twisted, and stretched their capacity for shame, but they seem less inclined to test the flexibility of their compassion. One of the principal underlying assumptions for border fortification, for asylum deterrence and denial, is that the survival of the state is threatened by extending the roof, by opening the gates. In Anna Seghers's novel *Transit*, the unnamed narrator, a Jew trying to flee occupied France, asks, "And what if some of these poor souls, still bleeding physically and spiritually, had fled to this house, what harm could it do to a giant nation if a few of these saved souls, worthy, half-worthy, or unworthy, were to join them in their country—how could it possibly harm such a big country?"

For asylum seekers, raison d'état—the motivations of the state —impinges upon raison d'être, upon being itself.

~

The "border" is more than a physical obstruction—more than a wall or a fence—more than a line on a map, more than a political organizing tool. The border produces and maintains extreme levels of inequality—some live, and live comfortably, and some suffer, and suffer miserably. For asylum seekers, the border is the knife-edge of the crisis—the turning point, as Hippocrates defined *crisis*, toward either recovery or death. Some shall live, is what the border says.

Some.

~

It's not possible for any one country to extend protection to everybody—a roof is only so large, can only be extended so far until it buckles and falls. But if we continue to organize the world according to nation-states—not by any means a given— we have to reassess refugee and asylum agreements. Otherwise, we have to be willing to consign millions upon millions of people to Untergang—to, in Adam Knowles's words, the "perdition, downfall, doom, extinction, and ruin" that denied asylum seekers are subjected to. Who are today's pirates for which we need agreements of asylos? Who is being plundered and dispossessed?

As hundreds of millions are left without homes, we must confront whether or not we are willing to live in an era of global apartheid—a world of comfort and wealth next to a world of fear and a constant clambering at the gates. We must decide if, as some hunker down and defend their privilege, we are willing to see more and more of humanity amassed along border walls into camps of squalor and desperation.

~

We're often told that the only long-term approach to stabilizing the modern refugee crises is improving the conditions in sending countries. But, besides curing humanity of our penchant for war and plunder, and ending carbon emissions, we should also be wary of "development." Honduras stands as a warning against careless injections of cash and arms. What was once pejoratively referred to as "USS *Honduras*" is, today, a high-crime paradise teetering on the verge of a failed state, annually expelling tens of thousands of refugees. Injecting a country with US-style "aid" is not vaccinating it against a virus; it is, too often, injecting it with one.

"The extraction and looting of natural resources by war machines," Achille Mbembe writes, "goes hand in hand with brutal attempts to immobilize and spatially fix whole categories of people."

~

Practically, asylum policy is an exercise in triage, that "gentle violence" of deciding who is worthy of protection and who is not. But decisions issued by judges and asylum officers reflect on them as much as on the seekers. Asylum triage, that is, exposes the heart of a nation as much as the individual welcomed or refused. Philosopher Christopher Yates calls these decisions "moments at the doorstep of our identity."

In their essay "The Truth from the Body: Medical Certificates as Ultimate Evidence for Asylum Seekers," anthropologists Didier Fassin and Estelle D'Halluin write: "Asylum seekers are expected to unveil themselves, to recount their histories, and to exhibit their wounds." And they do: that "moment at the doorstep" is a moment of unveiling as much as it is of arrival. But what about us—those doing the weighing, judging, and triaging? It would be naive to think that we remain unrevealed by the encounter. What about our history, our wounds, our veiled motivations?

What we ultimately fear, what we ultimately hate, is, so often, an outward manifestation of our own action or inaction. As Kristeva puts it, "The foreigner lives within us: he is the hidden face of our identity ... By recognizing him within ourselves, we are spared detesting him in himself." Dispossessing and denying the stranger or refugee does not keep us safe or in possession. It exposes us.

Before letting him take refuge in Colonus, Theseus asks Oedipus, "What is your worst fear?" Oedipus might have responded: What's yours?

~

"It is not we, as hosts, who are masters of the scene," Yates writes, "but we who are very much in question in a provocative way." The bravado of bordering is little more than exhibitionism, a manifestation of a nation's internal conflict or malady. Researcher Nick Megoran, in analyzing the political dispute at the Uzbekistan-Kyrgyzstan border, writes, "The state border, although physically at the extremities of the polity, can be at the heart of nationalist discourse about the meaning of the nation." Greg Grandin, channeling Freud, writes that America's "obsession with fortification against what's outside is symptomatic of trouble that exists inside."

Perhaps we can't extend our roof because the foundation is in shambles.

~

But how? we must ask—how do we make this world more habitable? How do we invoke and uphold, for everyone, the "right to the earth's surface," as Kant once exhorted? Gibney answers that "humanitarianism is a modest, sober, and painstakingly realistic criterion." Betts and Collier suggest turning refugee camps into "charter cities." Dana Leigh Marks pushes for an independent immigration court—breaking it out from the Department of Justice. Geographer Ruth Wilson Gilmore promotes the paradigm of abolition geography, which "starts from the homely premise that freedom is a place."

How do we arrive there?

~

It's easy to be outraged; it's hard to act, or even to come up with reasonable actions. Waiting for the government to offer to share its roof, or to implement any positive change, will be waiting too long. Meanwhile, instead of hoping for change or waiting for a radical rethink of refugee policies, we should open our churches, temples, mosques, schools, and homes. We should build communities that are willing and able to receive those in need, not merely incarcerate or expel them. Practically, this means boldly and emphatically resisting federal law. It means building on ICE-out-of-community efforts, and it means taking immediate, active steps toward offering sanctuary, offering love and welcome to people like Hilda and Ivan. It means fighting the transnational capitalists who are despoiling our planet, and building a more just and sustainable world.

The highest virtue, Emerson wrote, is always against the law. The highest virtue may also be impossible. Both should be spurs to action.

~

In Victor Hugo's *Les Misérables*, Monseigneur Bienvenu (a Pecksniffian name if there ever was one) offers welcome to Jean Valjean: "This is not my house; it is Christ's. It does not ask any guest his name but whether he has an affliction. You are suffering; you are hungry and thirsty; you are welcome. And don't thank me; don't tell me that I am taking you into my house. This is the home of no man, except the one who needs refuge. I tell you, a traveler, you are more at home here than I."

Bienvenu's speech recalls the Albanian proverb: Our home is first God's house, second our guest's house, and third our family's house.

~

In 2018 in The Hague, a church began holding a round-the-clock religious service in order to protect an Armenian asylum-seeking family from deportation. Under a centuries-old tradition, Dutch authorities can't enter a church while a service is underway, and so the church called out to religious leaders from around the country to come and hold mass. The continuous service lasted for ninety-six days, and only ended after the government agreed to review the case. One church member told a reporter, simply, "We have to be hosts."

~

This reality is that the world is uninhabitable for some of us. Politics, colonialism and neocolonialism, heedless greed, obscene waste, the centuries-long extravagant eructation of carbon dioxide, and forever wars have dispossessed millions of people across the globe. The credo of contemporary politics embodies the logic of the border: *some shall live.*

"Being a spectator of calamities taking place in another country is a quintessential modern experience," Sontag writes in *Regarding the Pain of Others*. But we are not just spectators. We—our way of life—are enactors of calamity.

If we are not actively working to curb the calamity, we are its participants, its instigators, its hellions.

What was unprecedented in the twentieth century's refugee crises was "not the loss of a home but the impossibility of finding a new one," Arendt wrote. Her former sweetheart, the philosopher Martin Heidegger, responded, in his way: "The real plight of dwelling does not lie merely in a lack of houses. The real plight of dwelling lies in this, that mortals ever search anew for the nature of dwelling, that they must learn to dwell."

What is the nature of dwelling? How do we learn to dwell? We might strive, in German poet Friedrich Hölderlin's words, to "dwell poetically on this earth." But what does it mean to dwell poetically? Derrida offers that "an act of hospitality can only be poetic."

Poetry—our stories, our shared narratives—is what ties the here to the hearth—is what forges a home. The root of the word *poetry*, poiesis, is to make. To dwell poetically is to make together, to raise a roof.

Empathy is not a passive act. It is listening to someone and then actively sharing in their story. The opposite of dispossession is a dwelling together.

~

Fifteen months after Meybelín and Arnovis were reunited, I went back to Corral de Mulas for another visit, to see how they were doing. Arnovis had gone back to his job—the same ranch, the same shitty pay, the same hot muck-buckets, and the same stubborn sun. He had been given a raise: eight dollars a day. He didn't have any other options. His father was recently diagnosed with kidney cancer. Meybelín needed school supplies. They all needed to eat. In short, the family needed money.

~

A new president had taken office in El Salvador a few months earlier, and the national murder rate had dropped significantly. Homicides dipped in Usulután as well, but not as much. In the last six weeks before I showed up again, there had been two murders in Corral de Mulas—both gang-related. The most recent was one of Arnovis's coworkers: shot to death after a cockfight at the nearby restaurant, El Delfín. The family had heard the gunshots. A few weeks before that, two of his other coworkers were driving their boss's car on an errand and were shot at. They escaped unharmed.

It's better than before, Arnovis told me, but it's still bad. The fear is always there, he said. It's constant.

Every time Mey hears someone mention the United States, Arnovis told me, she says, *I was there!* I was there but then they left me. They sent me back. They put me in prison. And, he said, to hear such a young child say that she was in prison, it's …

He didn't finish the sentence.

I feel ashamed, he said. For her, so young, to have that memory.

After talking for a while, I asked him if I could ask Meybelin some questions. We goofed around a lot together—played tic-tac-toe, drew, or kicked around a soccer ball—but I'd hardly asked her about the trip itself or the separation. He called her over and she plopped down in a plastic chair to my left. She was wearing a yellow Peppa Pig tank top, a small white bow on the breast, and short pink shorts. She had one outsize front tooth—broad toothless gaps on either side. There were little turtle earrings in her ears. Arnovis, shirtless, was in his hammock next to us.

I asked Meybelín if she sometimes thinks about the trip they took. She nodded. Arnovis told her to answer me out loud. Yes, she said. When do you think about it? I asked. She sighed … I remember, she said … crossing the river. I asked what sparks the memories, what she's doing when she remembers. She thought about it for a few moments, and then said, It makes me want to cry.

It's okay, I said, and asked if she wanted to talk to someone about it—her dad, or a friend, another adult. (Arnovis had told me he wanted her to see a psychologist, though accessing and paying for one was out of reach.) She didn't answer. She hardly even moved. I thanked her, and then she shifted from the chair to the hammock, sinking in with her father.

Later that day she showed me a sketchbook she kept to draw in and practice writing. There were childish doodles: a house, a volcano, stick figures, scribbles. On almost every page,

sometimes multiple times on the same page, she had written, Te amo Arnovis. Te amo Arnovis. Te amo Arnovis.

~

Arnovis and I were sitting under the single bare light bulb. There had been a storm that evening, and the air seemed scrubbed clean and redolent with life—bursting, damp, and green. There was a soft breeze, the quiet of roosting birds, the calm slap of distant water.

When I crossed the river into the US, Arnovis told me, I could feel it—I was less human.

He was talkative that night, but he was speaking quietly, almost whispering. I tried to hear every syllable.

JOHN WASHINGTON

It's shitty, he said softly. Está perro. But it's what I had to do. I felt an emptiness. It was like taking off in a plane, with nothing in your hands anymore, nothing in your control. My world was behind me. There was an emptiness. A separation.

Everybody else had gone to bed. I was leaving the next morning. It felt like he had something to say, and he was saying it, but there would always be something I wouldn't understand. I asked him what he was after in life. What he wanted. My only dream, he told me, is to wake up and be able to smile at my daughter. That's my dream.

Is that too much to ask?

Acknowledgments

This book would be a shell of itself without the courage, magnanimity, and hospitality of more people than I can thank here. I want to bow first to Arnovis, whose honesty, equanimity, fortitude, openness, humor, and kindness inspired much of this book. He and his family took me in and shared with me their stories, their roof, their hammocks, their hearth. Sonia and Pedro, his parents, trusted me and invited me into their lives. Meybelín, too, I want to thank for her spirit and her sweetness. Arnovis, gracias por compartir tanto. Estoy agradecido a toda tu familia por haberme recibido en su casa y abrirme sus corazones. Nunca olvidaré el tiempo que pasé con ustedes.

Dozens of other people—Hilda, Ivan, Martín, Gerber, Beto, Jesus, Edwin, Santos, Antonio, Javier, Sixto, Orlando, Antonio Montes, Nhemesis, Nestor, Nubia and Henry, Mako, Rolando, Sobe, Javier, Rosa, and others—shared their humanity and a piece of their lives, their stories and their spirit with me.

And then, too, there were those who helped me find, understand, and tell these stories. In El Salvador, Julia Gavarrete for her acumen, joy, and abundant hospitality. Zoraya for friendship and setting me up for my Olancho trip. Gabriela Castellón for the drives and the kindness. The whole El Faro crew, especially the Martínez brothers, Nelson Rauda, Victor Peña, Daniel Valencia, Carlos Barrera, Daniel Reyes, José Luis Sanz, Efren Lemus, Gabriela Cáceres, and Gabriel Labrador: thanks for the desk, for the beers, for your incredible and inspiring work.

Thanks to Bryan Avelar. Thanks to Beto for inviting me into his home, for being my Mejicanos cicerone, for his work, candor, and clarity.

In Honduras, Martín Calix and Jennifer Ávila from ContraCorrientes. My wonderful new friends Sandra and Gordo and Amelia in San Pedro Sula—thank you for the food, the insight, the spirit, the gifiti, and the dance.

In Guatemala, thank you to Mako for the trip to Xeatzán Alto and taking me into his home, even as it is nearly being washed away by the weather, as well as Fredy and Gerónimo, for crossing me twice, and tuk-tuking me around for a nervous, illuminating, and memorable day.

In Arizona, thanks to No More Deaths, and especially the abuse doc crew Sophie, Alicia, Adrian, Genevieve, Parker, Max, and Glen: such careful wisdom, dedication, and radical spirit continues to inspire from afar.

The El Paso folks who helped and guided me: Edith Tapia, Gloria Amesquita, Alan Dicker—incredible work—as well as Molly Molloy and Nancy Oretskin, especially for the night listening to the performance of Carmina Burana, the intensity of which, along that border, captured something of Juárez and El Paso for me that continues to resonate. In Juárez thanks to Julián Cardona and Sandra Rodriguez Nieto. In Austin, thanks to Jim Rigby and the whole team and parish of St. Andrews, as well as Alejandro Caceres of Grassroots Leadership and Amy Thompson. In Tapachula, Tenosique, Ixtepec, Nogales, Agua Prieta, and Juárez, I owe more thanks than I can muster to the teams of committed volunteers at the migrant shelters who offer the succor, reprieve, meals, and care to tens of thousands of migrants day in, day out, for years. You give life.

Other journalists whose work has inspired and informed me include Sarah Kinosian, who introduced me to Arnovis and brainstormed and palavered with me over rum in San Salvador; Jon Blitzer for the coffee, intros, and such fiercely good journalism; Todd Miller for pushing me to write a book and sharing his inspiring work and wisdom; Francisco Cantú for encouraging me to take on the pirates and write the book I want to write; Ryan Devereaux for friendship and covering stories—often that nobody else covers—with such heart and aplomb; Danielle Mackey for her wonderful work and grace; John Gibler whose work and integrity burns; also Sarah Stillman, Dawn Paley, Itamar Mann, Matthew Longo, Tracie Williams, Laura Gottesdiener, among many other whose work I've learned from and leaned on.

I also owe thanks more lawyers than I can remember: Heather Axford and Anne Pilsbury at CALA, Andrew Free, Carlos Spector, Ed Beckett, Matthew Lamberti, Jodi Ziesemer, Crystal Massey, Lenni Benson at New York Law, Deborah Anker at Harvard. Also Ian Philabaum at Innovation Law Lab for being such a badass, and Fred for the perennial boost of inspiration. Also Jordan Weiner for critical legal tips, as well as Ros, for opening Quiet Island to me.

Thanks to Frank Reynolds, a magnificent editor at the *Nation*, who has wisely chopped up and so improved so many articles. Also the shimmering expertise of Cora Currier and Ali Gharib at the *Intercept* who edited a few articles that got squeezed in various ways into the book.

Andy Hsiao, at Verso, for years of wisdom and support—for being a literary angel and polestar, a comrade and a dear friend. To Ben Mabie, who championed and trusted the book early on and gave me a terrific edit and expertly talked me through some narrative knots, for Brian Baughan with his terrific copy edits. Mark Martin for his classical expertise and artistic touch. Also Anne Rumberger and Natascha Elena Uhlmann, and for all the others behind the scene doing the necessary and beautiful work of publishing.

The folks at Saltonstall, for the peace you've cultivated.

John Granger, my aesthetic and spiritual mentor and dear friend, for the old fashioned–fueled close readings of early pieces of this book, and for teaching me to read the world, to write, to see—for the grammar lessons and the view and the wine and the soul. I owe you my sentences.

My family, of course, especially my sister for her daily love and ballast, my grandparents, George and Helen Blebea, who showed such faith and spirit all their lives, who taught me what it means to sweat and to work, who were themselves dispossessed and who fled Romania with my mother and uncle. My mother, a bulwark of love. My father, for constant respect and support and openness and love, and for slogging through a few early excerpts for me. Julian and Livia for their dose of joy. También agradezco con todo corazón a mis suegros, tan lindos y queridos, por darnos tanto apoyo y amor. Y, más que nadie, agradezco a Daniela, my heart, my spine, my monad. You've made so much possible, infusing daily reality with such light and love and beauty. And our son, Elías, one-day-old as I write these words, sleeping in a bassinet next to me in the hospital: may we offer you the welcome and the refuge—the right to grow, the right to blossom—such that you seek and fight to share it with others.

New York
January 2020